A Space Where Anything Can Happen

Creative Drama in a Middle School

by Rosilyn Wilder

Photographs by Burt.

New Plays Books, Trolley Place, Rowayton, Connecticut

*Dedicated with joy
to husband Ben
and daughters
Jeannie and Julie*

*All three
creative spirits
in their own rights*

Copyright 1977 Rosilyn Wilder
Library of Congress Catalog No. 77-828-55

Creative Drama in a Middle School

My Invitation to You	1
The Space	5
My Sequence: Experiences and Challenges	11
Involvement	13
Focus	31
Imagination	44
Improvisation	56
Conflict	69
Choices	77
Characterization	84
Critiquing	89
We Choose Projects	97
Models	99
Court	104
Adventures in Reading	115
Human Beings in Our World	122
"Let Us Be Free"	136
My Carpet Bag	144
Building an environment	145
Personal space; personal rhythms	147
Encouraging the individual within the group	149
Why start without words?	151
Why use the question?	153
Grading	155
What, no discipline problems?	159
Other people who can help	165
Surviving within the school system	172

FOREWORD

As a Superintendent of Schools, I was interested in ideas that motivated children. It had long been my opinion that motivation is *the* main essential to learning. Without motivation there is little purpose. Without purpose no learning occurs. My rural background had taught me that you can drive a horse to water, but you can't make him drink. There were things, however, that could be done to make him thirsty.

Ms. Roz Wilder came to me in the mid-60's with an idea to make kids thirsty for learning something new. She wanted to help urban kids be what they wanted to be; to forget their disadvantages; to develop their strengths; to encourage dreams; to use available materials to sail away on a "Magic Carpet" to any place at all.

I have always been glad I believed her.

You can't create and act out an idea and ever be quite the same. You can't lose yourself before your classmates and continue to be shy and withdrawn. You can't build a stage set and not use arithmetic, nor act out an original drama without doing a hundred things that we call education — reading, writing, cooperating in a group, developing the whole child, organizing ideas, seeking options.

That is Creative Drama! A device for creating the thirst that will help children do better those desirable things in a quicker, more pleasant, unpressured way.

Admittedly, not all teachers have the enthusiasm of a Roz Wilder, but not all teachers have seen the faces light up, the desire to stay in class longer, the self and group improvement that Creative Drama encourages. They should.

The modern technology that Creative Drama can use — video, tape recorders, cameras, film — allows the doers to hear or see their recorded deeds within seconds. They can look, listen, discuss, improve. They can see what they look like to others, and they can do all of this right where they are, with the materials they have, with limitations placed only on themselves by themselves.

Creative Drama is an idea whose time has come. I have seen the ideas described in this book used. They work. Children need this kind of motivation. The results are pleasantly surprising! Good luck.

Robert H. Seitzer, Former Regional Commissioner
U.S. Office of Education
Department of Health, Education, and Welfare

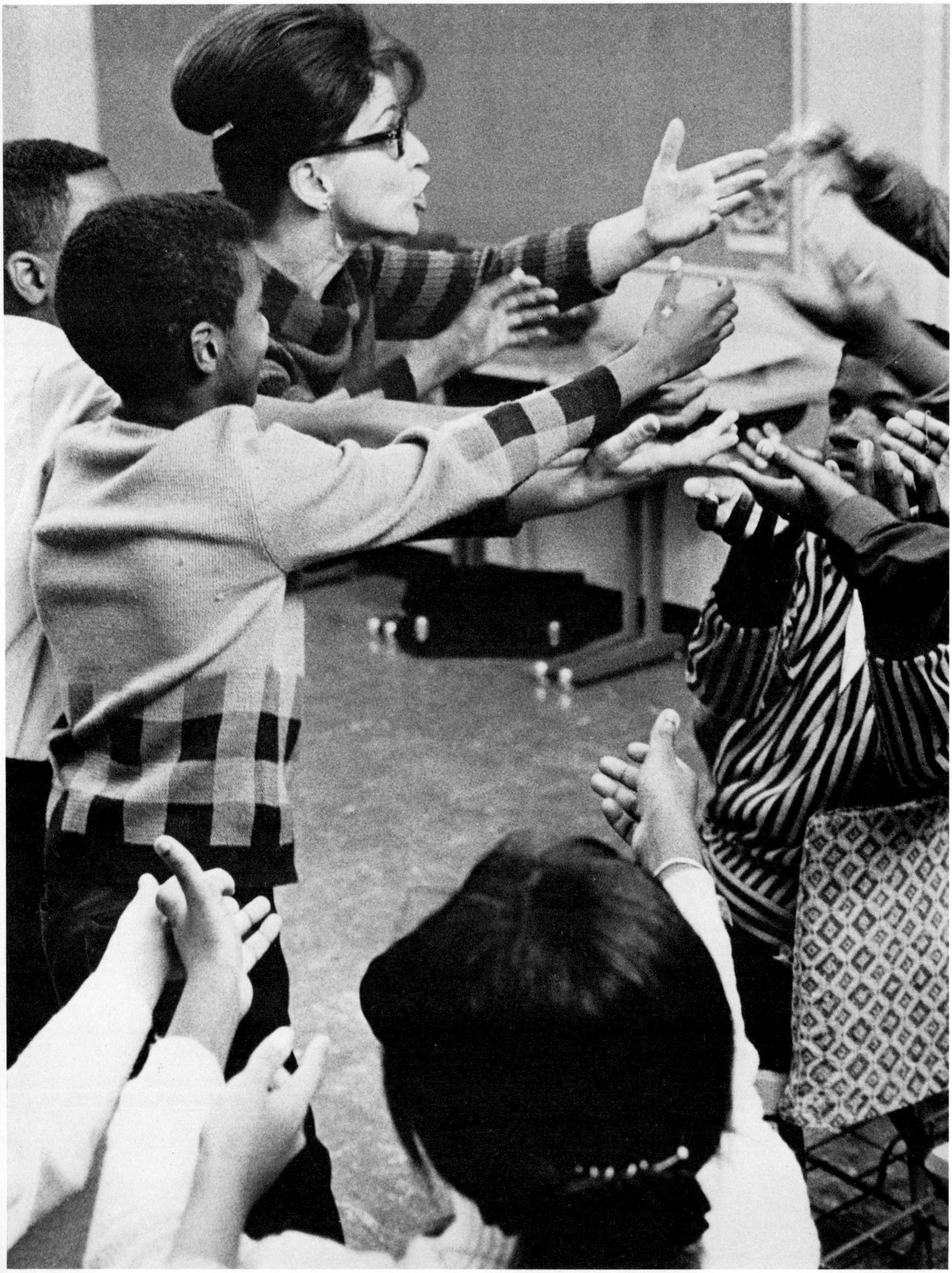

A SPACE WHERE ANYTHING CAN HAPPEN

A space where anything can happen:
a space to dream worlds
that we have yet to build;
a space to explore
the limitless feelings
we all share. . .
the bond
that binds us all together.

A space
I can change
with the experiences of my life. . .
the imagined,
the feared,
the loved,
the hoped for,
the possible,
and the impossible.

A space
where I can dare to be
the people I am
the people I see,
the people I fear to be
or
the person I might become.

A space
where choices
are there
for me to seize. . .
and dare!

          A group poem

MY INVITATION TO YOU

It's hard to teach today. It's also hard to grow up today. The numbers of high school students who read or write poorly are alarming; but beyond this we see the terrible boredom and despondency — so many youths with absolutely no idea of their own resources and capacities. So many wasted hours of classroom time.

How can we make education more meaningful on both sides?

I address myself to you who seek ways of making the classroom alive with the humanity of young people, a workshop rather than a drill shop, an area for personal search and discovery; not merely an environment for programmed curriculum.

As I've discovered over the years of meeting you at teachers' workshops, you are making changes. You are recognizing the different needs of your students. Above all, you CARE about your students and about the relevance of what you're offering them to their lives...as they are... as they can be.

Today, despite tightened educational budgets; despite larger classes and curriculum pressures back to basic skills, you are insisting that imaginative, relevant teaching can be maintained. Then come take a look at programs I've designed in creative teaching, and see how they may help you in your classroom.

Where do I speak from?

My way of working with young people in many subjects is through Creative Drama and the related arts. My main interest is humanistic education. For six years I developed a Creative Drama program in a new urban middle school, grades 5 through 8, with a black population mixed with hispanic and many white students of nearby university families. This book is based upon those years.

I continue to teach teachers, K-12, how to use the discoveries, innovations and techniques of Creative Drama in their own disciplines within their own spaces. I am sent about the state to introduce teachers to Creative Drama as a tool to teach Language Arts, Math, Social Studies, Guidance, Gym, and other subjects.

What is Creative Drama?

Children dramatize their lives from earliest ages...they recreate the images and characters and events about them as their way of selecting and learning. They express their own language in movement, sounds and words. You've seen them convert the staircase to a pirate ship; the space under the kitchen table to Pinocchio's whale. All this rich and natural use of dramatic involvement goes generally unrespected in most "ed methods" courses.

This is where our concept of Creative Drama starts. We say to young people, let's hold on to this wondrous ability and use it as one way to explore and discover ourselves...others...the world. It's a fun way. It's a natural way. Let's build upon it and make the most fruitful uses of it. We — the teacher in the classroom, the academic or arts specialist, the program leader working with drop-outs — have the opportunity to harness all this inherent creative energy and channel it to serve the child.

What I'm talking about for Creative Drama is not just a set of techniques and methods. There are enough of those. Creative Drama can provide an approach, a way to connect with something special each kid contains within him/herself. That is why Creative Drama is so important beyond early childhood; with young people ten to sixteen and over, so often the most turbulent and difficult years. It respects and encourages what each unique person can express. It extends a key — the key to unlock limitless feelings, dreams and possibilities. It can help lead a human being to become a creative ("capable of activating change"), productive, socialized adult.

We really can't measure most of this, or prove its values on a national test score, or change people who have other ways of teaching deeply ingrained in them. However, recognition of the values of this kind of Drama-in-Education is spreading. Creative Drama courses in universities and colleges, varying in appproaches and activities, but generally agreeing in basic philosophy and goals, are increasing. The hope, as Peter Slade in Birmingham, England, explained to me, is to train the classroom teacher to use Child Drama (his term for Creative Drama) as naturally as he/she uses numbers and letters. . .as a tool for learning in any academic discipline, and for the self-expression and personal growth of their students.

Creative Drama, by any name, implies:

- learning through using all the senses, including the kinesthetic,

- experiencing as well as talking about, reading about;

- making selective and imaginative choices;

- collaboration among individuals rather than teacher-direction;

- thinking/experiencing/evaluating/communicating

- group interaction rather than "I for myself."

As I have learned from experience, Creative Drama inside a school can include dramatizing anything within potential human experience and understanding. Anything? *Almost* anything one can think of, from mathematical concepts (not my strong area, but the students take the lead once they know the way) to matters like drug addiction, skin pigmentation, old-age homes, alternatives to violence, values, and career choices. Creative Drama helps students internalize learning through the unified physical, mental and emotional experience, and to integrate this experienced learning into human understanding.

Sometimes we culminate our experiences with a program for an audience, but that's not the primary goal. The process of discovery is its own reason for being.

Creativity can't be packaged

Some of the meanings of Creative Drama, I must caution, are diluted through carefully packaged "creative" manuals and activity packets. Some teachers explain that these are necessary inducements and aids for the teacher who doesn't trust his/her own creative ideas and abilities. But if it's packaged and programmed, can it still be creative? Whose creativity does it reflect?

If we want to promote the value of creative learning, let's expand the training of interested teachers and administrators. Let's pour these monies into the workshops and college courses, the in-service experiences. For Creative Drama is not a series of activities pulled out now and then — "rainy day projects when the kids are restless," as one teacher brightly explained.

This book does include activities, but mainly I want to share my philosophy and procedures. I'll try to explain to you what my goals are. I'll also describe my sequence of objectives, which is more important than the specific activities I use. What one does is less important than *how* it is handled and *why* it is chosen.

Why this book

I am attempting to re-create in print a living workshop experience by taking you along with me into my school. I've culled experiences from diaries, letters, memories, and from the innumerable written and taped notes of my students. These students are ever present as I write. I've changed their names, but I see them, each one: their eyes, shapes, laughter, misery, joys. They prod me to go on searching and re-examining. I hear them saying, "Oh Ms. Wilder, how'd you remember me doing that!"

They tell you, in the pages that follow, what it's all about, better than any descriptive words or academic syllabus. They are my motivating force for writing this journal — to try to show you how Creative Drama has worked in a real, urban schoolroom, and how some real youngsters, ages 10 to 16, responded at many different stages of their involvement with drama.

How to make this your own

These are only *my* experiences. You will need to adapt, change, and re-design activities to meet *your* purposes in your classroom or workshop. And that's the meaning of using Creative Drama as a process in teaching. Each teacher must make the process into an individual one.

I'd like to encourage you to feel safe in implementing this approach. I'll try to anticipate some of your questions, and help you over certain hurdles, discouragements, self-doubts. I'll try to explain my purposes in selecting certain activities at certain times with particular groups. An activity has little meaning, other than "just for the fun of it," unless it connects to your goal. As you put these ideas to work, start by asking yourself, "What am I reaching for today?" Warm-ups and sequence of activities will then fall into place in meaningful ways.

Listen carefully to your students. You may select something which appeals to you...but not to them. Draw upon their ideas more and more. The first expression of an idea from the class which is *heard* and *accepted* by a perceptive teacher, and *respected* by the group, will encourage more, and more.

Set an atmosphere for sharing and respect. Be consistent in setting your expectations, not just in words, but through your manner and behavior. Accept that which is different from "your way."

Above all, be courageous. Become a navigator with your students, setting out on an odyssey...a stimulator, a facilitator, an expeditor, a Pied Piper.

"A catalyst," one of my college students called me. "You use Creative Drama to connect us with ourselves and then with others." Yes, the word "catalyst" feels good...a catalyst connects but assumes little power alone. Let's add that to my list of roles. How much more exciting, this role. And fulfilling.

But remember...not all at once

It's not push button, or sure fire. Creative involvement is not where every kid "is at." It hasn't been a respected quality in too many lives. Not in many schools. Not in many homes.

You and I have a challenge to scratch through the outer coating, to lead a kid to value his/her own ideas and abilities. Yes, they may resist us. Some may sit sullenly in the corner, defying involvement. We may think they're showing us that they really need the security of a controlled classroom with spoon-fed knowledge which is to be regurgitated back to us, verbatim, on tests. Don't be fooled. There IS a human being there, capable of individuality, imagination, humor, cooperation, thought, learning, expressiveness. Each child knows within him/herself a microcosm of the world...waiting to be enticed forth. It takes lots of time...and patience...and belief...and insistence of a kind... but you'll reach it.

Why bother? I can't really answer that for you. But inside myself I know. Because only then is teaching exciting. When the light comes on behind the eyes, or an angry, hostile kid becomes involved in one moment of happy investigation, when Rona begins to volunteer ideas, or Sam discovers that others value his comments; when Fred shares his perceptive imagination, or Jeff starts coming to school regularly and staying late to work on our film...those are the nights I come home from school as though I've discovered a new planet.

THE SPACE

"What goes on in there?" used to be a question I dreaded from teachers whose rooms adjoined the Creative Drama area. It was a question implying censure and confusion. What happened to change drama from the nice, controlled, auditorium-program-kind-of-activity it should be?

But that was during the first year of the new Intermediate School, a pilot school under the East Orange Board of Education in the mid-1960's. The faculty were commissioned to try out new approaches in stimulating urban students to want to learn. "Make learning exciting. That's all you have to worry about," the administration urged us. All kinds of foundations were helping us. And companies producing new educational machinery.

I had been invited to join the faculty under a false expectation. The program design called for a "Speech-Drama teacher." My resume was deemed in order since it listed lots of Speech and Drama. That must have done it. For surely the interviewer to whom I spoke: "I want a chance to relate Creative Drama to kids...as a humanizing art form and as a tool for all kinds of teaching. Unless we have a full-time program in a school, we can't possibly know if it can work" — that interviewer was either involved in another sense of drama as I talked, or he was willing to take a risk.

For years I had taught Creative and formal drama in settlement houses, progressive creative arts centers, Y's and colleges. I had led workshops to demonstrate the values of the creative process of drama in education for teachers and administrators. Always the participants had chosen to attend. A public school would provide a different kind of challenge — and a test. The program in this new school would be the first full-time Creative Drama program in the state. If it worked, other school systems might be persuaded to open their doors to similar programs.

Preparing to open

For two months prior to the opening of the school, we teachers met in teams for three to five hours a day. My team included Vocal and Instrumental Music, Physical Education, Fine Arts, Industrial Arts, Family Living (an extension of Home Economics), and French/Spanish. Our first discovery was that we talked different languages with the same words. "Creativity," for example, meant something different to each one of us describing our programs. "Problem children" and how to handle them was an area that threatened to split us completely. Gradually we began to talk to each other over lunch more than in meetings. We began to talk as people-to-people, not as educators, and to respect why each had chosen to move into this school. We all felt a deep responsibility towards the students. What worked well with them would be the basis for the curriculum and methods used in the projected new Middle School for up to three thousand students, planned by a far-sighted superintendent, Robert H. Seitzer. For now, two hundred and fifty students from the two most overcrowded public schools would be transported by bus to our building at the western edge of the city.

Our school made educational history in its first three years. We started with traditional classrooms. In February we voted to tear the walls down and experiment with the "Open Floor" plan for academic areas. Core teams, combining a Math, Social Studies, Language Arts and Reading teacher, worked together at each end of the floor with a same group of students. A number of teacher aides provided ample planning time for them.

But I'm getting ahead of myself. When we opened that first October, almost all our students, we were to learn, resented being moved from neighborhood schools and friends. And they expressed it. They ripped up the bus seats, and within two weeks all the toilets were clogged. Fights and hostile behavior erupted all over the building. Some teachers retaliated — a kind of reflex action for some people — by severe disciplinary actions. Some teachers retained their "cool" and waited the period of adjustment out while extending a consistent open hand to their students. Firm but open.

As for me, I moved, with my trunk of display fabrics (donated by a local shoe store who used only Dazian theatrical fabrics) from room to room. A large multi-purpose room used for gym. A music room. A 12' by 13' Family Living room. A small attic room with peeling walls. Sheer optimism and unlimited energy were undoubtedly my greatest strengths.

I met in workshops with all the students twice a week. They appeared in groups of twenty-five every forty minutes. Then for several months we tried modular programming. Some groups would arrive for twenty minutes, go to lunch for twenty minutes, and return for another twenty minutes. The standing joke was "Was that you I saw before lunch?" We became mutually frustrated by this division of time.

Creative Drama as a menace!

That first year, I now realize, I "laid siege" to that school. I had so much accumulated passion for Creative Drama. I was sure that the faculty and students were going to embrace it too. It took a while before I really got the signals.

Creative Drama, as personified by me, was not only *not* embraced, but many teachers regarded it as a threat — a threat to good, programmed education. A teacher in a controlled Math area next to me abruptly stopped speaking to me. From the office I learned that she was horrified by the sounds emerging from the drama room. What *was* that woman encouraging the children to do? she had demanded. Creating chaos, over-exciting them so they did not concentrate in class in anticipation of their Creative Drama workshop! and they were so keyed up they could do little work after a class. I could see her point; many children do over-react when they are first let loose from a tight control into a situation inviting their ideas and expression.

The first time word got out that students were reading and then improvising from Chaucer — using their own words — an irate Reading teacher descended on me to say that *she* taught reading. She expected me to stop impinging on her territory in an area for which I was obviously not trained.

Incidentally, don't think that all the students were just "born" for Creative Drama either. Some had been told they were scheduled for drama, "where you'll learn how to act in plays." But I was not putting them in plays. "How come. . .why aren't we learning plays?" Others, during the first few months, were more like Fred, who came in as if entering a prize fighting ring. A small minority would clamor for the others to "shut up!" The first group would shout back, and I'd wonder whether I was there as referee or observer.

Discouragement and self-doubt? Of course. They gnawed at me on alternate Fridays. Monday mornings too. Sometimes I took it all personally. Maybe I was not sensitive enough to the real interests of the students.

Is it my middle-class values?

A colleague who was also enduring the early hostility of this student body ripped from their neighborhood schools in mid-term suggested it might be a "class thing." I was middle class and, she suggested, my theatre-trained speech might be a problem. As far as the middle class was concerned, I discovered that many of my students were more oriented to middle class values and aspirations than I. But I thought seriously about changing my speech.

I tried a period of emulating street speech. The kids knew me better by this time. They laughed at me. I laughed too. "Ms. Wilder, it just doesn't sound right out of you." "But what does sound like me?" We got into an imitating-Ms-Wilder thing. Then we began a really exciting exploration, and arrived at the recognition that street language is a separate language, and that many people need to speak two variations of English. "If we go on a TV show or get a job with the telephone company, we need to speak different," commented one girl. After that — and you can be sure they tried out many animated improvisations — a group volunteered to make up a book of street language, with definitions. Illustrated, too, with dialogues demonstrating usage.

Slowly, indiscernibly, a trust was growing as to what could be shared and expressed in Creative Drama and what gratifications would be received. Sometimes, when my stimuli really clicked, perhaps during the last twenty minutes of a forty minute session, all went well and everyone left the workshop with a taste of the pleasures of Creative Drama. Sometimes this pleasant taste would hold till the next session, and they'd come in raring to repeat what they'd done before. "Let's do that scene with me locked out of my house and crying. . .let's do that over. . .it felt go-o-d."

It's hard to realize, in retrospect, that many of the students you will read about on the following pages, initially among the most belligerent, were to become enthusiastic regulars of the Creative Drama space. Gido, who sat aloof for months, later improvised some passionately moving scenes in preparation for an original play on drug addiction. Keith, who was regularly suspended from school for his "disruptiveness and lack of cooperation in the halls," emerged as a self-disciplined participant intolerant of any inconsideration by others.

First year projects

In the peeling attic room, which the students and I painted blue, yellow, and orange as a "getting acquainted" project, I led small group sessions in special projects. I organized a UNICEF program on the similarities and differences of children of the world; assisted with an "all-Canada" day, an exciting inter-disciplinary, all-day program designed by a Language Arts teacher; led a program on the conquest of the Incas, hoping to show the Social Studies teachers how we might work together; developed the "Anti-Slurrvian Society" from an idea in an English book which I thought would interest the Language Arts teachers.

I did tread on toes, spurred by my enthusiasm and impatience. I had to learn, through anguish, the meaning of educational diplomacy. (In retrospect I apologize, dear Principal, for the day I took an eighth grade group to the plaza in front of the Town Hall to film one scene for our version of *Bye-Bye-Birdie*. The twenty-five students, with blank signs held overhead, were awaiting the arrival of "Birdie," while two other students were running our Super 8 camera. I noticed the Mayor looking out the fourth floor window of the Town Hall, and waved — facetiously, as it turned out. We were suddenly surrounded by police cars, sirens raging. The Mayor had interpreted our activities as a protest picket line, and called the police to disperse us.)

Yet at that year's end, this principal was perceptive enough to write in his report:

> Specifically, an atmosphere is created in Creative Drama which is conducive to imagination, involvement, enthusiasm and active participation. All the students are able to better develop verbal and physical means of communication. As the first year of this program draws to a close, we can begin to evaluate what has been accomplished. Always the best evaluation is made in terms of actual performance. In this case, we have definitely witnessed, on the parts of many, a change in attitude and an assumption of more responsibility.

Our second year

After the walls came down, we initiated an "open choice" program whereby each student had to make daily choices and assume responsibility for designing his/her daily program. Each teacher had a homebase group of 7 to 9 students. During the hour at the end of each day we discussed the students' experiences of the day and checked that he/she had achieved at least three hours a week in each academic area. A maximum of ten hours a week was left for the Related Arts. This allowed students to design interest groups in Creative Drama, meeting from three to five hours a week. I might have 14 in one group and 25 in another. Most of these students now had had a year in basic Creative Drama workshops, and were ready to develop interest areas for depth work.

One interest group stayed together from the first year, and continued for another three years. A tale from Aesop's Fables started us off on an investigation of the causes of slavery and experiences of enslaved people throughout history. Eventually all this material went into developing a documentary movie, designed, researched, improvised, characterized, written and filmed by the students. The development of that film, "Let us be Free," is described later in the book.

Another group concentrated on improvising original and folk tales which were shared outside school, with children in nurseries and shelters. Another group was excited by the film, "West Side Story," and wanted to develop their own parallel. After weeks of improvising relationships and meanings, a very personal modern story evolved. Shakespeare would have disavowed any relationship with our *Romeo and Juliet* — except for a few speeches lifted from his text because, as Herman commented, "His words are so beautiful. . .how could anyone think of such beautiful ways of talking?"

Choices

My personal theme the third year was "Choices." Choices of life style, choices of interests, behavior, friends and enemies. Choices of involvement and attitudes, of what we wanted of ourselves. . .all kinds of choices which might expand a student's self-concept and dreams and aspirations.

"Human Beings in Our World" was one interest group which formed to explore our options in life. With thirty students, and an inter-disciplinary faculty group, we combined research, improvisation, and field trips to meet with and interview people all over New Jersey. We spoke with people of many ages, backgrounds and involvements — as diverse as Puerto Rican physicists visiting at a solar system center, dock workers, architects of an international air terminal, a shoemaker, a day care center leader.

With the help of a state grant, we developed "Drugs and Other Cop-Outs" with fifty students. The Family Living teacher and I designed this program with assistance from DARE, a pioneering drug rehabilitation residential program of the area. Again, our focus was on the ways we could express our feelings, frustrations, and how we could boost or break ourselves.

A Math problem provided the basis for another group's efforts. Using the concept of the continuum and negative/positive numbers, the students developed "The Court of the Last Integer," examining negative and positive behavior in their lives. (Negative, as they agreed, denoted "behavior which is harmful or hurtful to others.")

Your space will be different, of course

All this gives you, I hope, a strong picture of where it all took place and how it developed, from commitment and struggle. I realize my space was special. I think you'll find, however, that much of what follows will adapt to any space.

Move with me now into actual workshop situations. Look in on the Creative Drama process as it has worked in one city's school, and may be incorporated by you into your work with children and youth almost anywhere.

MY SEQUENCE

For years I followed an orderly route which was determined by activities. I started with non-verbal activity and pantomime; then sense memory; then verbal activities into improvisation then characterization then emotions then voice and speech then dramatization of literature etcetera etcetera...

In public education I began to see an organic progression flowing from my objectives; not the activities. More and more, this has felt right with students of all ages.

It moves like this:

Group participation leads into

INVOLVEMENT — which allows for

FOCUS — concentration which frees

IMAGINATION — the release of ideas, feelings, and perceptions through the senses (which means more, by far, than five) which we use for

EXPRESSION AND COMMUNICATION through movement, voice, speech, attitude, action and reaction, using

IMPROVISATION — developed further by

CONFLICT

CHARACTERIZATION, and

CHOICE, refined by

CRITIQUING — or "Rap Time" to build insight, standards and self-expectation,

and spiralling around again toward

SELF-GROWTH!

I see it all starting from the environment we set and maintain from the first step into my space...the ambiance...the atmosphere.

The Ritual of my Workshops

(But nothing is all-the-time; nothing is static.)

- Warm-up — a time to "lubricate" the imaginations and bodies, to help make the transition from previous classes into Creative Drama. Warm-ups usually relate to the theme or problem of the workshop; they begin the flow of responsive ideas.

- Planning — after the stimuli for the session are presented, during this time individuals and groups share ideas, choose possibilities and plan their structure.

- Doing/Enacting — this is the time for sharing their plan in action and the time for others to observe and respond as an active audience.

- Rap Time — the time for critique for positive reinforcement, by those who did and those who observed. A critique should serve all involved to raise their awareness for future sessions.

Time table

It varies with the group. Surely there is no such thing in creative process as arbitrary time schedule. Some groups take longer to achieve involvement and need more time with it. Time spent on Focus is never wasted; it's a short cut to quality work later on. In everything we do we are reinforcing these objectives so we need never think "well, now I'm done with Focus," or "now I'm done with Imagination." All the efforts are spiraling to higher levels of expression.

EXPERIENCES I: INVOLVEMENT

They enter the space

EACH YEAR...EACH NEW GROUP...I AM READY WITH MANY IDEAS...ALL KINDS OF WAYS TO INTRODUCE THEM TO CREATIVE DRAMA...TO CAPTURE THEIR INTEREST... TO STIR UP THEIR BOLD IMAGINATIONS...THEIR COURAGE TO SHARE THOSE ABSURD AND WONDERFUL INNER THREADS OF FANTASY AND YEARNING. THERE'S SO MUCH TO EXTEND TO THEM. BUT, "NOT ALL AT ONCE," I REMIND MYSELF. LITTLE BY LITTLE LET OUT THE TREASURES OF DRAMA. FIRST FIND OUT WHERE THEY ARE...WHAT THEY LIKE, DESPISE, ADORE. FIND OUT WHAT WILL EVOKE A GLEAM IN THE EYE. AND SO I SET MY SIGHTS TENTATIVELY AND MOVE IN ON THEM SLOWLY...TOO MUCH TALKING AT ONCE WILL LOSE THEM. I TRY TO CREATE AN ATMOSPHERE OF ACCEPTANCE...RESPECT...AND EXPECTATION. GIVE THEM A GLIMPSE, ENOUGH TO CATCH HOLD OF. EXTEND MYSELF WITH A DIRECTNESS, HOPING THEY WILL SOON RESPOND IN THEIR WAYS, AS THEY BEGIN TO TRUST THAT WHAT THEY SHARE OF THEMSELVES, SERIOUSLY, IS OKAY. AND SO WE BEGIN.

Notes from a diary

The door opens and twenty-five fifth graders hurtle their bodies into the space of my room. They are responding to the openness and the two walls of glass and the folk-rock playing on the turn-table. Within two minutes everything has been handled, overturned, thrown in the air if it can be. I feel that words to call them to order will be futile — I won't be heard above the din. How else?

I pull out the "lumber jack," a wooden, hinged puppet which tap dances on a board. I hold the puppet by the back stick and rap on the board to make it dance.

As though for myself, I start him tapping out the beats of the music. Immediately a group gathers near. Then others join. Soon all twenty-five are pushing in around me. "What is it?" "Lemme use it, lemme!" "I'm here first; move over dope!" Together we examine how it was made. No one uses it, not yet. I tell them where I bought it...at a folk festival in New England...hand crafted by some wood carvers from Vermont. A few don't know where Vermont is. We get onto the subject of carving. One boy has carved something which he'll bring in tomorrow. "Listen to the music. Clap the beat of it." Some intuitively clap the off beats while others pick up the main 1-2-3-4. They take turns using the lumber jack to tap to the music.

"Can you move to the beat with your eyes?" They laugh...then try it. "How about your toes on both feet?" Instantly a few are on the floor, several on chairs. Some pull off shoes. Toes are keeping the beat. "How would you keep the beat if you were a worm or a caterpillar?" Some giggle, and soon all but one girl who is dressed in starched lavendar are busy keeping time with a "tail" or a "head." The process has begun.

YOU CAN EXPAND ON HOW THIS FIRST SESSION MAY HAVE PROCEEDED. THERE ARE MANY POSSIBILITIES. TEN MINUTES BEFORE THE END OF CLASS, THEY ALL GATHER TOGETHER TO EXCHANGE NAMES WITH ME AND TO THINK ALOUD WHAT THEY'VE USED FOR DRAMA, WHAT'S MADE IT WORK.

THEY WILL NEED SOME KEY QUESTIONS TO DRAW FORTH THEIR PERCEPTIONS: DID YOU ENJOY TODAY? WHY? IF THIS IS PART OF CREATIVE DRAMA, WHAT WOULD YOU SAY WE USED OF OURSELVES HERE? IF SOME OTHER STUDENTS HAD COME IN HERE AND LAUGHED AT YOU, WOULD IT HAVE BEEN THE SAME?

FROM THE TEACHER'S POINT OF VIEW, IT'S IMPORTANT TO POINT OUT WHY YOU HAVE ENJOYED WORKING WITH THEM, HOW THEIR IMAGINATION AND INTEREST STIMULATED YOU AS WELL.

An Eighth Grade class enters

"They're the toughest group in school," I was warned by a teacher who watched to see me flinch.

I set a mike on the table in the center of the room. A large posterboard sign was available, but not filled in. I put a James Brown record on the phono.

They straggled in. One or two threw a look at me which said, "Oh, that's her — she can stay if she don't bother us." The seats were in a large circle, so they sat noisily and talked to each other. Then I addressed myself to a few who weren't involved in conversation. They might just be amenable.

"What would you use the mike for? Something outside of a school?"

"I don't know," answered one. "For a walky-talky, I guess," responded another.

"That kind of mike, they use them on TV quiz shows. I know cause I watch every day when I eat," said Dina.

"I seen 'em on TV *interview* shows," said her girl friend.

We had a coterie now. They voted for an interview show. The "I-don't-know" boy, named James, agreed to letter a network sign: WIS-TV. A boy named Kevin volunteered to be the interviewer. Another girl joined in with "Whyz he wanna do everything?" I asked her to be the first interviewee.

Gradually, the interest had spread. I explained to the entire group what we were doing. Some saved face by sighing and mumbling, well, they couldn't care less, but if they had to they'd answer questions.

I set the tape recorder up so we could play the interviews back at the next workshop. We rearranged chairs. Dina conducted a vote to agree upon a topic: "Your Feelings about Coming to This New School." Some suggested interview questions, and others wrote them on the portable board.

When the tape recorder was turned on and Kevin said, "We're on the air," everyone became super quiet. Martin muttered, "That's for radio, not TV." Three others turned on him in a loud whisper, "We're being broadcast, you fink." And the stillness resumed.

Kevin asked; **"What's your name?"**
"Where d'ya live?"
"Where'd ya go to school before here?"
"How'd ya feel 'bout being switched?"

Only a few giggled their way through the interview. Once we stopped the tape because of a dispute. Then I asked whether we should go on together or stop because a few made too much noise. Again, Dina volunteered to take a vote. We went on.

Malcolm answered that he was called a retard every day because only retards are picked up by bus on his street. He hated being moved away from his friends. From then on, the answers rang with a too-long-suppressed resentment. Feelings, probably harbored for weeks, poured out in bitter phrases and humorous descriptions.

At the end of the workshop I told them I felt much better now than I had when they'd come in. "Why?" asked one of the last girls to join the interview. Briefly I told them. There was silence. Then Kevin said, "Oh, we're not all that bad. Most of us just don't like school and being made to come here. And we get into a lot of fights. This was fun today. Can we hear it back when we come next time?"

I looked at the faces. Most of them really looked like they'd like to hear themselves back. According to my "plan" I like to end a class by discussing what we'd done that made this a Creative Drama workshop. Nix on that, I realized, looking at them. They participated. They shared of themselves. They even controlled each other in order to keep the activity going. They want to come back. That's a good beginning. Better than words.

THE ACTIVITY OF INTERVIEWING IS MUCH USED IN SCHOOLS. FOR CREATIVE DRAMA. IT IS NOT THE ACTIVITY OF ITSELF WHICH IS IMPORTANT, BUT WHY WE USE IT AND HOW IT'S HANDLED. STUDENTS WHO ACT OUT THEIR HOSTILITIES IN SCHOOL USUALLY HAVE FEELINGS AND EXPERIENCES WHICH NEED OUTLET BEFORE ANYTHING ELSE. LACKING ANY RAPPORT WITH ME, THEY WANTED TO IGNORE ME. THEY COULD TALK TO EACH OTHER. THE MIKE BECAME A DEVICE

THROUGH WHICH THEY GRADUALLY REALIZED THEY COULD SPEAK OUT. A POETRY-WRITING SESSION MIGHT HAVE EVOKED SOME OF THIS, BUT THE GROUP INTERACTION WOULD NOT NECESSARILY HAVE BEEN AS POTENT A STIMULANT TO CANDOR.

A fifth-sixth grade group arrives!

I'm seated on the rug. No chairs. One girl sits next to me. As teachers, we "know" the student who immediately sits next to a new teacher. We hope we can strengthen her self-esteem in time.

I start a rhythmic beat going, hitting the floor. I signal a few to pick it up. A ritualistic beat. To a few others, I ask, "Can you pick this up?" A few late stragglers join us noisily. Rhythm has its own secret language with children and with adults who've maintained contact with their natural selves. The beat continues...then changes. Some students think, "That's it. She's trying to trick us," and they get that sly look on their faces. I may stop and simply wave the beat in the air for several phrases. They're all on to me and imitate exactly what I'm doing. After a period of sustained beat, increasing in volume, decreasing, but persisting at the same tempo, I'll add a sound and nod to them to echo it; or a word:

"Ta-ka kam ooom pah." Just whatever comes into the head.

"E-e-e-e-e-e-e-e," from very high traversing down to low.

"B-b-b-b-b-b." Mouthed sounds, breathy sounds, grunts, sighs; staccato, smooth.

Within the beat I'll address a question to a child. Usually he/she responds within the beat naturally. Some children are not yet comfortable enough and will demur, so the question will be moved on without any critical look.

"What/color/do you like?" Something simple, easy to answer.

"Purple."

"She/likes/purple. What color does she like?" (Still to beat.)

All: "She/likes/purple." And on to other students in the same manner.

From there, it's simple to move into uttering my name and something I like, to the same or a changed beat. To the girl next to me I whisper, "Repeat mine and add yours." A groan usually goes through the last ten members of the circle. Are they going to remember the likes of each person? (The names, at least the first names, they know.) "We'll help you if you forget." I try to reassure them in order to remove that old stigma of failure. Without that fear it's quite usual for a group of twenty-five to thirty to remember new names and what each one likes within fifteen minutes.

Hands are getting tired from clapping and beating, so we change to a light tapping on our thighs...just enough to express the beat which is now internalized. I start a story going. A made-up story. Very uncomplicated in order to encourage others to do the same.

I went for a walk.	**(They chant this after me.)**
I went down the lane.	(They chant this after me.)
and through a door	(They chant this after me.)
and up some stairs	(They chant this after me.)
and down a hall	(They chant this after me.)
until	(They chant this after me.)
I saw...	(They chant this after me.)
the strangest...	(They chant this after me.)

If the group seems ready, I'll now turn it over to a student to lead with his/her story, and then to another. Involvement is beginning. Concentration and effort. Team work. Some room for imagination is beginning. Above all, we're beginning to enjoy each other.

THE "PASS YOUR NAME AND SOMETHING YOU LIKE" IS, AS YOU'VE RECOGNIZED, ANOTHER VARIATION OF "MY GRANDMOTHER PACKED HER TRUNK." USE THIS KIND OF ACTIVITY ADAPTED TO YOUR OWN PURPOSES. IT ENCOURAGES INVOLVEMENT BY EVERYONE.

Notes on working in another teacher's room

There was pandemonium as I walked into the room. A substitute teacher was imploring them to get quiet. Again it was apparent that it would be useless for me to call them together. A few were staring at me, curiously, even pleasantly. As though hoping I might be a new diversion. Chaos gets boring too.

I approached a group of girls. "If you think you know what I'm doing, then join in and help me."

I started a simple pantomime, hammering a board. One girl, then a boy, lined up next to me and began hammering.

"You recognized right," I said. "What do you think you were hammering?"

"I don't know," answered the girl. "Maybe a board — like for a park bench."

"Then who might you be?"

"We might be builders...or maybe high school boys hired during the summer to fix benches in the parks." "Why not high school girls?" From the girl.

Now I asked for an action from them for others to guess. The others were interested now. Three girls conferred quickly and started tucking and pinning in the air. Someone called out, "She's fitting a dress on a store dummy." "You're observant; I didn't see that until you said it," I said sincerely.

Now the girls whispered together. Then they proceeded to wheel imaginary shopping carts through the room. Another girl understood and began shopping too. A boy joined as stock clerk. Another boy became a cashier. He began to ham it up. With a large grin across his face he began to shout, "Step right up, ladies and gentlemen and get the biggest bargains of the year...free panties for the ladies' bottoms...with every sale!"

Naturally, the others in class began to howl. That's all the encouragement he needed. His ideas were endless. He had an inherent sense of timing. The influences of TV were apparent. The shoppers were non-plussed; they'd lost their scene. As they later confided, they were enjoying this new kind of drama — no scripts to read — and they wanted to go on.

They started screaming at him. Others screamed back. Punching and smacking began. As though the stopper was pulled out of a fire hydrant, the action erupted all over the hot room.

What choices do we as Creative Drama leaders have at moments like that? I certainly had no real rank to pull with them. I, a stranger. The substitute teacher ran for the principal.

I knew he was there before I saw him. Push-button stop to all fighting, except for three in the back of the room. He was a man of great presence, at least six feet six. With a tired sound in his voice he called to those still fighting, "You're suspended again for a week." To me, "Who started this? Just point them out to me." Looking straight at the incendiaries, I said, "I really don't know."

It was quiet after he left. I remember sighing and saying something like, "Really, what was that all about?"

One boy said very candidly. "Nothing. We gotta have some excitement on a hot day." We all laughed. The bell rang. School was out. I was eager to return to that class again. With their passion and animation, a marvelous Creative Drama program should develop — in time.

IT CAN'T ALWAYS WORK. RARELY DO WE NEED OUTSIDE HELP. WE HAVE SO MANY, MANY RESOURCES WE CAN CALL UPON IN DEALING WITH FLARE-UPS. OUR GREATEST RESOURCE IS THE GROWING INVOLVEMENT AND INTEREST OF THE OVERALL GROUP. OFTEN, AFTER TRYING SEVERAL APPROACHES UNSUCCESSFULLY, I'LL SIT DOWN AND EXPRESS MY DISAPPOINTMENT AND TRY TO GET THEM JUST TO TALK *WITH* ME.

THE KIDS WHO REALLY WORRY ME ARE THE ONES WHO ARE BEATEN DOWN. NO SPARK. OBEDIENT. NEVER QUESTIONING.

NEVER TEASING. PLAYING THE GOODY GOOD STUDENTS. HOW TO STIR UP SOME FEELINGS. HOW TO REACH THEM TO DARE EXPRESS AN ORIGINAL THOUGHT!

THE "BAD" BOY OR GIRL USUALLY CARES. . .ABOUT SOMETHING, FOR OR AGAINST SOMETHING. LEAD THEM TO REDIRECT THEIR ENERGIES AND THEY CAN BE POWERFUL FORCES. THEY CAN MAKE WAVES. . .LEAD OTHERS.

Everyone doesn't have to participate

We worked as a group: to change the space of our room. "We can move furniture," Leda had suggested. "We can use our imaginations," shouted Jack, jumping with enthusiasm.

The lights were adjusted to dim blue gels. The room became a forest, a library; a tunnel being dug under the ocean, a church, a basement hideout in an abandoned building. What energy and imagination!

Suddenly there were loud, derogatory noises. Ted had jumped on Leda. "I don't care if she is bigger than I am. . .she can't tell me!"

Ted was small for his age, and handsome, with an angry chin and brooding eyes. He continued pummeling Leda, who was defending herself stoutly. I've been warned over and over not to get into the middle of a fight. Yet, after estimating the anger, I said, "Leda, get over by the door." And she did!

"Ted, if you're to stay in this room you will have to remove yourself to a far corner. You do not have the right to keep others from taking part in drama." I turned now to the others. "That's one thing I will *not* accept in this room. No one *has* to take part. But no one may interfere with the rights of others to take part. Am I clear?"

When I looked for Ted later, he was curled up under the pile of stacked plastic chairs at the far end of the room. For several weeks he retired to them on arrival in the room, without comment or looks exchanged between us. I did stop him in the hall one day and asked if he wanted his schedule changed to something else during his Creative Drama period. "No," he answered. I was glad.

Sometimes I wondered about him — why he came, what he thought about during the period, whether this quiet time he'd made for himself was in contrast to the rest of his life, and whether he'd rejoin the group.

One day we were dealing with slow-motion and speed-up in a shadow boxing situation. The group was preparing to emulate the boxing match which had been featured on TV the night before — at 11 p.m. The excitement was high. Without comment, Ted joined the action as a waterboy and masseur — competently, forthrightly. No one even exclaimed that he was "back." He had never left.

I INCLUDE THIS DESCRIPTION FOR TWO REASONS. ONE, THE GROUP MUST KNOW WHAT WILL BE ACCEPTED AND WHAT WILL NOT BE TOLERATED. RULES GENERALLY SHOULD EVOLVE FROM THE GROUP. BUT PART OF "SETTING THE ATMOSPHERE" IS THE TEACHER'S STRICT PROTECTION OF THE SENSITIVITIES OF THE GROUP MEMBERS. THIS NEEDS CONSISTENT REINFORCEMENT UNTIL IT IS THOROUGHLY UNDERSTOOD.

MY SECOND PURPOSE: IF I TRULY RESPECT INDIVIDUAL DIFFERENCES, I MUST RESPECT THE RIGHT OF THE INDIVIDUAL NOT TO BE "TURNED ON" BY A GIVEN PROGRAM OR ACTIVITY. BY LETTING THE YOUNG PEOPLE KNOW THAT THEY WILL NEVER BE COERCED INTO PARTICIPATING, I GIVE THEM A GREATER FREEDOM IN TAKING PART. THE STUDENT WHO CHOOSES TO SIT AND WATCH QUIETLY IS NOT REALLY AN ON-LOOKER. WHO IS TO SAY WHETHER AS MUCH, OR MORE, ISN'T HAPPENING WITHIN HIS/HER SENSIBILITIES AND INTELLECT?

Eighth graders

FINALLY, IN THIS SECTION, I WANT TO SHARE A GROUP WHO WERE READY TO ANALYZE AND PERCEIVE AND DARE SOME EARLY ELEMENTS OF ORIGINAL THINKING. THEIR RESPONSIVENESS LED ME.

They straggle in with that dull-eyed look of "summer's over. . .I don't know why I'm scheduled for this except I am." They sit in clusters. . . girls together, boys together. Blacks. . .whites. . .Spanish speaking. . . and there are the few loners. Two boys and a girl come over and greet me. A boy they call Sam is leaning against a far wall, whistling soundlessly. I say quietly, "Please place your books, purses, combs, picks, candy, or whatever you've got under the chair."

"Huh? What'd she say?" That's the class entertainer, starting the business-as-usual. Testing me out. I bypass him and go on.

"Including me, we're twenty-five. Can we just naturally fall into teams of two around this circle, starting with you two on my right? Consider yourself reporters now. You're on assignment to line up a thumbnail sketch of your partner. Of course full names, some family information; special interests — what he or she likes; maybe dislikes; maybe ambitions. A clever reporter can usually get information if he or she thinks through a few questions beforehand. You'll have about six minutes for this. Then you'll give your information to the class."

THIS IS ANOTHER APPROACH USING THE INTERVIEW. THE PURPOSE IS STILL TO START WITH THE PRESENT; TO LAUNCH A FORM OF SHARING ONESELF, EXPLORING ONESELF. IT'S EASIER TO HAVE SOMEONE ELSE TALK ABOUT YOU THAN TO HAVE TO INTRODUCE YOURSELF — AT ANY AGE.

A raucous laugh greets this assignment. Many of them have known each other for years. I realize there's a certain discomfort, coming into drama for the first time, not knowing what to expect.

"You're so sure you know each other?" I cross to the first boy. "How many names does the boy next to you have?"

From across the room someone shouts, "She's got you, Dutch. What's his real name?"

Dutch smiles sheepishly. The boy next to him also has a nickname. No one, it turns out, knows his real name. As I turn away I hear Dutch say in a stage whisper intended for my ears. "This is stupid. We come here for drah-mah, not to meet each other." Appreciative laughter erupts.

I EXPECT THEIR LAUGHTER. ABOVE ALL, DUTCH AND HIS FOLLOWERS ARE TRYING ME OUT. IF I'M SURE OF MYSELF, IF I DON'T GET UPSET OR "UP TIGHT". . .IF I MAINTAIN SOME EASY HUMOR, WE'LL GET ON FINE.

I give them the signal to start interviewing: "Action!" The odd student becomes my partner. Sam hasn't budged by the wall. After six minutes it's hard to get them to stop talking. Of course they're not all on the assignment.

Margie starts. "My friend here has six names." Overdone laughter; she snorts a little. "Honest. She only told me three, though — Debra Valerie Caretta. She does hairdressing in her building, even on ladies. Betcha no one knew that, she's so quiet. She gets paid too. Real good. She wants to have her own beauty parlor but she's gotta go to a school first. . ."

Suddenly everyone's pumping their teammate for some surprise information. They want to top Margie's. My partner introduces me. They exchange looks after they hear I "was a real actress — live." A few girls now smile shyly at me. I have an identity now for all of them other than just "teacher."

LET KIDS KNOW ABOUT YOU AS A HUMAN BEING. YOUR LIKES. YOUR DISLIKES. YOUR FAMILY. HOW YOU FEEL TODAY. THEN YOU AND THEY BREAK THROUGH THE STEREOTYPES. YOU BECOME SPECIAL.

We've gone around the circle with some interesting reports. They improve as they listen to each other. More details. Some lovely timid smiles break out on the faces of those who're being introduced as they hear about themselves. Even Dutch loses his "wise-guy" look and an eagerness shows as he hears his partner say, "And Dutch hopes to make the pros as soon as he gets out of school, and you all know he's *fast*."

I explain how I feel about knowing people by name. And how it helps to know some special things about each one. I ask them to stop at the end of the workshop to see if I can call them by the right name. "Your name is a very important part of you. It's your label. It's a shame so many people mumble their names, like rosemaryaronowitz, so nobody knows who she is." I hear others trying out mumbling names.

"We've started by sharing something of ourselves. That's where all drama starts. Now let's do something."

"I'm not going to act...you can't make me act," says Jill. This time, we break up into teams of five. I give an assignment to each group.

Group One: Explore the room for all the circular shapes you can find.

Group Two: Find an original way of measuring the width, length, and height of this room. No rulers or standard measuring tools.

Group Three: Discover what makes this room a Drama room and not a Science or Family Living or Reading room.

Group Four: Find ways of expressing the arrival here of your class — the moods and attitudes; also any changes since you've all entered.

Now, Group Four's assignment wasn't at all usual. Something about the faces of the four girls in this group attracted this suggestion. If they had looked stumped, I would have offered them a quick alternative.

"Action!" begins their searches. Sam still hasn't budged. "Sam, will you just turn on any spotlight if someone needs more light." A simple direction, uttered quickly with no time for him to say "yes" or "no." He'll either do it or not. If he doesn't, tomorrow I'll reach out to him some other way to get an idea of where he is.

"Cut!"

Many return to their seats, sitting or leaning against the backs. A few feel comfortable enough to sit on the rug.

Group One presents an awesome list of circles: "Doorknobs, clocks and watch faces, round spotlights, eyes, buttons, the chair arrangement when we came in, jar tops in the make-up drawer, the fire extinguisher, discs, the turn table, polka dots on Debra's shirt..."

"Did they fulfill their assignment?" A few mumble agreement. "What was needed for them to do even this simple an activity? For they used almost everything which we'll be using, in different ways, for Creative Drama." It was apparent to them that they used their bodies and their fingers to point. Eddie realized that they had to use their eyes and their heads. "They had to plan and talk too," added a deep-voiced fellow named Jesse. "That takes imagination."

Group Two starts off by giggling. Since they didn't have a yardstick, they decided on "new types of measurements." A sideward look at me. Are they "doing right?"

IT TAKES A LONG TIME TO ASSURE AND REASSURE STUDENTS THAT IN CREATIVE DRAMA THE EVALUATION IS NOT BY RIGHT OR WRONG. THERE IS NO FAILURE AS SUCH. APPRECIATION IS EXTENDED FOR ORIGINAL THINKING, FOR SERIOUS EFFORT, EVEN IF THE RESULTS ARE COMIC, FOR THE WAY A GROUP WORKS TOGETHER. THE TRYING IS MOST IMPORTANT.

Group Two measured using Janet and Robert's bodies for length and height. Plus a window pole. The width they measured by chairs. I don't know if any Math teacher would have accepted this, but the group could see that they had fulfilled the assignment imaginatively.

Dutch asked, "If they knew how tall they were, why couldn't they just break it down by feet and inches. They took the lazy way." Jesse cut it, "Man, that's dumb. There weren't always rulers. Didja ever hear anyone describe Cleopatra in inches?"

Group Three observed that the rug and the jazz record, playing when they came in, helped make this room different. But it could have been a music class. The blue lights and the costumes changed that. They found the drawer of make-up; the props drawer; the cameras and film, the large fish net, even sound effects records.

"They stuck their noses into every place," commented Linda, giggling. "That's what they were s'posed to do, idiot," said Margie, looking the room over a-fresh. Again I led a brief evaluation of their perceptiveness.

Group Four was a surprise. In that short time, they'd decided to each say what she thought when she came in, and Mattie, a short, guarded-looking girl, organized them into a choral reading. (An English teacher later told me Mattie wrote reams of poetry, but was a loner who never worked with others at all.)

First they all made the noises of students tearing through the halls. Then Frankie hummed to represent the Miles Davis record on the turntable.

Debra: Lights — soft blue

All: Soft, mysterious
        Blue, quiet. . .

Mattie: We become softer, quiet —
        Silence frightens me.
        When do we ever hear quiet?
        We sit.

All: We laugh a little.
        We don't know why we've come.

Debra: Why does she want to know my name?

They went on like that for a few more lines. At the end everyone clapped. "That was real good." "I never would've thought anything like that." "That took some thinking. That was original, wasn't it?" Everyone saw this last point. Also how well the four worked together.

The sixty-minute period was almost up. "One quick activity. Will Group Two get up again, please. Here in the center of this circle imagine that someone's spilled a box of thumb tacks. Some have fallen with the sharp points up. When Sam says 'Action!' will you collect every tack and put it here in this box."

"Huh?" says Sam.

"Would you just say a loud 'action!' please, Sam."

"Action," mumbles Sam.

The group starts, on all fours. Everyone hams it up, getting their fingers stuck by tacks and then acting like they're dying. Linda keeps giggling the whole time. Eddie keeps winking at Jesse. Some of those watching are rocking their chairs with laughter. I signal Sam, and he says "Cut!"

"That was perfect," I tell them. "Perfect for what we need to see now. How did you feel down on the floor collecting tacks? Did you really imagine any tacks?"

They weren't sure what I was after. They sensed I might be "putting them on," yet there was no displeasure in my voice. So they stalled for time. "Well," said Eddie, "I was acting like I was being stuck by tacks."

"Oh man, you were so corny," laughs Jesse.

"Why?" I insist.

"Cause they were no more picking up tacks than I'm sitting here eating. . .eating a pizza."

"Did you feel different before when you were doing the measuring so thoughtfully?"

"Before," said Eddie, "nobody was watching us. . .so we didn't have any reason to feel silly. Right?" Linda giggled and agreed. The others too.

"That was a perfect job of faked acting. You see, before, you were looking at real things. You weren't concerned about an audience watching you. You didn't feel the need to entertain anyone. It takes time to give the same concentration to an imagined scene as you were able to give naturally to a real problem. Do you begin to understand?"
From the responses, most of them did really see the difference, and

this was most significant. "I suggest you tune in to TV tonight and especially watch for actions which you believe, and those you recognize are faked. Someone might sign a check so fast that you know he only zig-zagged some lines across the paper. Or someone might say "You look beautiful" in the same way he'd say, 'There's a skunk eating the garbage.' Next time we'll try some imagined actions and find how they too can become believable."

In the hurry to leave, only two students forgot to stop to find out if I knew their names. And Sam, I noticed, found the switches and turned out the spotlights before tearing out the door and up the hall.

A GREAT DEAL HAPPENED IN THIS WORKSHOP UPON WHICH TO BUILD. YOU NOTICE HOW THE DOING AND THE DISCUSSION BEGIN TO DEVELOP THEIR CRITICAL FACULTIES AND SET STANDARDS FOR OUR WORKSHOPS.

DURING EARLY CLASSES, THE LEADER IS THE STABILIZER AS WELL AS THE STIMULATOR-FACILITATOR. I FIND THAT MY OWN PARTICIPATION IS OFTEN THE KEY WHICH SAYS TO THE STUDENT: IF SHE CAN TRY IT SO CAN I. IT'S IMPORTANT TO TAKE PART RATHER THAN REMAIN REMOTE AND DIRECTOR-LIKE, BUT ONLY AS FAR AS IS COMFORTABLE FOR YOU. THERE ARE SOME ACTIVITIES IN WHICH YOU MAY NOT BE COMFORTABLE. YOU CAN SAY SO. LET THE GROUP KNOW, AT THE SAME TIME, THAT YOU APPRECIATE HOW WELL THEY CAN PARTICIPATE.

IT'S ALSO IMPORTANT NOT TO OVERSHADOW THE STUDENTS WHEN YOU ARE PARTICIPATING. WE ALL REMEMBER SOME TEACHER SOMEWHERE WHO INHIBITED THE REST OF US BY THE PASSION OF HER READING OF LADY MACBETH, OR HER LEAPS THROUGH SPACE AS PETER PAN. INHIBITED AND, UNFORTUNATELY, AMUSED. IF YOU CENTER YOUR AWARENESS ON THE RESPONSES OF YOUR GROUP, YOU'RE GENERALLY SAFE.

CHALLENGES I: INVOLVEMENT

Warm-ups and Games

All of the following activities can be adapted and changed according to your needs. The goal, of course, is group involvement and transition into creative drama. These can be used for early workshop warm-ups when they are directly related to your purpose and theme. I cannot reiterate enough that *what* you use is of less significance than *why* you choose and *how* you present and develop it. The *how* includes your manner, your interest, and your presentation of the ideas.

Use all kinds of old and new games which allow for some ideas, suspense or surprise, movement, and growing group unity. Games, to children and adults, imply fun. Many games also imply competition. Let's replace competition and "win or lose" with "involvement by all" and cooperation.

Adapt games...DARE to change them. Have two people as "it" instead of one; replace punitive aspects of being "out" with new challenges to keep each individual involved in some way.

I include magic tricks too. And some of those marvelous group tricks which require everyone to discover what the central "trick" is. Like SCISSORS, CROSSED OR UNCROSSED. Be sure you have two assistants who know the secret. You hold and then pass a pair of scissors in a circle. You say, "I am passing the scissors crossed." The next person says, "I receive the scissors crossed; I pass the scissors uncrossed." The position of your legs is the secret; if you cross your knees the scissors are "crossed;" when you uncross your knees the scissors are "uncrossed." Keep it going until almost everyone catches on.

Here are some more I like:

WHO'S LEADING: Send two people out of the room; the others stand in a large circle. Choose one person to lead a simple action for about ten repeats and then change to a second action.

The two who are "it" try to discover who is leading the action. The group want to disguise this leadership — without making it impossible for the "its." (Having two "its" protects a shy child from feeling completely alone against the group.) Encourage movement ideas to extend beyond gym type.

HUMAN TIC-TAC-TOE. You need nine chairs, arranged in rows of three in tic-tac-toe line-up. Two teams stand facing the chairs about ten feet apart. Team 1 is "O." They agree on a physical way to express their symbol. Team 2 is "X." They also find a physical way to express "X." They decide which team starts. The first player, in position of the team's symbol, takes a chair.

As in tic-tac-toe on paper, the first team to complete a line horizontally, vertically or diagonally through the playing field scores a point. A tie results in no score. The team that wins one set starts the next set.

STRESS THAT WINNING OR LOSING IS NOT IMPORTANT. THINKING TOGETHER AS A TEAM IS IMPORTANT!

NUMBER MIX-UP. Stand in a circle, well spaced. Count off around circle. Check that everyone knows his/her number. Start a 4-beat count going: clap on thigh, hand clap, two thumb clicks in the air. The leader, starting and maintaining this beat, calls his/her number: then the number of another person in the circle, "One-Five!"

Five calls, within the next beat sequence, "Five-Eleven!"

No one can fall asleep in case his/her number is called, since there is no sequence. Above all, once a group gets the idea, the aim is not to break the beat, and not to call a number more than once until everyone has been included.

Go slowly at first. It's amazing how tongue-tied someone can get when he/she hears the number called. Sometimes, in the eagerness to keep the beat going, you can't think of another number to call out.

COME SEVEN. Still in a circle, count off around the circle. Whenever anyone comes to a number that includes a seven or a multiple of seven, he/she says "Buzz!" and the game continues with the next number. For example 1/2/3/4/5/6/Buzz! 8/9/10/11/12/13/Buzz! 15/16/Buzz!

Reverse Buzz: When a player says "Buzz," the player to his right instead of his left resumes the count with the next number. We don't eliminate anyone. If someone goofs, then he/she starts the process all over again with number one. The game ends when the group reaches sixty without missing.

DO YOU NOTICE THAT THESE GAMES ARE BEGINNING TO FLOW MORE SMOOTHLY AS YOUR CLASS MEMBERS LEARN HOW TO WORK WITH EACH OTHER?

GEOMETRICS. You need some open space for this Dalcroze Eurythmic exercize re-designed to fit different Creative Drama purposes. It's good for any age.

Start by urging students to identify the major shapes to be found in their area, implied or defined. For example, a wall may be made up of defined rectangular blocks. A hand may imply a rectangular shape if you outline it. A window can be looked at as a series of triangles.

The first time through, when you say "Action!" all of the students are to assemble from the outer edges of the room to form, as a collective group, the shape you have called. Allow them about one minute to form a square, a rectangle, a triangle, an oval, etc.

STAND BACK AND SMILE AT THE COMPLICATIONS THAT OCCUR. SEVERAL BEGIN TO BOSS. SOME CAN'T SEE WHERE THEY FIT INTO THE SHAPE.

YOUR OBJECTIVE IS GROUP GIVE AND TAKE: PROBLEM SOLVING; PHYSICAL AND MENTAL INVOLVEMENT. THE GAME IS ALSO A WAY TO LEAD CHILDREN TO PHYSICALIZE GEOMETRIC AND OTHER SHAPES, AND THEREBY TO INTERNALIZE RECOGNITION OF A SHAPE RELATING TO ITS NAME. IN OTHER WORDS, IT IS EXPERIENCING AN ABSTRACT.

They finally do get together as a standing or lying or sitting representation of the geometric shape. Now add a time limitation. In 25 counts, can they form a group shape?

The third time, add the element of personal time. Knowing they have 25 counts in which to achieve the group shape, add more details to the action.

"Individually, touch something red which is not on a person; cross the room sideways from here to there; make the smallest possible shape with your body, then leap up to the tallest stretch of your body; then join with the entire group to shape a polygon."

That's one possibility. It doesn't really matter what you ask them to do as individuals. You're giving them a problem of planning out their time so that they can re-join the group and accomplish the group shape within a limited period. Beat out the 25 counts — slowly — so they can hear them.

I've led groups of adults who get quite flustered by this challenge; they all become directors and nothing gets accomplished. Some children, under the pressure of time, idle their movements. When the group finds mutual agreement and the ability to work together for a common goal, you can show them, in this fairly simple way, what they have achieved, and how they can extend this to deal with more complex problems.

Initially, you might appoint one or two students to help the group assemble into the shape. When the groups are ready, go beyond geometric shapes into: the shape of a ladder; the peace symbol, puntuation marks.

SOUND-ON: The group faces you in a semi-circle, sitting or standing. You are the conductor, armed with a slender stick if you like. Let the group choose a well-known, uncomplicated folk tale, which most of the group knows, for a start.

You start the tale with just two or three sentences. In the middle of a sentence, point to a student to continue; then to one at another point of the semi-circle. Vary the time you allow each. You're using the tale merely as a base — each individual's imagination can add all kinds of decoration and expansion.

If someone falters, everyone shouts, "Sound On!" and that person steps forth to present a television commercial for a suggested or original product or service. (He or she can choose one other person to help with it.) As he/she proceeds, the audience can call out "Sound Off!" and the commercial proceeds in action only; "Picture Off" and he/she continues to talk but not to move. Space the instructions. The entire commercial should not be more than two minutes in order to continue the interrupted story from the exact words where the break occurred.

The "Announcer" is then included back in the story telling, with full praise for his/her abilities in doing the commercial. Please make sure they understand this is the fun of the game, not the punishment. You'll find some students purposely stumbling in order to be able to do a commercial.

At the end of each section I'm listing some of the books that have been useful to me through the years.

CREATIVE DRAMA AND IMPROVISED MOVEMENT FOR CHILDREN. Janet Goodridge. Plays, Inc. Boston. 1971

HANDBOOK OF RECREATIONAL GAMES. Neva L. Boyd. Dover Publications, N.Y. 1973

GAMES FOR YOUNG AND OLD. Frank W. Harris. The Eastern Cooperative Recreation School, Philadelphia. Order from Mr. Harris, 14597 Warwick, Detroit 48223. He gives a point of view as well as good games.

GAMES ENJOYED BY CHILDREN AROUND THE WORLD. The American Friends Service Committee, Inc., 160 N. 15th St., Philadelphia, 19102. Emphasis on collaborative as well as competitive games.

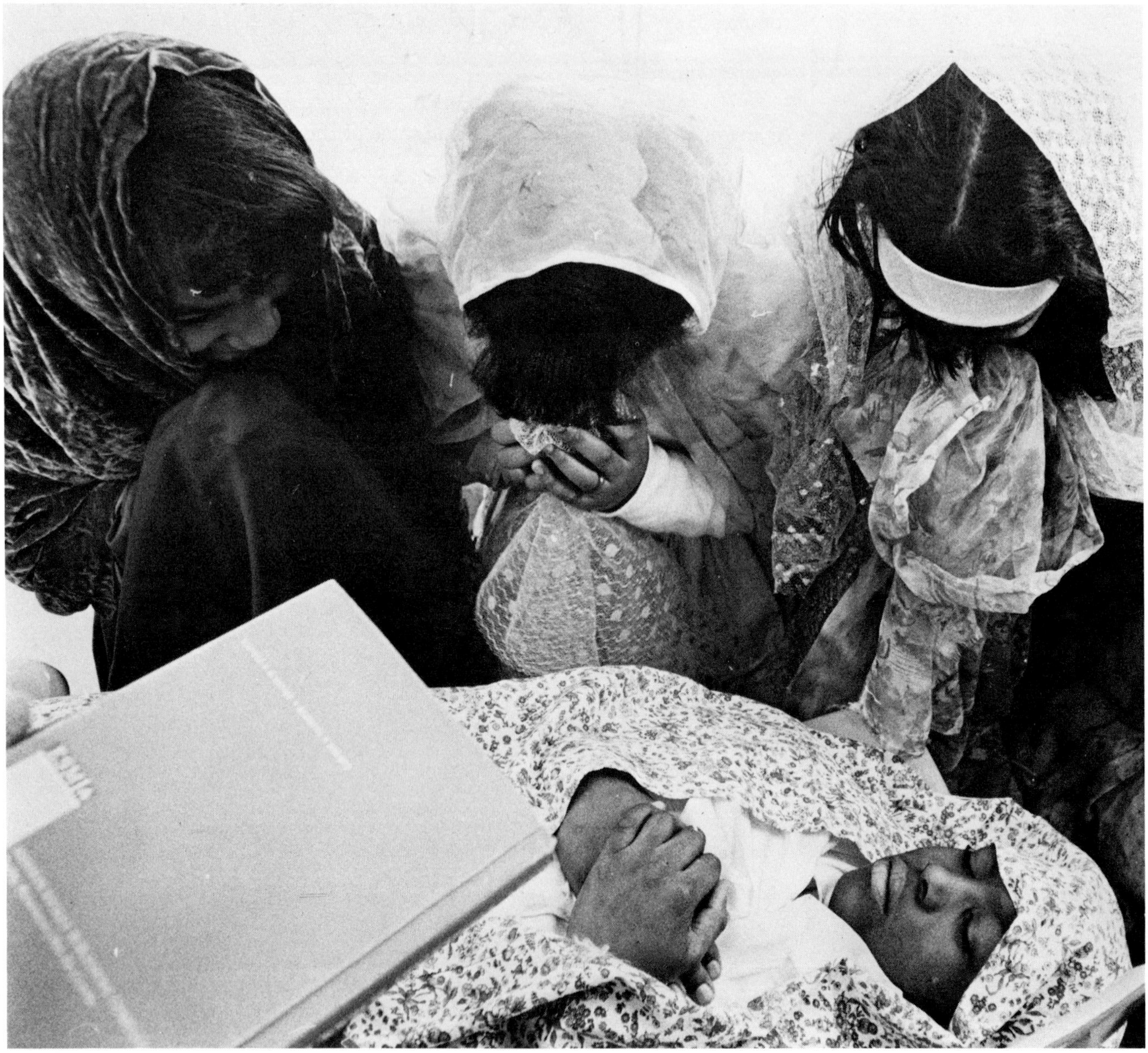

EXPERIENCES II: FOCUS

From Involvement...into Focus

"MY MAJOR PROBLEM IS THAT THE CHILDREN DON'T KNOW HOW TO CONCENTRATE," SAID A TEACHER AT A MEETING. "IF THEY COULD PUT THEIR MINDS ON ONE THING AT A TIME, THEY'D BE ABLE TO DO SOME ORIGINAL THINKING."

OBSERVE YOUNG CHILDREN ABSORBED IN THEIR PLAY ACTIVITIES. IT SEEMS SO NATURAL TO THEM. WHAT *IS* THIS ABILITY TO ACHIEVE TOTAL ABSORPTION? WHAT HAPPENS TO DISSIPATE THIS ABILITY?

IT TAKES INTEREST AND SELF-DISCIPLINE TO FOCUS OUR MINDS, OUR IMAGINATIONS, OUR PERCEPTIONS AND OUR BODIES. GIVING OUR FULL ATTENTION TO A TASK OR AN IDEA IS A KIND OF LIBERATION. CONCENTRATION CAN SET US FREE TO BE CREATIVE...AS WELL AS TO REALIZE CURRICULUM OR LIFE GOALS.

TO ENABLE YOUNG PEOPLE TO BRING THEIR CREATIVE ENERGIES TO "CREATIVE DRAMA," I'VE FOUND IT VALUABLE TO SPEND TIME — AS MUCH AS NECESSARY — IN ISOLATING "FOCUS" WITH THEM SO THEY CAN RECOGNIZE IT, USE IT, AND DIRECT IT.

Keith

At teachers' meetings someone inevitably begged that something be done about Keith. He never lighted in one spot long enough to study anything. He was like quicksilver; now you had him, now he was gone. He ranged through the halls, looking in at classes, picking fights, bullying younger students. For long hours he sat in the office — as punishment, but performing as unofficial receptionist when strangers walked in.

In Drama it was seldom better. An idea might catch his interest. In a loud voice he would direct others what to do. He didn't see or hear me or anyone else. Fifteen minutes later he was gone.

The others in class shrugged when asked their suggestions. "Oh, that's Keith. He doesn't put his mind to anything." Put his mind to — they

had caught it. How to entice him into an experience of commitment. An experience which didn't allow him to boss others, swagger, or duck out. To capture his imagination for one session in a way so gratifying to him that it would awaken his desire to repeat it.

It happened unexpectedly. We had invited Pearl Primus to give an African dance demonstration at school. The three students handling arrangements were called to the office phone. Five minutes later their desolate faces were at the door. "She's dead. She's being buried tomorrow," they uttered in one wail.

No, it turned out, it wasn't the dancer, but her aged mother. The funeral would be at the hour we had scheduled for the workshop. I explained the situation to the class. "What an unusual funeral that will be," I mused. "There'll probably be artists and dancers, musicians, dramatists and diplomats attending from all over the world. The mother was a great lady herself."

"Couldn't we hold the funeral here?"

Keith was speaking. Not with bluster and sarcasm. His voice was soft, eager, responding to the picture my words had summoned up for him, responding to some inner association all his own.

I looked around in surprise as agreement sounded from all over the room. The next day we would hold a funeral at the same hour as the real one.

"We'll need a corpse. . .or should we just use a bundle?" asked James. "Can I. . .can I be the corpse?" Again from Keith. He was serious. His eyes looked directly at me, as though seeing me for the first time. Everyone sensed the intensity of his request.

I compelled myself to ask the class for "any other volunteers." No one volunteered.

To be "foreign dignitaries," each eighth grader in the group wrapped fabric about themselves in styles considered "international." Some covered their heads. Eugene was the preacher, carrying a large book and wearing our choir robe. Three girls were the dancer-daughter and her sisters. William was the choir, in his beautiful husky voice, softly singing church songs. And there lay Keith along a gym bench, swathed in pieces of lace and silk, all carefully arranged, his eyes closed, his arms crossed upon his chest.

There he lay for one hour — not stirring. Relaxed. . .serious. . .involved. Twice he "shushed" some mourners who giggled slightly as they approached to "view the body." As players knelt in front of his coffin, his face became a shade more serious. Once I caught him gazing serenely as the preacher spoke of the love everyone felt for this "adored woman."

At the end, when we held our critique, the class was enthusiastic about how real it had felt. "It was scary. . ." "I forgot we were only in the gym." "Do you think it was really like that in New York today?" "Get off; they were in a real church in Harlem." "I thought Keith was a good corpse." There was a murmur of agreement, some of it reluctant. Keith's face slowly expanded into a grin, then he chortled. He said nothing. He sat and listened.

Who can guess what need was filled for Keith that day? Sometimes we may have an indication of causes. There I had none. Nor did it matter. It was a chance happening that we held the funeral. It served to catch his interest.

I talked to Keith after class, about what his concentration as the corpse had done for the entire class. "You helped hold the improvisation together by your seriousness," I told him. He listened, his face in a half smile containing his own inner meaning. I resisted the temptation to delve. How tenuous is that moment of self-discovery. How private. Too many words, the wrong intonation — and a teacher has "blown it."

He came early to the next class. He sat down near me in the circle, keeping an eye on the others. If someone whispered or giggled he glared at them. He was ready now to assume involvement in Creative Drama. He had found his way to begin to focus his imagination and his energies.

IT'S NOT ALWAYS SO DRAMATIC. NOR DO WE ALWAYS STUMBLE ON THE NEEDED IDEA OR CHARACTERIZATION SO EASILY. BUT THE IMPERATIVE REMAINS: TO LEAD AN INDIVIDUAL TO FIND HIS/HER WAY TO FOCUS MIND AND BODY, FANTASY AND INTELLECT, AS PREREQUISITE FOR LEARNING, AND FOR DOING. HOW EXHILARATING IS THE EXPERIENCE OF GETTING TOTALLY INVOLVED IN A BOOK, A PROBLEM OF LOGIC, MAKING SOMETHING, WORKING IN AN ART FORM. TO LOSE ONESELF IS, IN A SENSE, TO FIND ONESELF.

One way in to Focus

"How many of you have cameras at home?" Almost every hand is in the air.

"Have you a photo print which is blurred?" Half the hands are up again.

"Why is that photo blurred?"

Sam answers flatly, "Cuz you moved...or the camera moved...when you took it."

"Okay. Sam's given one reason. Any others?"

"The lens wasn't focused," comments Daryl.

"Let's try both these reasons out for ourselves." I have a polaroid camera in class for the occasion. We quickly turn on the spot lights, pose a few self-conscious students, and take turns having different students adjust the action of the camera; and then take a roll of pictures. For some shots they steady their aim. For other shots, they move slightly on purpose. So we get sharp shots and blurred shots.

I also have some small instamatics and box cameras, vintage 1930, available. Each team of three takes a camera, without film. Individually, a student focuses on a single object in the room. I tell them

> Decide upon and focus on one object only: a shoe, a clock, a light source. Eliminate as many extraneous details from the camera frame as possible. Focus so that the object of your choice is sharp.

This takes some doing. Some understanding. Next I ask each person what he or she is focusing upon.

> You make the decision for the eye of the camera. Therefore, first you have to select. The camera doesn't have the brain. You do.

It takes time to help each person understand what they're doing. I ask if they can describe what it means to focus — in words. Gradually we list some responses on the portable board (the only real touch of academia I need in the space):

> Put your eye to it
> Put your mind on it
> See something as though it's all that's there.

Now I ask each person to make the smallest possible aperture with his fingers or through a piece of paper. Looking through this tiny opening, they focus on one small object again. This time they will focus their minds further. "Put your mind to work thinking about that object...what it's made of; where its materials are from; how it was made; how it felt in each place of its life. Build a story of its history, in your mind, as though you *are* the object. Then we'll ask each other questions to build a kind of biography."

Sheila says it's silly for her to be an electric switch. Everyone laughs. "A lot of people can use their imaginations more easily when they think of themselves *in* a situation, or *as* something or someone. If you try this and it doesn't work for you, then just try to think as much about your object as you can. The questions by the class may help you later."

After five or six minutes the student director calls "Time!" James offers to start. I ask the first questions. As soon as the way is opened, the others eagerly take over. James is not to tell what he is. The class will try to accumulate the evidence and guess. But not before he asks them to.

"Where are you from?" I ask.

"Canada, I think. Yes, the Canadian Rockies."

"How long were you there and why'd you leave?" asks Janis.

"One day I was chopped down by people wearing metal hats."

From continuing suggestions we learn that he moved from Canada by truck with some relatives to a big building on a river. He fainted. When he came to all his bark was gone. Then came a trip by water.

Another factory. Coffee being spilled on him. Nails driven through him. He was bundled into four tight walls, "real comfy," bounced, thrown, until he heard his walls rip apart and saw sunlight. Placed on a floor. Greeted by relatives in the floor. Something round and heavy edged on top of him. Wriggled. Something sticky and sweet stuck under him. "What am I?"

Every student's hand shot into the air. "He's a chair."

The session ended by measuring other experiences against the definitions on the board. Did you put your eye to it? Did you put your mind on it? Your imagination? As you were thinking, were you able to focus with no other thoughts intruding?

BY LEARNING TO FOCUS OUR ENERGIES, OUR IMAGINATIONS, OUR WHOLE BEING, WE CAN FIND WAYS TO SOLVE MANY PROBLEMS THROUGHOUT EDUCATION. IN CREATIVE DRAMA AND THE OTHER ARTS, THIS ABILITY OPENS THE WAY TO FULLEST PARTICIPATION. IF TIME HAD ALLOWED IN THE ABOVE CLASS, I WOULD HAVE LIKED TO HAVE THEM DO AN IMPROVISATION IN WHICH NOBODY WAS FOCUSED, NO ONE LISTENED, OR ANSWERED WHAT WAS ASKED. THEN TO REPEAT THE SAME SCENE IN FULL "FOCUS." BUT ALL THAT'S AHEAD, AND WILL GRADUALLY COME CLEAR. WE'RE BUILDING THE STANDARDS, THE PROGRESSION, THE EXPECTATIONS — AND THE PLEASURES OF GROUP SHARING.

Differentiating between real and fake

"I'm mad. I'm so mad. . .I could just throw everything around. I hate every single one of you. I hate this building. . .I hate this rug. . .I hate. . ." As I spoke, I smiled, swung my crossed legs casually and used a super-sweet voice.

"You don't sound mad to me," ventured Chris.

"You mean I don't sound real?" I threw off the guise.

Others laughed. "Course not. People sound different when they're mad, like. . ."

"Like what? Cross the room, anyone, as you do when you're furious about something."

Jackie threw herself into it first, clenching her fists and her jaw as she stalked across the room to the door. Suddenly she took it in both hands, and, uttering an oath in a low, controlled voice, she swung it open and banged it shut.

I'd made my point about "fake" and "real." They all had quick associations with people who seemed "fake" — dentists and nurses scored low because they could say so nicely, "This isn't going to hurt you." The students were more careful not to name names as they imitated certain teachers doling out punishment, certain students putting on fake airs. The class howled at John's imitation of a lady he delivers newspapers to, talking to him as though he were her French Poodle.

We began to talk about plastic products and "plastic" behavior in people who hide their real feelings. We got into artificial foods and fabrics. From there it was easy to move to "real" and "fake" in our workshops. Students began to see that when an action or a characterization is done to impress others, it tends to be fake. The player, in that case, is concerned with how it looks to others rather than what he/she is doing, and why. We tried a few out together, first really doing the action, then faking it.

- Unlock your front door
- Untie a shoelace
- Write a check
- Eat an ice cream cone

We analyzed the actions for their truth in terms of (1) shape, (2) weight, (3) texture, (4) muscle involvement, and (5) details of action that are needed. Next, in groups of two, I asked them to plan and share a simple action, once fake, once real:

- playing a game
- eating
- repairing something
- making something
- cleaning something

Our critique after each action centered on the focus evidenced in dealing with the size of an object, its shape, weight, texture, placement, operating the object, and working together with teammates.

We explored voices for "real" and "fake." I assigned literary paragraphs for quick interpretation in groups of twos and threes. Privately they analyzed the real feeling of the selection. They presented it to the group once as real. Then they burlesqued it, playing against it. A tragic tale was told as though it were a weather report. A poem by John Ciardi was delivered as a mystery story. "Friends, Romans, Countrymen" was presented as though it were whispered gossip.

Larry suggested real and fake in facial expressions. A new idea. He showed how he looks interested to get the teacher off his back about homework, "but really it's fake because I'm thinking about a game after school."

We spent the remaining time preparing a pantomime to be tried out at home and brought to the next class. What pantomime is; what it isn't; how it differs from the traditional art of mime, how it requires intense focus. As they left, I noticed three boys taking gigantic steps across the room. "We're faking climbing through mud puddles to get to the door," they explained.

CHALLENGES II: FOCUSING MIND AND BODY

Breathing — for focus and for life

"Everyone breathes. . .to live. Why give it special attention in Creative Drama?" many teachers ask.

To which I must answer, in a more serious tutorial manner than usual, "Ancient civilizations recognized that proper exercise and breathing served physical and mental health, alertness, and self-awareness. Today natural processes like breathing, walking and speaking often become *un*natural, affected by the pace and tensions of our lives and by our lack of strenuous physical activity. Can we who are concerned about young people afford to ignore these prerequisites for mental and physical re-conditioning?"

Watch a young girl in seventh grade. She's constantly tensed as though school dismissal is two seconds off. She's quick in gym but her movements are stiff and unyielding. In class, she rarely puts her mind to anything. Her breathing is shallow; she never takes long, deep breaths filling her lungs. She never stops long enough, even to breathe. Six months of daily work in Gym — and breathing in Drama — can help her health and study habits.

Let me introduce breathing here for FOCUSING the attention of mind and body, but also as a way toward invigorating the body and relaxing nervous tension. Try these for several weeks, a few minutes a day, and see what you think.

INITIATING AWARENESS: Observe animals and babies for one week to see how they breathe. Have each person share an imitation of what he/she observed. They will probably recognize the baby's stomach moves in and out; so, too, does the lying-down dog's, cat's, cow's.

On hands and knees, pant like a dog. Rapidly breathe in and out. Place one hand on the stomach to check its action on inhalation and exhalation.

Take a deep breath. Many people immediately raise their shoulders and tighten their throats. This indicates shallow breathing. . .too little air to supply oxygen to the brain and other organs. And tension in the throat affects the voice box and the spine, generating tension up into the skull.

Exploring inhalation/exhalation through imagery

- Take an empty balloon. Blow in a little air. Let it seep out. Blow it full. Let it out in one energetic gasp. Compare this balloon to our lungs and to the diaphragm, a muscle under the lungs which moves down and forward to allow air into the lungs, and contracts back in to press the air out of the body.

- Concentrate on picturing the air entering your nostrils. Sense it moving through the nose, down the throat, past the vocal chords, pushing into the lower cavities of the lungs, shoving out the disphragm muscles. Think of the oxygen coursing through the veins of the feet and arms and brain. Then, as you exhale, try to sense the gradual emptying of all air from your body. Notice that without air in the body you can't even speak your name.

For the "cleansing breath" (best seated crosslegged on the floor):

- Inhale about a third of a lungful of air, expanding abdomen.

- Forcefully pull in abdomen, quickly pushing air out through your nose.

- Immediately take another partial breath through the nose while expanding abdomen outward again.

- Again, force air out through nose with same quick forcefulness; pull abdomen in.

Establish a steady rhythm as this is repeated ten times. The emphasis is upon the forceful EXPULSION of air through the nose and the contraction of stomach muscles. Try this before beginning any activities in class.

MY YOGA EXPERT, RUTH GOLDEN SAYS, "WHEN ONE'S MIND IS INTENT ON THE BREATH, THERE'S NO ROOM TO THINK OF ANYTHING ELSE. THIS EQUALS RELAXATION...THE OPENING OF THE MIND AND THE BODY."

For a morning wakeup, have everyone sit back on their haunches, toes turned under. Breathe in on four to six counts. Hold breath for six counts. Let it out on a sustained "Hoooooo....." (sounding like the waterfront at dusk) as slowly as each person can. They may reach ten seconds, or twenty, or more.

Next, replace the "Hooooo" with a whispered tongue twister, a nonsense rhyme, numbers, or an ancient chant. Or, let one student lead with a sentence while the others echo on the outgoing breath:

> A tooter who tooted a flute tried to tutor two tooters to toot; said the two to the tooter, is it harder to toot, or to tutor two tooters to toot?

(Yes, all on one exhaled breath.)

If the class begins to yawn, it's not a sign of boredom. Rather it shows that they are, indeed, breathing more deeply and focusing their attention on what they're doing. It's the extra oxygen coursing through their bodies which is relaxing them.

Notice, too, how stooped bodies have to straighten to allow the diaphragm muscle to stretch. Extend these, and other, exercises to include flowing movements of the arm, torso, and legs; i.e., stretching to pull down a bell rope on the exhalation; inhale as the rope pulls you back up. Start observing breathing patterns of others. People do express themselves as much by their breathing as by their rhythm, movements, and mannerisms.

Focusing through movement: Labyrinth

"Imagine that we are all in a gigantic building, full of corridors and stairways, secret passageways, doors, and crawl-spaces. Each one of us is lost in this maze. We want to find each other or just to find our way out. it is dark. We can barely see; sometimes we can't see at all, and move only by feeling the walls with our hands.

"Will you each start at a point of the outer limits and design of your own corridor, moving straight ahead, turning curving, zig-zagging. Go under, over; include angles. After you set up your route, go back and forth along it several times to be sure you can repeat it exactly. Know exactly where you go straight; where you turn. Because you are alone, you have no reason to talk or laugh. If you meet another person at a junction, give way for each other without seeing each other. Maintain your aloneness. In silence, then, let's start."

Twenty-five bodies are soon creating a maze of linear patterns about the room. When I feel that most of them are sure of their routes, I will add suggestions:

- Move in very slow motion (a drum beat can help).

- Go over your route in speed-up.

- Go backwards for ten counts; forward, fifteen counts. Keep your hands on a low ceiling you imagine overhead.

- The walls are getting closer; push against them as you move sideways.

- You think you see something in the shadows moving toward you; you are frightened.

Another day I might approach this a little differently. For example:

- Ruth, walk your route moving two beats; stopping two beats.

- Marie, walk your route with one stiff leg; sit down every twelve beats for sixteen beats.

- Dennis, walk your route: sixteen fast steps, then a pose, a different one each time you stop, for ten counts.

Each person counts his own beats. All are moving simultaneously again. Sounds can also be added when they are ready to maintain their focus.

MUSIC IS HELPFUL TO SET AND SUSTAIN A MOOD FOR THIS ACTIVITY. THE STUDENT WHO IS NOT ABLE TO REMEMBER A ROUTE OR SUSTAIN SERIOUSNESS SHOULD BE TAKEN ASIDE SO THAT THE GROUP IS UNDISTURBED. GIVE THAT STUDENT SOMETHING ELSE TO DO WHICH WILL NOT MAKE HIM/HER SELF-CONSCIOUS, LIKE HANDLING THE RECORD PLAYER AT

YOUR SIGNAL, OR PROVIDING SUBTLE INTERFERENCE TO TEST THE CONCENTRATION OF OTHERS, SUCH AS WALKING UP TO SOMEONE TO CHECK IF HE/SHE WILL GO AROUND THE INTERFERENCE.

Labyrinth can be developed in many ways, as you will find. Our main purpose, at this time, is building conscious focus by having individuals working at the same time, but alone. Later, as an extension of Labyrinth, have students, when they encounter another person along the route, instead of ignoring each other, find a non-verbal way of greeting each other.

Mirror

This largely non-verbal activity between two or more people encourages all kinds of movement with lessening self-consciousness and increasing daring. The focus between leader and follower is the meaning.

Start with the entire group mirroring you. In this way you can set the concept of reflected image — a right hand reflects your left, etc. — and check out who needs assistance. Move slowly. Don't get too tricky. Use large fluid movements of the arms and the legs, posture changes of the torso. Have fun with it. When each individual understands how a mirror reflects him/her, then divide up. Explain that the objective is to develop such a flow between leader and follower that a casual observer won't be able to tell who is leading. The leader must time his movements carefully, in consideration for the follower.

In Twos and Fours

You call: "Lead only with the right arm;" "Lead only with legs;" "Lead only with arms and upper torso." This helps the leaders begin to explore what they can do with each part of the body. It also helps them become more inventive. When you feel they're ready, release them to use full bodies: symmetrical movements, assymetrical, abstract or natural actions.

As the students become adept, one team can mirror another team. This takes a lot of practice by the four involved. It's an achievement in coordination when one team has so absorbed the flow of action of another team that they move as one.

For example, the first member of the mirror team follows the first member of the leader team; the second follows the second. Try an action requiring two people: At a soda fountain, a waiter serving a customer. Shopping in a large store. Forming letters of the alphabet, slow motion. Air sculpture.

In the full group again, PASS THE MASK. In twos, students tend to fall apart with mirth. It's a bit threatening to look someone else full in the face all at once.

Sit in a circle. All together, explore the muscles that move on the face: brows, forehead, cheeks, jaws, chin, nostrils, lips. Up down, around, left and right. Then, the first person slowly assumes a facial expression: a grumpy look, a surprised look, etc. The second person watches and copies it; holds it briefly, and slowly changes it into a different expression which in turn is assumed by the third person.

After going around once or twice, they are ready to try this in teams.

Some Mirror variations

- Mirror styles of fighting: dueling, boxing, wrestling, swords, judo. (For safety, state loud and clear that a subject and its mirror *never* touch!)

- "Fun House" exaggeration mirrors. There is all measure of opportunity here. Leader does a simple, confined action; mirror must exaggerate or distort the action into a caricature.

- Mirrored characterizations. The mirror(s) gradually discover WHO he/she is becoming as a result of details added by leader. For example, in action, in putting on items of clothing, in hair styling or other accoutrements; in change of posture. Santa might be revealed by beard, nose, fattened belly, boots, sack over shoulders, jolly expression, silent laugh; a cat by ears, fur, tail, whiskers, getting on four paws, cleaning itself.

- Rear-view car mirrors. One person is the "car." He/she initiates the action which the person in front (the car mirror) reflects. The "car" behind reflects the car mirror.

- Mirror sounds. First have the group explore the many tones, inflections, variations which the voice can produce. Try them all out. A high, thin sound, elongated. A bubbling sound. A ticking sound. A guttural sound. You will lead to start.

After lots of experiment with sounds, add combinations of words expressed in many variations of tonal pattern. Rising and falling. Questioning. Monotone. Elongated vowels. Clicking consonants. Nasalized n's and m's.

Next, try story telling — with a student leading and the group mirroring a few words at a time. The timing cannot be as precise when they are waiting to hear what word to produce. But the unity of effort can be maintained, even extended, as they wonder what the leader will add next.

ALLOW OPPORTUNITIES FOR THE TEAMS TO SHARE EACH OTHER'S EFFORTS AFTER A WHILE. DISCUSS HOW THEY FEEL. ARE THEY WORKING TOGETHER? CAN ONE REALLY SEE THE FLOW OF MOVEMENT BETWEEN THEM AS THOUGH THEY'RE BOTH LEADING AND BOTH FOLLOWING. ABOVE ALL, CONSTANTLY REINFORCE THAT A TEAM IS WORKING WELL TOGETHER DUE TO THEIR *INTENSE FOCUS* ON EACH OTHER.

MIRROR IS AN ACTIVITY WHICH CAN BE REPEATED REGULARLY THROUGH THE YEAR FOR DIFFERENT PURPOSES. SOMETIMES IT'S A WARMUP WHEN YOU FEEL THAT FOCUS IS WEAKENING. SOMETIMES IT'S JUST A WAY OF GETTING THE BODIES MOVING IN FREE, FLOWING WAYS. OTHER TIMES YOU MAY WANT TO USE IT TO EXPLORE MOVEMENT POSSIBILITIES RELATED TO A PARTICULAR PROBLEM.

CHILD DRAMA. Peter Slade. University of London Press, Ltd., London, 1954.
  Also INTRODUCTION TO CHILD DRAMA, 1958; EXPERIENCES OF SPONTANEITY, 1968.
YOGA U.S.A. Richard Hittleman. A Bantam Minibook, New York, 1968.

A good source for the British and other hard-to-find drama books is The Drama Bookshop, 152 West 52nd St., New York City

A Poem

The door closes
I am hidden now
Hidden from all life
For I have been hurt
I am not like everyone else
I dont have a doorbell.

Gretchen Henry

EXPERIENCES III: IMAGINATION

> One of the roles of the arts in education is to give people the capacity to imagine beyond the scope of their daily existence...to see the things to be put together differently, in order that relationships between people might be different.
> John C. Pittinger
> Secretary of Education,
> Pennsylvania

With young children it is still easy to stir up the imaginations. A fanciful story, a selection of music, a wishing feather, a magic cloth...and all the world and all the people in it can change.

With older students the barriers are up; the images are programmed; the responses are more predictable. Imagination is there — but harder to unlock.

The hunger to express oneself

> Dear Ms. Wilder: I have loved making improvisations and I have loved being in Drama. I think Creative Drama like you make us do it should be in every school because we use our imaginations and it lets us be lots of different people and because it lets us say what we feel. Thank you.
> Karen

That note was slipped into my drawer by Karen at graduation time. Karen, two years earlier: good, obedient, quiet, dull. Karen, eyes cast down, face guarded, body hunched over into a perpetual S-shape. Her cumulative folder said, next to each subject, "Fair." "Fair." "Fair." One teacher in fourth grade had written: "Never offers an idea of her own. No imagination."

Our guidance counselor seized upon that comment and sent Karen to Special Drama — a group of eleven students meeting with me twice weekly. All were good/obedient/quiet/dull/ students. Each had a communication problem serious enough to be detected in the school testing. I was to work with them on "Speech" until a Remedial Speech Therapist was hired.

We stood in the doorway of our small attic room, contemplating the peeling walls, dirty windows, and accumulated academic discards of many years. One boy eased our dismay. "Can't this be like having our own clubhouse? Up here...nobody'll know what we're doing."

Everyone plunged into moving and cleaning. All but Karen, who slumped on a box staring out the window. When others prodded her to lift something, she did it. When we sat down in the cleared space to plan what to do next, she stared at the floor and said nothing.

"What colors can we paint this room?" They first responded with colors they thought a teacher would like: beige, green; white. I was non-committal. They got bolder. A bright blue like Kevin's shirt. A bright orange on the wall that arched into the ceiling. And the ceiling? "Black," mumbled Karen.

With their hands occupied with paint brushes and their muscles busy reaching and bending, the inner language began to pour forth. They all began to share ideas, dreams, fears, family situations. Even some ghost stories and superstitions. Occasionally they giggled.

I heard Karen, wielding a paint brush, confide to another girl, "If you see a man with a black hat at night, do you know what that means?" Dressed in a freshly pressed smock each time, she painted slowly and painstakingly. I saw her laugh once when someone tripped over the paint can. She laughed again when the room was finished. She stared at the ceiling and giggled, as if in surprise that it was really done.

But the curriculum calls for speech classes

I felt pressured into starting them by the expectations of the other teachers. The students froze. The special ambiance of their "clubhouse" was ruptured. The stuttering was back. Karen returned to sit and stare out the window.

I threw out my lesson plans, and explained my reasons to the school psychologist and the guidance counselor. I told them what I wanted to try. Later that week I brought in a puppet stage, placed it on a table, and went downstairs.

When I returned, I heard voices arguing and screaming. The door was slightly open. Peeking in, I saw only Karen standing behind the stage. On her right hand was stuck a ball of twine. An empty film carton was on two fingers of her left hand. With these as puppets, she was holding an impassioned argument. Her face, showing above it all, was alternately pleading and furious.

I made lots of noise in the hall as though I'd dropped all my books. Then I entered the room barely looking her way. Already the "puppets" were back on my desk. Karen sat, slumped, on the stool. The only give-away was the flush on her cheeks and the lingering animation in her eyes.

WHY WAS KAREN UNABLE TO SHARE OF HERSELF IN HER SCHOOL LIFE? ARE WE INVADERS WHEN WE TRY TO WOO A STUDENT TO SHARE IMAGINATIVE IDEAS?

WHEN A PERSON ANSWERS A THOUGHT OR FEELING QUESTION WITH "I DON'T KNOW" ARE THEY REALLY SAYING "I'M AFRAID TO RISK LETTING YOU KNOW. . .YOU MIGHT LAUGH AT ME. I'LL JUST STAY HIDDEN WHERE I'M SAFE."

BY USING THE INFINITE POSSIBILITIES OF CREATIVE DRAMA, WE ARE OFFERING TEMPTING MORSELS TO THE EXPRESSIVE IMAGINATIONS OF EACH YOUNG PERSON...TRYING TO ENCOURAGE THEM GENTLY TO COME FORTH, TO DARE EXPRESS THEMSELVES, TO DARE BECOME SELF-ACTUALIZING PEOPLE SHARING RESPONSIBLY WITH OTHERS.

Imagination is coupled with feelings

> I liked when we showed our feelings best. It was scarey how Ruth screamed at me because her dog was hit in that improvisation. She was too real. I wish I could act like that. Once my dog was hit and I know how she felt.
> Daryl

Thank goodness, educational theory today encourages the recognition and expression of feelings within your classroom in many ways. Confluent education, I think it's now called, dealing with both the intellectual and the emotional needs of the child.

Drama has to make way for feelings. But it takes time for people, at any age, to trust each other enough to express more than obvious emotions in stereotyped ways.

When Ruth let out that piercing scream in her improvisation, we all knew, without saying it, that she trusted us enough to *risk* revealing her deeper feelings. There were one or two self-conscious giggles which were quickly shushed by the other students. Three months into drama, this group was, generally, ready to be sensitive to each other.

SO OFTEN TODAY WE ENCOUNTER THE ATTITUDE: PLAY IT COOL. DON'T RISK SHOWING HOW YOU FEEL. HERE IS ONE WAY I LEAD INTO THE RECOGNITION AND EXPRESSION OF FEELINGS. IT'S OUR LINK, I TRY TO SUGGEST, TO ALL OF HUMANITY.

Priming the imagination: a class of 7th and 8th graders

I hold up a large blank canvas or sheet of paper. A box of vivid crapas and pastels are near me on the table. I ask everyone to empty their minds and just sit staring at some spot of the room.

"Your faces right now are like this blank canvas. Can you see why?" Several will take a chance with some guesses. Each one is right, in a way. They're sensing my drift.

"Does this canvas tell you anything? What happens to it when I add a stroke of purple?"

Several think it looks more interesting. I ask a student to add another stroke of color upon the canvas. She adds a blob of red. Again we respond to the change of the canvas. Dots of gold are added. A swirling movement of green. Other tones of green.

Isn't this what emotions do to a blank face? Emotions are the colors, the lines, masses and spots which make you alive. Your emotions start deep inside you. You can't just slap them on, like the crapas.

We try some of this out by discussing the colors each person associates with different emotions. Soon we have a lengthy list. We represent the external stereotypes of anger, sorrow, joy, surprise, grumpiness, etc.

Next we relate the emotions to the human voice. What colors can be added to a blank voice? How? We read sentences DEAD PAN (the way too many people read naturally and don't even hear.) We exchange DEAD PAN jokes. We "pass" a mystery story, telling it DEAD PAN. We're ready to try out some DEAD PAN scenes.

BE SURE THE WINDOWS AND THE DOOR ARE CLOSED. THIS CAN BE AN HILARIOUS WORKSHOP.

What is a dead pan scene?

Start with a trial group. Ask for a suggestion of an emergency situation — i.e., awakening in your home one morning to find the floors are under several feet of water. Or any other catastrophic problem. Improvise it with absolutely no feeling, no expression. Speak in a monotone. Be DEAD PAN.

Someone comments that some news commentators talk this way. "Fifteen hundred people killed in an earthquake" is spoken in the same voice as "the weather today is sunny and humid."

They improvise the DEAD PAN scene once in a toneless, unanimated manner. Then they redo this improvisation a second time, using animation, playing it "real."

THE RESTRICTIVE QUALITY OF DEAD PAN OFTEN RELEASES A NEED FOR ANIMATION. THE SECOND TIME EMOTIONS TEND TO FLOW EASILY.

Relating the emotions to literary characters

An 8th grade class asked to improvise Shakespeare's *Romeo and Juliet*. Not to enact the script, but to start from the characterizations and the conflicts and the feelings. I asked Marlene to improvise Juliet one day.

"How do I know how Juliet feels in this scene? I'm not her," she answered, reneging. "But you are her," I maintained earnestly. "Let's find out in what moment of your own life you are Juliet. Has there ever been a time when you've disobeyed your parents? In any way?"

She thinks a moment. A mischievous look comes into her eyes. She nods.

"Have you ever liked a boy, even though you knew your parents wouldn't approve of him?" Without a pause, she nods. "I never even let him walk near my block for that reason."

"But you met him anyway?"

She laughs. Then she pulls back, on guard. "Well, for a little while."

"All these feelings and experiences are part of Juliet. She met Romeo, who was from a family at war with hers. She was thirteen at the time."

"I'm thirteen."

"Juliet disobeyed her parents more than you might dream. She married Romeo."

"At thirteen!" Marlene looks disbelieving. "I wouldn't go that far!"

OF COURSE THE POINT HAS BEEN MADE. YOU MAY HAVE RECOGNIZED THAT THIS WAY OF WORKING STEMS FROM THE RUSSIAN THEATRE DIRECTOR, STANISLAVSKI. IT'S USEFUL FOR THE ACTOR; IT'S EVERY BIT AS USEFUL IN THE CREATIVE DRAMA WORKSHOP TO LEAD STUDENTS TO DIG OUT OF THEIR OWN FEELINGS AND REACH EMPATHY WITH THE LIFE OF ANOTHER.

Can a person imagine beyond the known?

Through our roles as guide and catalyst, we have the additional responsibility of priming the fantasy to consider other ways, other lives, other aesthetics, other combinations. We can begin where the student is, with interests, appetites, possibilities which are known. Then, by offering stimuli from literature and the arts, and from pure conjecture, we can try to stretch into the realms of the original, the creative, opening the way for new values and hopeful future possibilities.

THE HEADLINE NEWS COMING INTO THE SCHOOL PROMPTED THIS EXPLORATION. WE'RE EXPOSED TO SO MUCH VIOLENCE AND CRIME. DO YOUNG PEOPLE STOP TO QUESTION CAUSES? TO ASK HOW THEY MIGHT REACT THEMSELVES IF TRAPPED BY THE SAME SITUATIONS?

Our class arrived after reading headlines on the Attica prison riots in New York. Said one boy, "Ugh, they're all crazy...criminals!" Janice wasn't sure. "I wonder what it's like to be in a prison. Can they have visitors?" A few had relatives in jail; they remained silent.

I sent some of them to check on the size of the cells at Attica. Our librarian had clipped information from many papers. "Eight by eight! For two men!" was the information they brought back. We moved our portable screens to shape an area 8' by 8'. Two feet longer than a bed. Low ceiling. Toilet: a hole in the floor. Bars all around.

Two students were placed in the space at a time. Others marched up and down shouting, the way they thought guards might do.

"Human beings have to live in THAT! I thought I was crowded sharing a bedroom three times that size with my brother. And we only go in there to sleep." "That would drive me crazy." With imaginations stimulated, we improvised the feelings of caged human beings.

The next day, three students showed me a letter they'd written to the governor. If people were treated like caged animals, they wrote, how could they ever be helped by prisons to become human beings again?

Testing the social fabric

After imagining the prison space at Attica as it affected the prisoners, the students initiated a file of profiles on the inmates, based on TV, radio, and newspaper reports. They wanted to know what kind of people these were who dared to organize and rebel against authorities in a maximum security prison; and what they had done to be sentenced there in the first place. The concept of "political prisoners" puzzled them, as they questioned why so many prisoners were black and came from poverty.

Our workshop improvisations shifted: imagined situations in the lives of some of these people; situations in which they had no choices or in which they made a "wrong" choice. In many improvs, they were evidently testing social and anti-social acts. Chris concluded one day, "If what I do hurts only me; it's okay — it's social. BUT if it hurts another person, it's not okay; it's anti-social."

I continued to provide no answers and few opinions, just responsiveness to the directions of their thinking.

Another headline announces the incredible — a walk on the moon

"Landing in outer space. I wonder what it's like. . .to be in space, landing on the moon," said Danielle. That set us loose upon our own voyage. Following some outside research into space conditions and the preparation of the astronauts, we imagined the sensations they could be having "out there."

Before the next workshop, a student committee worked with me to clear the room. We dragged in gym mats to cover the floor. We ripped muslin into blindfolds. I brought several electronic records which contained "out-of-this-world" sounds. We attached a mike to our auxiliary speakers and enlisted the collaboration of a college intern with a fine bass voice.

The class convened in the hall. They were asked to remove their shoes and blindfold their eyes. We requested absolute silence. "You are entering outer space. . .alone. . .you are encased in a spacesuit. You remain totally silent within your space helmet, giving all your attention to the directives from the earth space station. Follow these directives exactly. May we have your solemn vow that you will not make a move on your own, lest you injure yourself. . .irreparably." So went the briefing.

One by one they were led into the darkened room. A committee member steered each one in, at one-minute intervals. Electronic sounds penetrated the air. The deep voice sounded hollowly over the amplifier as if from thousands of miles away:

> Move forward four steps. . .straight ahead. Carefully lower your body. Stretch out with arms extended overhead. Roll four turns to your left. Lie absolutely still for OM-30 counts. Reach out with your right hand perpendicular to your shoulder, until you grasp something. NO. . .STOP! PULL YOUR HAND BACK BEFORE YOU GET HURT. Crawl backwards on hands and knees eight paces. Curl forward over your knees. . .

And on. And on. Sometimes committee people provided barriers for "space-people," blocking their impending collision with one another. There were moments of total silence when you could hear only the heavy breathing of our space travelers. Then an electronic whine would cut through the air, enhancing the intensity and the mystery of the environment.

> Jump in place twelve times, preparing to spring over that mound in front of you. No, you won't make it. Wait, try another. . . six times. . .you might. . .you might just. . .

The gym mats were springy. The space voyagers were having difficulty maintaining their balance. Yet they remained totally serious.

At the end of twenty minutes, all recorded sounds grew fainter and fainter, until there was total silence. The silence held for almost a minute. Then the voice said, softly, "You may sit down. Put your head between your knees. Count sixty and remove your blindfolds. Do not stand up until you are instructed."

Blinking eyes adjusted to the lights of the room. Blinking and disoriented. Dazed. Who can measure to what extent the effects we created were overbalanced by the power of the imaginations of the blindfolded spacepeople?

STUDENTS WERE AGAIN PRIMED BY SENSE STIMULI WHICH LED THEM TO "EXPERIENCE" BEYOND THEIR OWN ENVIRONMENT. THIS KIND OF ADVENTURE ISN'T COMPLETE WITHOUT LOTS OF OPPORTUNITY FOR THE MEMBERS TO SHARE HOW THEY FELT. AFTERWARD, SHARED RESPONSES MIGHT TAKE THE FORM OF A WORD COLLAGE, A GROUP MURAL, A TAPED DISCUSSION.

How do we deal with the assertive imagination that disturbs our own expectations? Can we move with it? Can we accept diversity which is blatant?

Matt was scored a liar, a fabricator, and a general nuisance. You can't believe anything he says, was the common denunciation. And he said a lot. About all manner of things. He knew what to do when the lights blew. When your lock froze. When the keys of the piano stuck. When a notice needed to be sent around the building. When you were burglarized, vandalized, immobilized, Matt could take care of it. He had done it all. He knew what needed doing.

The disconcerting thing was, if you could get past the swagger and the boasts, he really could do a lot of things. Anything that required his hands. His hands had magic in them.

But he specialized in appearing at that precise moment of exasperation when the last thing one could abide was Matt's wide blinking eyes topping his pounding voice, "LET ME. . .I CAN DO IT!"

What is creative imagination anyway? Is it only viable when it appears, all golden and haloed, within the recognizable confines of a prize-winning composition or a painting worthy of the principal's office? Why could we not deal with the energetic imagination of 14-year-old Matt?

> "If he weren't so noisy. . ." said one colleague.

> "If he weren't so nosey. . ." said another.

> ". . .so messy. . .so repulsive. . ." said his peers.

"Matt just takes off on his own ideas. . .he's totally undisciplined. . .doesn't read through his assignments. . .ignores his outlines. . . doesn't turn homework in on time. . ." wrote a science teacher.

One day he arrived in Creative Drama with a light board he'd designed, without checking manuals or getting adult advice. It worked. A week later, he overheard me say we could use a small bell board for sound effects. He pestered me hourly until I got him some wood and money for the hardware. This time he went first to the shop teacher, then to the library. He arranged three bells on that board. They all rang.

MATT IS AT THE OTHER END OF THE CONTINUUM FROM KAREN, WHO OPENS THIS SECTION. HE INSISTS ON GETTING ATTENTION. THE MORE RESISTANCE HE ENCOUNTERS, THE MORE HE INSISTS. HE CAN BE HELPED TO INVEST ALL THIS ENERGY INTO STRETCHING AND APPLYING HIS INVENTIVENESS. HAVE WE THE PATIENCE TO APPRECIATE HIS INNATE IMAGINATIVE AND CREATIVE ABILITIES; TO HELP HIM CHANNEL THEM; HELP SOCIALIZE HIS BEHAVIOR WITHOUT SEEKING TO SQUELCH HIS ORIGINALITY?

CHALLENGES III: PRIMING THE IMAGINATION

Flow-charting

In one way or another, I'm sure you do this. I refer to the dynamic process of stimulating a group to find many imaginative possibilities during a planning session. Instead of stopping at the first idea expressed, they stretch for all the ideas they can gather, and then choose one to work with.

Here's how it might unfold:

As an activity by itself, to introduce a group to the procedure, give a word: "Green. What does it make you think of?" Responses start coming: Grass; leaves; pen; skirt; writing board; Greenhouse; evergreen; golf green; Pistachio ice cream. Elves in green caps.

Sometimes, instead of staying with the central word or theme, you may encourage the group to move in any direction their imaginations fancy. Elves in green caps might lead to goblins, pranks, mysteries, UFO's, planets, orbits. Ideas flow from each other. If you see them bogging down, you might pick up one of the central ideas or images and try to move it in another direction. "What else does greenhouse make you think of?"

Before improvisations, student groups will begin to use this process naturally. Instead of "Okay, what's your idea?" and then the interminable pause when no one has an idea because their concern is your approval, "flow-charting" makes it a stimulating free-for-all.

One day I might hold up a single object — let's say a stick. "What could this be. . .other than a short stick? Think about its physical shape, not its material. Make it shorter or longer in your imaginations."

The responses will start slowly and gain momentum:

"A thermometer."

"A spear."

"A pendulum on a clock."

"An electric cord."

"A dog's tail."

"A divining rod."

A recorder lists them all. Next, in teams of two, they decide which idea to use as *central* to a simple improvisation. It may be one that's been mentioned, or a completely new idea.

Flow charting for movement

"In how many ways can I get a heavy object across the room?"

"In how many ways can I come into a room?"

"How can you greet someone without using any words?"

"How many different ways can a person sit, stand, walk, fall, show pleasure, show anger, boredom, anticipation. . .?"

Flow charting, which some people call "Sun Bursting" and a dozen other names, is useful for a multitude of purposes. We'll use it again for *Choices* and *Conflict*. This procedure is a guarantee that a teacher doesn't stop at one answer, an answer that pre-exists in his/her own mind.

Animating the inanimate with imagination

Let me illustrate how you might proceed. We were having difficulty with the new doors in the building. Knobs torn off. Doors kicked open, kicked shut. All kinds of notices pasted or tacked on doors instead of bulletin boards. We tried a workshop on "how it feels to be a door."

First we flow-charted; all the kinds of doors in our world. Front doors, back doors, side doors, screen doors, wooden doors, glass doors, revolving doors, refrigerator doors, folding closet doors, louvered doors you can see through. We added adjectives: a broken glass door or a stuck screen door. An amazing list emerged.

For warm-ups, each person focused on the door of his/her choice. They found ways of opening and closing according to the situations I called out. "Someone's coming through you with a large package." "A kid who lives in your house can't get a key into your lock." "You just got jabbed with the wrong keys." "You were just slammed open against a back wall which smashed you closed. How do you feel?"

Later, we asked doors to speak about how they felt as people opened and closed them in different ways. I remember a revolving door screaming that it was getting dizzy as a little boy spun it round and round. And an arrogant aluminum door which opened itself with great reluctance for all sorts of riff-raff to go through.

I CAN'T PROVE THAT THIS WORKSHOP HELPED DOOR-HANDLING IN OUR BUILDING. BUT KIDS DID DISCOVER THAT, THROUGH THEIR IMAGINATIONS, THEY WERE ABLE TO SYMPATHIZE WITH DOORS. WITH IMAGINATION, WE CAN BREATHE LIFE INTO ANYTHING WE FOCUS ON. . .ANTHROPOMORPHIZE.

Nonsense makes sense too

LET ME PRONOUNCE LOUD AND CLEAR: I BELIEVE TOO IN WHIMSY, FANTASY, NONSENSE, CAPRICIOUSNESS, FLIGHTINESS, LIGHTHEARTEDNESS, HUMOR AND FRIVOLITY. IMAGINATION CAN PROVIDE THE MEANS FOR LAUGHTER, FUN FOR FUN'S SAKE, OR JUST LETTING OFF STEAM. I ENJOY A MIS-

CHIEVOUS PRANK WHEN IT'S TIMELY. I LOVE TAKING A GROUP OUT ON MYSTERY RIDES. SO YOU WILL SCARCELY BE SURPRISED THAT I HAVE EVOLVED EVENTS CALLED "FAR FETCHED DAYS," PRESCRIBED FOR HALLOWE'EN OR ANY OTHER 31ST DAY OF THE YEAR OR, FOR THAT MATTER, ANY DAYS IN BETWEEN.

Far-Fetched Day One — building an environment

When they arrive the room is somewhat awry. Some chairs are upside down. Some unusual object, like a refrigerator box, is in the center. I may be wearing a "kooky" hat or a home-made mask. The fabrics are all available. Also props which can be used in many ways: a hoop, a fish net or a volley ball net, paper bags, rope, hats, tubular jersey sacks, and stuff with which to make sounds — a washboard, roller skate wheels tied together, a bunch of tea strainers with coins inside, covered coffee cans. (The maintenance people look worried, but we do clean up.)

My first challenge to them: choose two pieces of fabric. No more, no less. Decorate yourself with them in your own way. Next, make yourself an unusual mask which feels right with your costume. Materials are on a side table: bits and pieces of cardboard, paper, string, glue, clips, pin, wool, feathers and tinsel.

In teams of two they discover ways they can move together — original ways. They experiment with sounds or voices that go with the mask, the fabrics, and their ways of moving. They start circulating about the space, exploring the rearrangement of things, using the large box and the other props placed around the room. They act and react with others. Two people, for example, may stop to hold a conversation with tea strainers. Another four or five may explore ways of shaping shadows behind a stretched, lighted piece of muslin (shadow play.)

Either they produce their own eerie music and rhythms, or use records. Often periods of silence can be the most far-fetched.

I may channel behavior by calling out "Cross the hot desert sands;" "Find your way through thick mists;" "Over there...it's speed up village, and at this side of the room everything moves in slow motion."

Eventually we begin a spontaneous improvisation started with a sentence from me and added to by others. The students know how to work now. All this nonsense is fun without falling into sheer silliness which would spoil it. They know this. A look into the room reveals a Dr. Seuss world in which A.A. Milne's heffalump would feel quite ordinary. Seuss and Milne have done much to lend sanction to the logical illogic which the imagination can produce. Which is why they and Lear and Carroll and Ciardi and others of this ilk are so loved.

Far-Fetched Day Two: Extending a Tall Tale

Here is an "Improbable Tale" from *An African Genesis* (Leo Frobenius and Douglass C. Fox). Any American tall tales can be used as well. Tell the story, then extend imaginatively beyond the story, casting the group as humans, animals, and inanimate objects.

Divide the class, for the following tale, into groups of five. In each group, three students play the three characters; the fourth provides sounds, and the fifth handles all special effects — the sack of millet, the river, or whatever the group adds to the tale.

> Three people set out on a journey. They've been turned out of their home because one heard too well, one saw too well, and one counted too well.
>
> They have a sack of millet. They cross a river. They load the grain on the boat. At midstream, one says: "A grain of millet has fallen into the water." And he jumps overboard. The one who counts so well counts all the grains in the sack and says, "He's right. There is one grain missing."
>
> In the same second, the person who sees so well reappears on the surface of the water and says, "Here it is."

Station the groups about the room. Simultaneously all groups are going to act the story as you or a student tell it. The fun of it comes from the hubbub of all the groups playing at the same time. It's also fun to give each character just one line to say at several points of the story, or a characteristic exclamation like "Humph!"

After trying out a tale this way, let the class start designing improbable tales of their own. . .building on each others' ideas. . .and acting them out in movement, sounds or words.

This becomes even more fun when they dress up in improbable ways to become improbable characters. Encourage lots of gobbledegook words and large, clumsy, gangly, gawky and outlandish movements.

AWARENESS: EXPLORING, EXPERIMENTING, EXPERIENCING. John O. Stevens. Real People Press, Box F, Moab, Utah 84532.
AFRICAN GENESIS. Leo Frobenius and Douglas C. Fox. Blom Publishing Company, New York, 1966. "Improbable Tales," pp. 153-158.
THE CREATIVE PROCESS. Ed. by Brewster Ghiselin. A Mentor Book, University of California. 1952. Read "The Biological Basis of Imagination" by R. W. Berard, pp. 226-261. Then read further into this symposium of revelations by thirty-eight creative men and women on how they create.
FANTASY AND FEELING IN EDUCATION. Richard M. Jones. Harper Colophon Books, New York. 1968.

EXPERIENCES IV: EXPRESSING AND COMMUNICATING THROUGH IMPROVISATION

WE'VE BEEN PRIMING THE IMAGINATION; WE'VE ALSO BEEN EXPANDING OUR ABILITIES TO STRUCTURE FEELINGS AND IDEAS. IT'S TIME NOW TO EXPLORE BOLDER CHALLENGES TO GROUP PLANNING AND EXPRESSION, SHAPED BY THE FORMS OF DRAMATIC IMPROVISATION.

MANY TIMES PEOPLE ASK, WHY DO YOU TAKE SO LONG IN LEADING INTO IMPROVISATION? THE STUDENTS ARE MAKING THINGS UP ALONG THE WAY...WHY CAN'T THEY JUST PLUNGE IN AND IMPROVISE FULL SCENES? WHAT'S ALL THE MYSTERY ABOUT?

An improvisation is not a skit

Let's compare the skit to an improvisation: as a tune switched on a carnival carousel playing its one-dimensional tune to a skilled musician improvising a complex jazz number with others.

When we throw students into making up a scene without all these steps of preparation, we get a skit — entertaining, obvious, and predictably superficial. To improvise in any art form requires a high level of conscious skill and a freedom to use the instrument fully, aware of all its possibilities. It'd be ridiculous to think of someone who's never studied music improvising on the French horn, for example. For drama, the instrument includes all the dimensions of ourselves.

My training sequence has evolved as part of my effort to develop a student's self-awareness, skills, and sensitive interaction with others. Above all, I hope to encourage high expectations and a taste for the genuine. By now, they will reject mere "show-off stuff" unless that's the order of the day. By now, I hope they are savoring a taste for quality and a keen critical eye — benefits for life.

> When you improvise, you can choose to be anyone, doing anything, anywhere and for any reason. Anything we can think up in our heads or read about. And believe in. We never know beforehand how it's going to end. We plan. The rest just happens. That way, it's always a surprise for me. Which is one of the reasons I like to improvise.
> 12-year-old Andy

Getting started: a sixth grade class after 2½ months of drama

Me: There are words which we use hundreds of times a day. They always sound different. Each time we say them, they mean different things. Can you think of some?

Jessee: 'Hey.' Isn't 'hey' one? You can say it like 'Hey, that's great!' or 'Hey, get outta there!'

Ruthy: (Her face lighting up) How about 'Oh?'

Rita: Or 'No.'

Delira: Or 'Yes?'

Brian: Yeah, I say 'yeah' lots of different ways. And 'Wow!' too.

We pass a single word around the circle for each person to say it with another feeling. They recognize when "No" implies "maybe;" and "please" sounds like a command.

Margie: It's really not the word that says something, is it. The word only tells what you feel inside.

SOMETIMES I START WITH GIVEN LANGUAGE SO THAT THE ENERGIES CAN GO INTO THE THINKING AND INTERACTING RATHER THAN THE SPOKEN WORDS. THEY ALSO ENCOURAGE MORE EXPRESSION THROUGH THE BODY, FACE AND EYES.

Expressing the meaning through the body — "Please/No"

I ask everyone to extend an arm. Then to withdraw it. Then to say "please" with just that arm.

"Now let's say 'Please' with our eyes; with our heads; with the entire body."

I divide the class. Half approach the others, who are seated, to implore them to do something, using just the body. The faces may be covered by paper plate masks we keep in a drawer.

We try expressing other words and meanings through the body. Some music is on the turntable to help set a mood. Sometimes the silence is enough.

Half the class are expressing refusal, now definitely, reprovingly, or with exasperation — using a foot, a shoulder, a finger, or through their backs. They're ready now for that ever adaptable exercise I learned from Grace Stanistreet many years ago.

I ask for two volunteers. "Can you learn an entire script in one minute?" I ask Brian. "Sure," he grins, confident I'm joking. "Okay, Brian, your script is — Please." He looks at me quizzically. "Just — Please?"

I turn to Margie. "Your script is — No." Brian is to move about Margie, changing his physical position before each "Please."

They first try a "neutral scene"...no identity, no purpose or action. They're just responding to each other. If either one seems afraid to start, I may briefly do the role — but only enough to reassure them.

Brian starts with a plaintive "Pleee-zz." Margie responds with a brisk "No!" The scene continues for about forty seconds. "Cut!" The audience agrees that Brian has used many different colorings for the word "please." When he got down on his knees in front of Margie of course everyone approved.

Deepening the neutral scene with Who and What and Why

"WHO could you be, Brian?" I ask.

The audience calls out suggestions. He refuses them all; he has his own ideas. "I'm myself, trying to get my mother to drive me to a basketball game." He's put himself into a total situation naturally. He's anticipated the next question, WHAT DO YOU WANT? He's also indicated a role to Margie, which she accepts.

Me: As the mother, what do you want?

Margie: I want him to stay home and study; he's got an exam tomorrow. That's important. Besides, I don't feel like taking the car out again today.

Me: (to Brian) Why do you want to go to the game if you have an exam tomorrow?

Brian: (as he winks at his friend, Jesse) Because. . .Jess and I make the most baskets so our team needs us; besides, I did enough studying in study hall.

We start the scene again. Still limited to "Please" and "No." Brian has a purpose (Why), an objective (What he wants) and an identity (Who.) Margie too. They also have a relationship.

But, as Margie's son, Brian shows he's uncomfortable. He fakes it, whining and begging and wheedling. It's all for laughs. We cut the scene and ask him what needs improving to make the scene believable? By now he knows the difference between "faked" and "real."

Brian: I just can't help laughing; she looks so upset. Just like my mother. (Others volunteer to take his place. That sobers him) No, I'll do it. I can do it now.

Afterward, we have a brief discussion about how much the original improvisation has changed.

Where, What (again), When and How

It's time to add more ingredients to animate the scene further.

WHERE is this scene taking place? They decide it's an apartment house kitchen with lots of dinner dishes.

WHAT are you doing? (A second use of the WHAT to stir up physical action) They are rushing to clean off the table and wash the dishes. Brian says he's helping so his mother'll want to help him.

WHEN is the scene taking place? They agree the term "dinner" sets it. About 6:30 p.m. A week night. The game is due to start at 7:30 p.m. This adds urgency to the improv when they next try it.

HOW are you trying to achieve your purpose? The group helps Brian realize he can use good humor, politeness, pleading, whining, cajoling, pouting and self-pity, indignation, anger, or any other feeling he used earlier. He has a rich supply of emotional colors available to him.

They repeat the improvisation a third time. The audience recognizes how sharp the scene has grown, even with only two words. They see the relationship between mother and son. They see the kitchen. They see how badly the son wants to get to the game and the mother's suspicion of his preparation for the exam. How far we've come from the initial "neutral" scene.

I DIVIDE THE CLASS INTO TEAMS OF TWO AND GIVE THEM TIME TO PLAN PRIVATELY BEFORE SHARING THEIR "PLEASE AND NO" IMPROVISATION. AFTER EACH SCENE, THE AUDIENCE TRIES TO GUESS WHO THEY ARE AND WHAT THEY WANT. IT DOESN'T MATTER IF THEY GUESS THE PRECISE PLAN. USUALLY RELATIONSHIP, AGE, GENERAL ATTITUDES AND CONFLICT WILL BE APPARENT. STUDENTS BEGIN TO RECOGNIZE HOW THEIR BEHAVIOR REALLY CHANGES ALONG WITH SPECIFIC IDEAS IN THEIR HEADS. IT'S NOT ENOUGH TO DO WHATEVER COMES NATURALLY. LATER ON, THIS EXTENSIVE ATTENTION TO PLANNING WILL NOT BE AS NECESSARY. BY THEN, THIS PREPARATION WILL BE INTERNALIZED, SERVING AS A SPRINGBOARD FOR THE INTUITION.

> I think of it like this. Improvisation is like going out on an adventure. You start out one Saturday morning thinking you've got it all planned. Right? You know just what you're going to do. You're going to meet your friend and bike ride up to the mountains. But in a second, everything can change. You slip in the street, rip your slacks, cut your knee bad and go to the hospital. Or those guys from the next street decide that today they're going to let a girl into their baseball game and you really want to play, so you accept. What I mean is in life you have to take your chances. You change as the adventure changes. You don't fight it. Except once in a while. We're all always improvising. An adventure may turn our real cool, or a surprise, or even dangerous. Or it might fizzle all together. Which is okay too. That's all part of it. It's the same, improvising in Drama. The only difference I can see is, in life, situations just happen to us. Unexpected. In Creative Drama we make up our situations.
> 13½-year-old Janis

Improvising a folk tale, and Philip the Scapegoat

My notes read: "...an extremely active, restless group, mostly boys, accustomed to being told what to do every moment of their school day, not accustomed to assuming responsibility for their actions or behavior. I find that they need lots of reassurance before they'll try anything new. They're really afraid of what the others think."

A group like this can easily force a teacher into an authoritative role. They're asking for it. Philip is the scapegoat of the class. He's small, wears obvious hand-me-downs, and the short trousers reveal that one ankle is excessively thin. Before long I learn that he has a wooden leg fastened to one knee. He seems accustomed to the abuse of others, and wears the abuse, even plays into it, with an air of resignation.

I want to introduce improvisation. I also want to begin presenting Philip to himself in other roles; to get his tormenters to see him as an equal, and to treat him better. A giant task. I could start them improvising from life situations, or from fiction. I decide to use a folk tale instead, which may lead them safely through the lives and feelings of others.

For a warmup, I extract sense memories relating to the tale I've selected, *Stone Soup*. With the entire class, I suggest: climb over rocks; sit down with great fatigue; get up with hope or anticipation; open doors, smell different kinds of foods; prepare vegetables for cooking; pump water; build a fire, etc.

I explain that for this first experience improvising a story, I will narrate it as they act it. "Okay? Or do you prefer that I tell the story today, and you dramatize it next week?" I am ready to go by their decision since I'm eager to have them begin to make choices.

They agree on "today for the telling *and* the doing." But they look perplexed about just how we'll do all this.

"When a character is needed for the story, I'll point to the next person in the circle to play it. In action. If I stop talking you may talk as the character — if you feel like it. Focus on your character and what's happening. Grab one piece of fabric from the costume trunk and use it in any way which *feels* right for you as your character."

AS I BEGIN, I KEEP MY EYES ON THEIR FACES. THEY WILL LET ME KNOW WHEN THE STORY IS INTERESTING, WHERE SOME DETAILS ARE NEEDED TO INCREASE THEIR INTEREST, AND WHEN I'M GETTING TOO WORDY, ADULT-STYLE. WE SIT IN A CIRCLE.

"Three soldiers are on their way home from a distant war. They've been away from their homes for many years. They're lost in the mountains trying to find their route." I stop to hear a comment about how "I got lost onct in the mountains" by Gregory, class bully and leading antagonist against Philip.

"The soldiers' clothes are torn by brambles and rocks. Often they've had to crawl on their bellies along sharp cliffs of rock. The first soldier wears his arm in a sling; the second has a limp from a leg wound which pains him; the third is so weary that when he speaks his voice can hardly be heard."

Philip, sitting to my left, has become the first soldier with a bad arm; Gregory has become the second soldier with the leg wound; and for Richard, a boy who can never talk without screaming, I've designed a third soldier. The three boys grab three pieces of fabric. Philip wears his as a cape, tucking his "sore" arm inside his shirt. Gregory binds up his leg in his piece of green burlap; Richard winds his piece of gold chiffon across his chest and about his waist like a school crossing guard. Of course Gregory receives advice from the sidelines to "limp like Philip."

I lead them over steep mountains, across dangerous rapids and down slippery rock where they need to help each other. If one falls, they all will. Suddenly, through the clouds and mist they see, in the distance, a church spire, tall and gleaming. It's a village! With the little strength they have left, they hasten down the mountain. They can already taste the warm food they'll be given; they long for the soft beds and the kindness of considerate people who will listen way into the night to their tales of misery.

"Two ladies are standing on the porch of a freshly painted little house. They're talking to two children."

I SIGNAL TO THE NEXT FOUR STUDENTS IN THE CIRCLE TO BECOME THESE CHARACTERS. THEY HURRY TO GRAB FABRIC AND TAKE UP THE ACTION.

"The first lady stands very stiffly. She agrees with everything the second lady says. The second lady, in a high shrill voice, is scolding the children for getting so dirty. The children, pouting, examine the mud on their clothes. The soldiers approach to ask, politely, for help." I nod to the threesome.

"Excuse us," bellows Richard as the soldier-whose-voice-can-hardly-be-heard. "We're soldiers and we're hungry," says Gregory pompously.

I continue. "The children look at the soldiers and then scream to the ladies, 'Look at them! They're much dirtier than we are. Why don't you scold them?'"

WITH LITTLE ENCOURAGEMENT, THE CHILDREN PICK UP ON THIS CUE AND START POKING FUN AT THE SOLDIERS. NOW TO LEAD THE SOLDIERS TO RESPOND — WITHOUT VIOLENCE.

"The soldiers were tired; they were hungry; they were dirty and ragged. But they would not accept insult. The first soldier looked the villagers in the eyes and told them that they were willing to work for some food; they didn't want charity."

Philip stands frozen; for a second it looks like he won't be able to say anything. Gregory starts to speak for him. "It's me," Philip says to him. "It's for me...to talk." And, word for word, Philip repeats what I said, adding in his own words, "If you give us work to do, you'll see. We're strong."

IT'S HARD FOR US TEACHERS TO REMAIN CASUAL AT SUCH MOMENTS. TO AN OUTSIDER IT WOULD SEEM SUCH A LITTLE THING: A BOY SAID A FEW WORDS IN A STORY. BUT WE KNOW WHAT IT IS FOR A YOUNGSTER TO SPEAK UP IN CHARACTER WHO RARELY SPEAKS UP IN CLASS. IF PHILIP DARES TO SPEAK UP TODAY, TOMORROW HE MAY FIND HIS OWN LANGUAGE, HIS OWN VOICE. IT'S VITAL THAT I NOT ISOLATE HIM AT THIS POINT, THAT I ACCEPT THAT HE HAS FULFILLED THE MOMENT. THE EXPERIENCE IS HIS. I GRIN AT HIM WHEN HE LOOKS MY WAY A MOMENT LATER. HIS DARK SKIN IS FLUSHED WITH EXCITEMENT.

Other students around the circle become the villagers. A few adjectives suggest quickly who each one is. The soldiers are refused food by everyone. They arrive at the last house. Gregory stops the others with his idea for making soup — from a stone. "We'll just ask for a pot and some water. If they give us that much as a start, we'll get 'em to loan us meat and vegetables too. Just watch."

The story proceeds well as a father sends his daughter for water from the pump. Suddenly the soldiers realize they need wood for a fire. They ask the men for firewood. A voice across the room calls out, "Even a wooden leg will do!" The entire class erupts into laughter. And Philip shrivels into himself.

I BLEW! I EXPLODED WITH ANGER. IT'S VERY RARE THAT THIS HAPPENS TO ME. OF COURSE I WAS EXPECTING TOO MUCH TOO SOON. IT HAD ALL BEEN GOING SO WELL. THE POWER OF A STORY HAD TEMPORARILY CHARMED THEM INTO ANOTHER REALITY. BUT REALITIES ARE NOT CHANGED SO FAST. I DON'T REMEMBER MUCH OF WHAT I SAID. THEY LOOKED GENUINELY SURPRISED AT MY OUTBURST.

THE PROBLEM AFTER SUCH AN EMOTIONAL REACTION IS HOW TO REGAIN ONE'S POISE AND HOW TO CONTINUE OR WHETHER TO TRY TO CONTINUE AT ALL. I WAS QUIET FOR A MOMENT. I FELT THE ANSWERING QUIET OF THE ROOM AS ALL EYES REMAINED ON ME. MY RESPONSIBILITY WAS TO GIVE THEM A CHANCE TO RESPOND.

In an attempt at a controlled voice I said, "All right. I got angry. I've told you why. Does it make any sense to you? Do you understand what got to me?"

Silence. Many faces are veiled against me. "Do you ever get angry? Any of you? What makes you angry? Do you ever just explode?"

Still no response. A few eyes look as if they'd like to speak. I don't want to let it end like this. I have to pave a way for going on. But how? A voice from a far point of the room says, "Can we go on with the story now, ma'am?"

"Do you want to? How many want to go on?" All but one hand is raised. I'm about to say, we'll go on as long as what happened never happens again. But I realize that's unnecessary. They've gotten the message; don't underestimate them. The soldiers are back on their feet. . .even Philip. The air feels cleared. And I thought they couldn't make choices.

We complete the story. Original dialogue begins. The townsfolk volunteer all kinds of meat and vegetables for the soup; they run with imaginary bowls to taste it when its ready. When the soldiers leave town, after presenting their stone to the cooperative father, the entire group, without any suggestion from me, cheers the soldiers, urging them to return.

As they leave the room at the end of this session, I overhear Gregory say to Philip, "My foot got tired having to limp so much; doesn't yours?" There's no apparent answer from Philip. But I see them walk out together.

YES, THE NARRATED STORY SERVED TO INTRODUCE THEM TO THEIR ABILITIES AT IMPROVISATION. THEY PROJECTED INTO ANOTHER TIME AND PLACE WITH OTHER CHARACTERS AND OTHER RELATIONSHIPS. THEY BEGAN TO EXPRESS THEMSELVES IN ACTION AND APPROPRIATE LANGUAGE. BUT REALLY, WAS THIS ALL?

Emergency situations — a compelling way into improvisation

EVERY PERSON AT ANY AGE HAS EXPERIENCED SOME KIND OF EMERGENCY. IN CREATIVE DRAMA THIS THEME IMPELS ACTIVE PARTICIPATION AND STRONG FEELING — THAT'S WHY YOU FIND ME SUGGESTING URGENT SITUATIONS AND STRONG MOTIVATIONS.

Mary, Alicia and Norman blew into my room looking damp and breathless. The school bus had broken down. All the students had to wait forty minutes in the October drizzle for a relief bus to arrive.

This experience was too good to just hear about and then abandon. My plan for the workshop couldn't equal this. I asked Mary, Alicia and several others who'd been on the broken bus if, just in movement, they could re-enact the experience. Quickly they placed chairs for a bus; three girls crowded into two seats, combing their hair and sharing an imaginary bottle of soda — their breakfast. Two boys stretched out, asleep, on a back seat. Norman became bus driver. Spirits were high during all this preparation. The experience had been a rare adventure, out of the ordinary routine. Arriving at school late and not being penalized was special. . .that nice feeling of finding everyone worried about you and eager to hear what had happened.

The scene was a silent melodrama. They toppled from side to side until the bus collapsed, pitching them all on top of each other. They re-enacted it with the seriousness of a sacred mission. Their alarm and bewilderment until they got off the bus contrasted with their growing annoyance at having to stand in the rain watching for a relief bus.

"Let 'em talk it now!" urged the audience as their laughter quieted. "Not yet," I resisted. "Let's get all of you into this. What happens to people in buildings or on foot when they hear an accident or a siren?"

"Everybody's curious." "They want to be able to say at suppertable *they* saw it happen!" Quickly we organized the curious bystanders; policemen trying to clear the traffic; a drunk (eighth graders place a drunk in almost any scene at any hour of the day). Some became drivers passing by who didn't care what was happening; they had to get to work. There was a boy on a bike who recognized some girls on the bus and tried to help them get off.

Alicia suddenly let out her special chortle as she remembered a man who knew-it-all; he's tried to give everyone advice about how to handle the bus, the traffic, where to wait, and how to keep dry.

We started the scene again from the moment before it happened. "Remember," I cautioned, "this time it can't be exactly the way it really was. We're adding people who were not there. They will imagine the situation and respond to what you show them in different ways. We're now taking life and recreating it as a dramatic improvisation."

This improvisation served as the start of a series of scenes exploring emergency situations they had experienced, heard about, imagined or dreaded. Today I was able to take advantage of a real situation and lead from the real into the imaginary, drawing upon many real thoughts and feelings. The bus riders discovered that they had been improvising out there on the street. They'd been doing something without realizing it.

The theme of emergencies really sparked interest. We continued it for four workshops. Groups of three and four planned all kinds of emergencies. Fred was a pregnant mother in labor and unable to get a cab to the hospital. A family found a flooded kitchen at midnight; a car broke down in the country and the driver was refused help at the nearest farmhouse because of his color; two sisters arrived home three hours later than they were supposed to and found themselves locked out. We had fires, street muggings, robbers in the night, a monkey stuck in a tree.

IT IS OFTEN GRATUITOUS AND UNNEEDED FOR A TEACHER TO OFFER TOPICS AND SPECIFIC IDEAS. TODAY'S KIDS HAVE EXPERIENCES WE COULDN'T DREAM OF. THESE NEED TO BE SHARED, EXAMINED AND EXPRESSED. OUR WORKSHOP IS NOT JUST ABOUT THE APPROACHES AND SKILLS OF IMPROVISATION, BUT IMPROVISATION PUT TO USE IN RECOGNIZING THE VITALITY OF OUR LIVES.

CHALLENGES IV: LEAD-INS TO IMPROVISATION

AS YOU'VE NOTED, THE 5 W'S AND THE H ARE MY WAY IN. LET'S ISOLATE EACH QUESTION, FIND OUT HOW IT CAN DEEPEN INVOLVEMENT AND HELP STRUCTURE THE PLANNING OF IMPROVISATIONS.

What am I doing? (without speech)

Start a simple action, in pantomime. Tell your group, "If you think you recognize what I'm doing, don't say a word. Just come join me with another action that helps mine."

You may start digging, as an example. One boy may start wheeling a wheelbarrow toward you with fertilizer. A girl may pull a hose toward the area to water the soil; another student may start raking another garden bed across from yours. They are helping to expand the basic action, not to imitate you.

A student may be ready to initiate the next action. Here are some actions which show up regularly in my classes: fixing hair in a beauty parlor; building a shed; serving food in a cafeteria; washing a car. Your students will think of many other ideas.

Where am I? (with or without speech)

You can approach this the same way as "What am I doing?" changing the focus to suggest WHERE an action may be happening.

Or, start by flow charting the many different places people can be. In groups of four or five, students pre-plan one WHERE from the chart, then share it for the class to guess.

A third approach: a variation on the television format, *You Are There*. Ask the students to bring in suggestions on paper, with several clues about the WHERE to help those who will dramatize them.

Example: An anthropological dig in Israel.
Clues: Hot, dusty, noisy with drills and picks;
Dangerous if loose dirt caves in on you.

Example: In a fish tank, as the fish.
Clues: Ferny plants floating; food sprinkled on top of water;
Each fish is a prize specimen.

A fourth approach to WHERE: set up four chairs...in a row; facing each other, as at a card table; or any other arrangement. Let the arrangement suggest to the students, in groups of four, places they could be. Re-arrange the chairs and start again.

When is it? (with speech)

Ask your students how the time of day, day of the week, week of the year, year of the century affects their lives? Do they behave differently on a holiday? Or in winter? Or summer?

Here are several examples to whet your students' ideas:

> Schoolchildren in a one-room school house, 200 years ago; boys on one side; girls on the other.
>
> Playing outdoors in midsummer, 110°.
>
> Playing outdoors in midwinter, after a snow fall.
>
> Awakening late on a Sunday.
>
> Awakening late on a school day — test day!

Why am I doing what I'm doing? (without speech)

Set up a simple action, such as carrying an object across the room; unlocking a door and entering a room; going to a phone booth to make a call.

Simultaneously, have all the students do the action — individually — to recreate it exactly. Now, one at a time, each student repeats the action, motivated by an internal WHY.

Ask for important reasons to build strong motivation. "I've got to call my girl friend just to talk to her," will not demand the same energies and attitude as "I'm locked out of my house and I want to know if I can stay at my friend's house until my mother comes home."

Who am I? (with speech)

A scene changes drastically by changing the people in it. Select a location which can involve all members of your class. Examples: an airline terminal, a carnival, a toy store before the holidays, a hospital waiting room.

Ask each student to choose a character, to decide why the character is at this location, and such details as age, occupation, and manner.

At this stage of development, the students may enact only a stereotype, a generalization of a character type. Point out that later on they'll find how they can probe deeper in building a characterization.

Start the scene with several people. Others enter gradually. After a few minutes, cut the scene, and ask everyone to choose a different character. Repeat the scene. Then discuss how the scene changed as the people changed.

Another approach to WHO: select photographs, slides and prints which feature groups of people. Students, in small groups, plan interpretations of WHAT the people in the picture are doing and WHO they are. They also try to recognize HOW each person feels, from physical position and facial expression.

"Please/No" leads into persuasion improvisations (with speech)

Divide the class into two's. Initially ask all teams to plan an improvisation of one basic situation. Examples: persuading a relative to advance some money; persuading a parent or teacher to let you go somewhere.

In their teams, the students plan the WHO I AM, WHAT I WANT, WHY, WHERE WE ARE, and WHEN. Urge the "persuader" to use all the "colors" of persuasion previously described, and the "resister" to find many ways to resist being persuaded. Conflict will emerge only if each person has very different wants.

Later, let the teams pick their own situations. Encourage imaginative ideas and important motivations. Stress that the ending of an improvisation is never planned. It evolves — and is often a total surprise to the participants.

Seven hundred and seventy possibilities
    or
A plot unfurls

After doing "lead-ins to improvisation," your students are ready to juggle the 5 W's to plan an unlimited range of improvisations, much as a mathematician does with permutations.

As a start, set up a basic plot such as: one person is at work. A second, and possibly a third, person arrives, stays a short while, and then leaves. The first person ends the scene.

This basic plot can become a tragedy, a comedy, a mystery, or a farce — determined by the characters and the circumstances planned to animate it. One group of eighth graders designed the following three possibilities before casting and improvising each scene. Your students will think of many more.

For person #1:	Scene A	Scene B	Scene C
WHO ARE YOU?	An old woman, friendly and trusting	A businessman, about 25, opinionated	A 16-year-old from a farm town, serious
WHERE ARE YOU WORKING?	hospital laundry room	employment agency	farm stable

	Scene A	Scene B	Scene C
WHAT ARE YOU DOING?	washing piles of linens	phoning to fill a job	nursing sick race horse

WHAT DO YOU WANT and WHY grew out of the interaction.

For persons #2 and #3:

	Scene A	Scene B	Scene C
WHO ARRIVES?	hospital VIP, with telegram, and reporter	employee just fired from job the agency got her	horse's owner and jockey who rides horse
WHAT DOES #2 (AND #3) WANT? WHY?	#2 wants to tell woman she's won state lottery, and to get into photo with woman; #3 wants news story	revenge against employer and new job for more money	a miracle: the horse's recovery. And a scapegoat for the illness
WHEN IS IT?	3 a.m. the hottest night of summer.	two minutes before closing time on Friday, Dec. 31.	three days before biggest race of the century, midnight.

Before improvising from this kind of diagram, students should be encouraged to discuss details of the WHERE, such as location of doors, placement of important objects, and the size and weight of the objects all three characters will use. They should consider, also, the relationships between people in the scene, and the attitudes toward what a person is doing. How does #1 feel, working alone; how does he react to #2 and #3? These questions ready the students for future work with improvisation and characterization.

REMEMBER — THE SITUATIONS ARE PLANNED. NOT THE DIALOGUE. NOR THE ENDING. A REHEARSED IMPROVISATION IS NO LONGER AN IMPROVISATION, SO RUN-THROUGHS IN THE HALL ARE DISCOURAGED. STUDENTS WILL BEGIN TO TRUST THAT THEIR INVOLVEMENT, FOCUS, IMAGINATION AND INTERACTION WILL SUPPORT THEIR EXPRESSIVE — AND INTUITIVE — ABILITIES WITH ACTIONS AND REACTIONS, AND HELP THEM FIND WORDS TO SPEAK.

IMPROVISATION. John Hodgson and Ernest Richards. Eyre Methuen, Ltd. London. 1967.
Other sources for stories to improvise:
  POINT OF DEPARTURE. Ed. Robert S. Gold. Dell Publishing, New York. 1967. Stories about teenagers.
  BLACK AND WHITE: STORIES OF AMERICAN LIFE. Ed. Carol Anselment and Donald B. Gibson. Washington Square Press, New York. 1971.
  AMERICAN INDIAN TALES AND LEGENDS. Vladimir Hulpach. Printed in Czechoslovakia. Published in London by Paul Hamlyn, 1967.
  STORIES TO DRAMATIZE. Ed. Winifred Ward. The Children's Theatre Press, New Orleans. 1952.

EXPERIENCES V: CONFLICT

HAVING INTRODUCED THE STRUCTURE OF IMPROVISATION, WE NOW NEED WAYS TO DEEPEN INSIGHT INTO ONESELF AND INTO OTHERS...INTO LIFE SITUATIONS AND HUMAN INTERACTION, THROUGH WHAT I CALL THE FOUR C'S:
> CONFLICT
> CHOICES
> CHARACTERIZATION
> CRITIQUING

> **The world exists as a conflict and tension of opposites.**
> Heraclitus, as quoted by Robert Pirsig in *Zen and the Art of Motorcycle Maintenance*

Conflict is a natural element in all of life. Observe it — in the insect and animal world, throughout our environment, in our society and within each of us human beings.

Conflict is integral as well to all the arts. The climax of a musical composition is the resolution of tensions within the cadences. A sculptural piece achieves balance by the tensions within it. Examine a sampling of fiction: characters emerge in their struggles to overcome obstacles.

Without conflict between two or more forces, internal or external, drama lacks its dramatic surge. Try this out in a very simple way:

> Approach a student, without forewarning of your intent. Demand something: a pencil, a chair, a ring or a sneaker. If the student readily turns the item over to you, your improvised scene collapses abruptly before it's begun.

> If there's resistance: "I can't, I need it." Or, "Why should I? It's mine!" — ah, that's the beginning of conflict and of drama. Your want versus your student's.

Through our uses of the drama process, we can lead our students to recognize and examine the existence of conflict as an ingredient of life and of drama. In all our lives. In a positive sense. NOT as a "bad" trait to be kept hidden within our gut.

Through improvisation we can try out alternative solutions available to us in the resolution of conflicts. A violent confrontation, so often portrayed as the only way out by TV and movies, can be seen as one of many ways. As we look for alternatives, we are already moving into the next major area of consideration...CHOICES. But first, CONFLICT!

Eighth graders in the 4th month

"What is conflict?" I asked, when I had everyone's attention. "Wanting something your parents won't agree to and you get into an argument?"

"Sometimes...sometimes it's conflict when someone, like a teacher's got it in for you and nothin' you do or say changes it. Even if you do all your work," offered Brad.

"I think conflict is people being pushed around by other people; there's no conflict if they just take it. BUT, if they stand up for themselves, defend themselves...like those Indians at Wounded Knee...there's conflict." Greg always sees a world view.

"Riots are conflict, aren't they?" "And fights between my brothers and me over who walks the dog," Vanessa spoke with authority: "I think it's me having one point of view and you having another, and we just won't listen to each other."

"Sometimes...sometimes I have conflict in my own head," said Sandy timidly. "Whadaya mean?" "Well, you know. There's something I want to do...really want to do...but inside me I think I shouldn't do it. Then I have a whole argument...inside my head."

Jesse and Eddie jumped up. "We'll show you conflict." They grabbed a thick rope from the prop drawer and started a tug-o-war. Everyone started to cheer them on. They pulled harder. It was an old rope. It snapped in the middle, pitching them both onto the floor. "That's resolved conflict." I laughed with everyone else.

It was time to extend into dramatic improvisations. We divided into groups of two, three, or four. This class was capable at structuring simple improvisations. Today I asked that they give special attention to selecting a situation and placing in it characters with diverse "wants."

In about ten minutes, they were ready to share situations of conflict. I checked with each group to see if they had amply planned their w's and h. The rest was to remain spontaneous. Because Sam enjoyed taping, I have the following scenes as examples of their efforts that day.

Group One

Who: Carey, about 15, a student; Mr. Morgan, the Shop teacher

Where: In Mr. Morgan's office

What: Carey wants opportunity to join a Shop class.
         Mr. Morgan wants to keep girls out.

Why: Carey enjoys working with her hands and wants to learn carpentry. Mr. Morgan believes girls don't need this kind of training; it should be given to boys who will use it in their lives.

When: A school day at the beginning of a term.

How: Carey — persuasive, insistent, angry, indignant.
         Mr. Morgan — amused at first, then annoyed, impatient, authoritative.

The scene developed easily and was cut when Mr. Morgan walked out of the room saying, "Well, honey, you'll have to excuse me. I've got to get my boys back to work. I'll get in touch with you. . .next month sometime," and Carey called after him, "But you don't know my name. Or my home room. . .Mr. Morgan!"

During the Rap Time:

Diana: I really liked the scene. But don't you think (to Carey) you would have been angrier than that. . .to show the conflict more?

Dennis: I don't think that mattered.

Larry: You did the scene real good. But it's far fetched. Girls don't need shop.

Bengie: Well I've always wanted to cook so I could get out of the house as soon as I graduated high school and make my own meals. . .but boys aren't scheduled for Family Living except at this school.

No one mocks Bengie because he's a VIP with the football team. Everyone starts talking at once about what is woman's work and what is men's. I finally interrupt the discussion to remind them to get back to the task of evaluating the planning and development of the conflict between Carey and Mr. Morgan. The discussion is important even if it's away from the main focus. Then we move on to the next improvisation.

Group Two

Who: Pete Chen, high school student; the Coach (done in voice only); several admirers (for which they borrow people.)

Where: The bench outside Coach's office.

What: Pete wants a chance to be on the team despite his height. Coach wants an impressive winning team.

Why: Pete has spent the year in body-building in order to qualify; this is his biggest dream, to make the team.
Coach has to have a winning team or he loses his job, so he takes no chances.

When: After school, in the Fall.

This improvisation obviously was planned to include a dream sequence. Pete is sitting on the bench, talking his thoughts aloud. Gradually the sounds of cheering are heard, getting louder and louder. He stands up on the bench smiling and waving as fans greet him and ask for his autograph. He talks about what he'd done to become such a big American star. "No one's a runt to me. It's what's inside you that counts," he says. The cheers subside. The dream is over as the coach calls out from his office: "Is Pete Chen out there?" Pete starts to answer, but instead he turns the other way and walks out.

Rap Time:

The discussion started with questions: had they pre-planned their ending? No, Pete answered, it just happened; it felt right for the situation. The scene is praised highly. The dream sequence was great, different. "I have dreams like that all the time," said Eddie. Ruth is impressed: "Pete really showed how a person feels. . .inside. He made me feel like crying."

"In other words," I suggest, "you found the scene believable? Pete was real to you. . .involved. . .focused?" There is agreement. "But I don't understand something. This was supposed to show conflict. Right? But where was the conflict?" A dozen kids were ready to answer her. "I think this was the inside-your-head conflict we talked about before," said Marcella.

"Couldn't he have told the coach off or fought for his rights at the end?"

"Sure," answered Marcella. "But that would have been your scene. This was Pete and Jim's. He walked off like he was saying, I'm not going to take a chance. . .he's not going to put me down any more. Notice how his chin was up. . .he didn't sneak off.'

Pete and Jim and the "admirers" listened to this discussion with grins on their faces. It was difficult for them to believe they had done all this.

Group Three

Who: Mary, about fourteen; Linda, her friend, same age.

Where: In the living room of the Stevens' house.

What: Mary is baby-sitting to earn money; Linda is telephoning her.

Why: Linda wants a place for a party.

When: 10 p.m. on a Saturday.

How: Linda has a "secret weapon" in hand.

I'M INCLUDING THE ACTUAL DIALOGUE AS IT WAS TAPED AS AN ILLUSTRATION OF THE WAY YOUNG PEOPLE, BY STRUCTURING CAREFULLY AND INTERACTING WITH FOCUS AND IMAGINATION, CAN DEVELOP THE DIALOGUE AND DIRECTION OF AN IMPROVISATION SPONTANEOUSLY.

Mary: (Watching TV when telephone rings) Hello. Stevens' residence. Oh, Linda, I was almost falling asleep. There's nothing good on TV tonight.

Linda: Hey, Mary, guess who's standing here with me. . .

Mary: Where are you?

Linda: I'm in a phone booth across from the Texaco. Can you guess?

Mary: It's a Saturday so it's got to be Tim.

Linda: That's right...for one. Keep guessing...

Mary: How many guys you need for one night?

Linda: Well, Craig and Louisa are here too. AND someone else...

Mary: I hate guessing games. I don't know who you've got there.

Linda: It's Aaron!

Mary: AARON! How'd you get him? Linda you double-timer, you know I've had my eye on Aaron for a month.

Linda: Shhh listen, that's why I'm calling. I thought we'd all come over...so he could get to know you a little. No reason for you to sit it out alone on a Saturday. Is there?

Mary: (Still squealing) Oh, Linda...you're not to be believed. How'd you stumble over him? Come right over...quick... I can't stand it. Oh I look a mess...I gotta comb my hair... those kids were tumbling all over me before I got them to sleep....OH LINDA!

Linda: What's the matter?

Mary: I can't...I can't....Oooooh...I just can't...

Linda: Mary, quiet down long enough to tell me what's the matter?

Mary: I can't let you come here!

Linda: Why not? You can't look that bad...

Mary: No, that's not it. I promised...I promised I wouldn't have any friends up. That's something Mr. Stevens told me right off. They don't want any more sitters who bring their friends over and neglect the children. And it'll be a regular job if I keep it.

Linda: That's silly...we'll all take care of the brats. He should consider himself lucky. He'll have six baby sitters for the price of one.

Mary: Oh, Linda, I can't. What if they come back early?

Linda: What time did they tell you?

Mary: They were going to a friend's house for dinner...early... they left at five. They could be back anytime.

73 Conflict

Linda: Who ever heard of coming home before midnight on a Saturday!

Mary: But what if they did?

Linda: Are you chicken? Here's your big opportunity. I did this just for you.

Mary: I know...I know...but I can't...I just can't...

Linda: (Sounding put out) Okay...it's your choice, but it's stupid. Make up your mind, my money's almost out...

Mary: (Softly) I'm sorry...honest I am...give my regards to... everyone...especially...(her voice peters out.)

At Rap Time Karen started off, "How did Linda know where Mary was baby sitting in the first place?" "How does that matter?" asked Guy. "What'd you think of the scene?"

HE SAVED ME THE TROUBLE OF FOCUSING THE CRITIQUE FIRST ON THE POSITIVE ASPECTS OF THE PLANNING. SOMEONE LIKE KAREN CAN DIVERT THE THINKING FROM THE GOALS OF THE ASSIGNMENT, AND DESTROY THE MOMENT FOR THE PARTICIPANTS.

Pete: I see two kinds of conflict...inside the head, like mine... and between Linda and Mary...and...and Linda had the upper hand for a while...with what's his name in tow...

Rita: I think Mary was the winner...

Jim: Maybe she's the loser, too; she didn't get to meet Aaron.

Me: Was this conflict resolved or unresolved?

Carey: Oh, definitely resolved. Mary made a hard choice...but she made it.

Mary: You know, I forgot you were all here...I just knew the feelings...

Linda: Me too...I used to babysit a lot.

Me: Did each girl stay with her stated purpose: Linda wanting to find a place for a party; Mary wanting to hold down a job according to her own ways of doing it...not being forced by the values of a friend?

The discussion could have continued, but the time was up and everyone grabbed their things and rushed out the door. I just remember the warmest smile from Pete before he left; he had scored that day and felt good, inside. Chances were that he would not retreat into his shyness...not in that class.

CHALLENGES V: CONFLICT

Arguments in numbers

First set up a demonstration team of two, who stand about five feet apart. Ask them to build an argument — slowly — using only numbers, one to infinity, for their dialogue. No touching is allowed (although they'll probably end up face-to-face with fists clenched). It might develop as follows:

Person I:(starts softly) 3. . . .17. . .444. . .409. . .

Person II:(cuts in) 89. . .88. . .4. . .945. . .!

Person I:(a little louder) 666. . .666. . .4. . .6 hundred AND 66!

Person II:(still stronger) 40, 335, 2, 2, 2, 2, 2. . .ZERO!

And so on, building tension and conflict between them in tone, volume, stress, attitude, and timing. Next, have the class divide into two's. Space them about the room. The teams will develop their arguments simultaneously (and the room will be quite a hubbub!)

Arguments in movement

Two lines of equal numbers face each other across the room. The class has agreed in advance WHO each line represents and WHAT each side wants.

Line I could be collie dogs; Line II, Fox Terriers. In the center is a trough of food. They approach each other warily, with caution and suspicion.

Or Line I represents starving villagers; Line II the militia. In the center are bags of food.

SUPPORT MOVEMENT ARGUMENTS WITH MUSIC WHICH BUILDS TENSION GRADUALLY TO THE CLIMAX.

"Please and No" with a new focus (See p. 57.)

The focus this time is not just on the persuasive aspects of the exercise, but on building conflict situations in which real struggle develops between opposing ideas and wants. Have them structure the scenes now from historical, literary, or current events situations in which they can readily recognize the conflict of personalities or ideas:

- King Solomon's Chalk Circle (or Bertolt Brecht's)
- The demand for recantation from an accused "witch" in Salem
- Tom Sawyer trying to convince his Aunt Polly that he's sick
- Washington and Franklin trying to resolve ouster of Jefferson

Abstract conflict

When your students seem ready to conceptualize through movement or sounds, suggest that they dramatize abstract ideas that contain inner conflict, like

- Gravity
- Splitting the atom
- The change of seasons
- Hatching an egg
- Barriers between people, like fear, prejudice, language, etc.
- "Oil and water don't mix"
- Anti-biotics fighting infection

AS NEGATIVE AS I FEEL ABOUT MOST TV COMMERCIALS, THEY HAVE SERVED US IN ONE WAY: AFTER SEEING INNUMERABLE VISUALIZATIONS OF ASPIRIN OR ALKA SELTZER ACTING UPON THE BODY, IT IS EASIER TO SUGGEST TO STUDENTS THAT THEY ENACT IDEAS SUCH AS THE ABOVE.

Shadow play — movement behind a rear-lighted sheet — lends itself to some of these conflicts.

The many voices inside me

Many of my older students choose to dramatize inner conflict by having one person at the center, another at the right, and another at the left. They are not so much the angels of good and evil, but the representatives of two different solutions to a central problem.

As an extension of this, it is interesting to have a central person — a contemporary figure or a character from history or literature — state a problem. Set positions A, B, C around this central figure. The first group of students which occupies these positions sets the three points of view. Then selecting from the class, rotate the students. You will tap a person on the shoulder and whisper which position is to be taken — A, B, or C.

EXPERIENCES VI: CHOICES

> There can be no choices if there are no alternatives from which to choose.
>
> Louis Raths, *Values*

TO BE CREATIVE IMPLIES BEING ABLE TO SEE OTHER WAYS AND DARE TRY SOME OF THEM. THROUGH DRAMA WE CAN EXAMINE CHOICES. . .OF BEHAVIOR, OF ATTITUDE, OF ACTIVITIES, OF FRIENDS AND ENEMIES. . .CHOICES OF LIFE STYLE, OF INVOLVEMENTS AND INTERESTS, OF JOBS, OF EXPLORATION AND PLEASURES.

Many young people do not dream there are any choices or alternatives for their lives. For some, poverty breeds a sense of powerlessness which denies opportunities to change one's existence. Others find too many choices equally stultifying: I can be anything, do anything, go anywhere, but how do I make up my mind? Mass media imposes programmed concepts of the "one way" to dress, behave, gain acceptance . . .many feel inhibited from even considering other ways. And still others respond to a general malaise called "apathy."

In the drama room, the child who answers when offered a choice, "I don't know. . .I don't care" is often one who sees no real options or is afraid to risk choosing the "wrong" way. By eliminating that stigma of "right" and "wrong," we can help free many to try walking new routes. Then their imaginations and ability to take risks show them their options, and they may reach for them.

Reinforcing the ability to make choices

Through enactment, students can experience the choice and evaluate the consequences. We offer activities; they supply ideas to think through and test out, with imagination and challenge, without fear of our judgments. Drama provides a natural arena in which to connect with our real lives and their joyous and not so joyous possibilities. "If I do this, maybe this will happen, but if I choose that. . ." To see alternatives and try them out is to have some sense of self-worth, a first step toward becoming self-actualizing.

With a fifth grade group

I started a session with everyone seated on the rug in a circle. "Let's pass an IF." Randy, next to me, started clowning. "IF I were a bear I'd. . ."

"Let's set it differently today. If I were something NOT Beast, Bird, or Fish, what might I be?" We went around the circle, each starting with a repeat of the basic "If I were a. . ." and adding an idea.

When a category was repeated more than twice, I'd suggest shifting to another. Marvelous ideas — If I were an antenna on a rooftop, I could get all the best music. . .If I were a puddle I could reflect girls walking through me.

Second round: "If I could stop the clock at any hour. . ."

After projecting nonsense "If's" and dealing with them verbally, we go into "ways I could move if I were. . .a line; a dot; a small circle; a musical note; a melting icicle; a lawn mower that goes beserk.

Later still, we deal with possibilities for shaping patterns in space and on large sheets of paper; or ways of arranging numbers, or of cardboard blocks.

Finally, having dealt with permutations in space, we deal with permutations in situations. In groups of two, ways of getting assistance; ways of approaching a new person; ways of cleaning up after dinner, ways of re-arranging a bedroom, etc.

HERE I IMPOSED MY LIFE STYLE IN A VERY SUBTLE WAY. BUT LET'S LOOK AT IT. I MADE THE ASSUMPTION THAT EVERYONE HAS A ROOM TO RE-ARRANGE. BUT MANY SHARE A ROOM WITH ONE OR MORE PEOPLE, SHARE A BED WITH OTHER SIBLINGS. THIS IS A SMALL EXAMPLE OF SOMETHING WE, AS TEACHERS, DO UNTHINKINGLY, WHICH IMPOSES A LIMITATION UPON THE OPEN SHARING OF DIFFERENCES IN THE WORKSHOP.

With a seventh grade group

"What do you do after school?" I began one day.

"Aw nuthin," answered Linda glumly. "There's never nuthin to do where I live."

"How do you do nothing? Can you show us?"

Diffidently, she pantomimed carrying her books up the stairs, unlocking the apartment door, entering and switching on the TV, then grabbing some soda and snacks and slouching before "the set."

"How many of you recognize yourself in Linda's scene?" Half a dozen hands went up. "What else do you do after school? What else can you do?"

Some called out their activities. We started a flow-chart for other possibilities: a newspaper route; an errand job; reading in the library; volunteer work in a hospital or agency; athletics of all kinds; dance, drama or music lessons; practicing and/or homework; "Y" clubs and activities; babysitting; helping at home; riding a bike.

One said, "Smoking in the lot." "Smoking what?" taunted a friend. A whisper and a snicker as they scanned my face to see if I'd heard.

IN ASKING FOR OTHER CHOICES, IT'S ESSENTIAL THAT WE MEAN IT. WHEN WE SAY WE CAN ACCEPT ANY IDEAS AND LIFE EXPERIENCES, WE'RE NOT LOOKING ONLY FOR RESPONSES GROOMED TO PLEASE US. VALUES AND CONSEQUENCES WILL EMERGE THROUGH THE EVALUATIONS DURING "RAP TIME" LATER.

After flow charting, I ask everyone to take his/her space about the room. Simultaneously, as a physical and imaginative warm-up, they try out individual responses to some of the suggested possibilities. "You are using something large which you've wanted for your birthday. What is it?" Or, "You have a special appointment after school; what is it?"

Several students help me call out suggestions. Ten minutes later, we're ready to move into small group improvisations of "Choices for After-School Activity." The scenes are planned and shared. At "Rap Time" afterward, we discuss the planning and structure of the scenes; believability; focus; use of imagined environment; interaction of characters; the choice of character; and the ramifications of the activities they chose. A lot. But these students have been at work in Creative Drama at least a term.

A girl who enacted a shopping scene in which she shoplifted explained that she doesn't take stuff herself. "But I know lots of kids who do. . . just for fun." A boy answers, "Yeah, I used to do things like that. . . made me feel real tough. It's kid stuff, that's all. . .stupid."

Chance versus choice

"When I'm mad I. . ." was the launching point for this session.

"When I'm mad I go sit in my room and stare out the window," said Molly. "When I'm mad, I gotta hit somebody," said James. "I hit the person who made me mad — PAM!" said Ricky, punching his palm.

"How about you, Ronnie?" I turned to a girl who rarely volunteered her thoughts, but, when solicited, was always ready.

"I never get mad," she answered quietly. Mary whirled at her. "Yeah, what about when you get teased for being so fat. Don't you get mad then?"

Ronnie stopped and then answered, "Nope."

"She don't care 'bout being fat," John explained. "She just grins when you say something like 'all that candy must make you awful sweet,' or 'how're you goin' to get through the door.'"

"Yeah," chimed in Daryl. "She just rolls in like a chocolate marshmallow." The class roared.

It was gang-up time on Ronnie again. Ways of expressing anger suddenly seemed of secondary importance. I did an about-face, made a quick choice myself. "I read a story you might like to act out today." Immediate interest from the class. "It's a pretty strange story; I've never tried it in drama before. It's called *The Lottery*. It takes place in a village in the United States. Each year for over fifty years they've been holding a lottery on the town green. Everyone pulls a slip. The person who draws a marked slip is then stoned by the townsfolk, young and old. It's their tradition."

Quietly I told them Shirley Jackson's story, watching the humor on their faces slowly dissolve into absorption and then to horror. The sheer starkness of the tale may have served to highlight our lesser abuses against each other.

IN THIS CASE I MADE AN INTUITIVE CHOICE IN RELATION TO THIS PARTICULAR CLASS. A SIMPLER TALE LIKE *THE UGLY DUCKLING* WOULD HAVE INSPIRED LAUGHTER NO MATTER HOW WELL I ADAPTED IT. AFTER MONTHS OF HEARING VERBAL AND EMOTIONAL ASSAULTS AGAINST SEVERAL VULNERABLE MEMBERS OF THIS GROUP, I HOPED TO LEAD THEM TO CONFRONT THEMSELVES.

We discussed the meanings of the story. Lamont recognized it as a parable, like some he knew in the Bible. "Did they really kill Tessie with the stones?" asked Gerry, still filled with the shock of the story. "Does it matter?"

"But. . .but she didn't even do anything wrong. She only pulled the slip with the mark on it." He wanted to change the ending.

"She didn't have any choice," said Amon.

"Sure she did," said Jerry. "She could've refused to draw a slip, or she could've just walked away. She didn't just have to stand there so they could stone her."

"Do you think the members of the crowd had any choices?" I asked. "Just because the lottery had been held for years and years, did each person have to join in? Even her friends and neighbors and their kids?"

Several students prepared the lottery slips while everyone else chose roles and outlined the development of the story. They enacted the story spontaneously, my narration filling only as needed. They developed the gleeful anticipation of the lottery. Some matter-of-factly piled up stones, "like a butcher sharpening his knives to quarter a chicken," as Gladys later commented.

We got to the drawing. We had decided not to follow the story at that point. They felt it didn't have to be Tessie; it could be anyone present who happened to draw the marked slip. "Unfold your slips!" called the boy holding the lottery box. Everyone looked around. Ronnie stood holding the slip marked with an X. Her face showed apprehension and fear, behind a self-conscious grin. I called "Cut!" A few students looked at me with disbelief and sudden understanding. "Do you realize what made me switch to this story today?" I asked.

THE DRAMATIC EXPERIENCE CAN REVEAL HUMAN CHOICES AND POSSIBLE CONSEQUENCES. AS THE WHITE HOUSE CONFERENCE ON CHILDREN AND YOUTH OF 1960 SAID IN ITS MAJOR STATEMENT, "DRAMA IS A MEANS OF HELPING CHILDREN GAIN POSITIVE HUMAN VALUES, SELF-AWARENESS AND TO PROVIDE CONSTRUCTIVE EMOTIONAL OUTLET."

CHALLENGES VI: CHOICES

Work Collage

One person chooses a work pattern associated with a particular job, such as *shoveling*. He goes to the center and establishes and maintains a rhythm for the job. Then a second person chooses another job with a different rhythm, a different physical pattern, such as *rapid typing,* and places himself near the first person. A third joins in doing a third job, such as checking out books in a library. Sounds which underline the rhythm of the job can accompany each activity.

When all are involved, the leader calls out "Change!" Participants immediately change to a contrasting job and rhythm.

The *role collage* is developed in a similar way. Students choose a role and make up a sentence for the role, and individually enter the space. For example, one sits in a tantrum, repeating, "I'm a baby and I want attention!" A second person enters and takes an adjoining space: "I'm a policeman and I want law and order." The third person: "I am a nurse and I want to take care of you." This can involve half the class or the entire class at a time. Their only relationship is physical proximity. As in work collage, call out "Change!" to switch roles.

After these warm-ups, discuss the jobs or roles performed, and what each might involve in life. You or the students may take an idea from this into improvisation.

How else?

Use this phase so often that it becomes a natural part of everyone's vocabulary. For all kinds of activities. . .first to do it; then to ask, "How else can it be done?"

A variation is to use a prop. Choose something which has a certain universality. . .a stick, a box, a flat board, a picture frame. "What could this picture frame be used as, other than to frame pictures?" Some responses —

>   A doorway
>   A window; a mirror
>   The house for my inner self
>   A book cover; a buckle; a table top
>   An underground mine entrance
>   An animal trap

Then develop an improvisation, using the prop as central to the improvisation, not a mere ornament. After a minute or so, call out, "How else?" The participants change the prop to be something else, and change themselves accordingly. If the frame was a window through which they were peering to see their new neighbors moving in, they might change it to an underground mine entrance, and themselves to rescue workers.

"How else" can extend to situations like making a date or responding to a drug pusher. In these situations, the students keep their identity and their problem, but change their attitude or perception.

"HOW ELSE?" IS USEFUL FOR STRETCH IN PERCEIVING OTHER WAYS, AND FLEXIBILITY IN EMPLOYING OPTIONS.

Diary of choices

Assign students to keep a log for a full day of the choices they make, little and large. Some students will say, "I never get to make any choices." Encourage them to recognize that they make a choice when they decide to put on another shirt, eat breakfast, walk another route, greet someone.

In class, draw from the logs to find simple activities to be improvised in different ways. Encourage class members to enact "how else" a situation might have been handled — what other choices might have been made.

VALUES AND TEACHING. Louis E. Raths, Merrill Harmin, Sidney B. Simon. Charles E. Merrill Co., Ohio. 1966.
VALUE EXPLORATION THROUGH ROLE PLAYING. Robert C. Hawley. Educational Research Press, Amherst, Mass. 1974.

EXPERIENCES VII: CHARACTERIZATION

> Son: (long-haired, in jeans) But Ma, I made $8.00 an hour singing.
> Ma: My darling boy, you're wonderful. I love you more than my son the doctor.
>
> From an evening TV show, prime time

We are inundated today with stereotypes: of people, of values, relationships, aspirations, occupations, causes...almost everything.

- An egghead is the student who likes school and wears glasses;

- Women libbers wear flat shoes, study karate, and don't like men — much;

- Women gossip a lot on phones; men (fathers) are always tired at the end of the day;

- An artist is usually a social outcast, an isolate, a crackpot.

Laughter, so healthy when it helps people look at themselves with some objectivity, is used instead to minimize serious efforts and the needs of other people. If our young people are exposed to three or five hours daily of media stereotypes, what can we expect in drama when we introduce characterization? Stereotypes!

What does this shorthand knowledge of the world do to each young mind? What limitations does it place upon their thinking and imagining, their capacity to relate to others and to empathize? How can we break through these myriads of cliches and little boxes to begin to perceive each other as individuals? How do we lead into honest portrayals of individuals through understanding and sensitivity?

Moving from stereotypes to observation

A second-term class started the session by portraying their ideas of old age — with their hands, their legs, their backs, through walking and through speech. Then I asked, "What is aging? What causes it? How is it manifest? In different people, will aging be shown in the same ways?"

Ralph answered my first question quickly. "It's being smart!" The class was puzzled. Hadn't most of them just expressed old age as bent, doddering, myopic, whining, forgetful, and generally senile? Ralph ignored their responses. "It's true. My grandfather knows everything. You just think of something and come ask him. He'll know...*and he isn't sick! And he can see as good as you 'r me!*"

His comments led us into a study of elderly people around us: relatives ...people on the streets. Each student kept a small notebook during this study, jotting down his observations, and then sharing them in class by "doing." They gave studies of feet, of hands, of gestures; linear drawings of backs; the pacing of movements, responses to questions; notes on physical capacities. The science teacher cooperated by spending time with us explaining the aging process in humans and in nature.

I arranged a class visit to a Senior Housing Center. Preparing for it, we planned an interview show with the residents. Our question: what was YOUR life like at our ages of thirteen and fourteen? (or fifteen, to accommodate Tracey.) We carefully rehearsed the show in our classroom, analyzed it, and improvised it again with new participants. Each time ten students portrayed the elderly citizens. "You shouldn't use slang; they won't understand you!" cautioned Roger. "And don't talk too fast," urged Linda. "And talk loud so they'll hear you."

On the afternoon of our visit, we brought dozens of cookies baked in our Family Living classes. The students were all dressed in Sunday finery. We walked the ten blocks quickly.

At the Center, a suddenly shy group of twenty-five teenagers sought refuge by the wall. Within seconds that changed! Fifty or sixty elderly folk were swarming about, eagerly welcoming the students. It became an animated experience of giving and taking, taking and giving. Intense and heart-warming. Our young people, many of whom knew no grandparents, found such welcome of their youthfulness, and they responded instinctively to the warmth and interest being showered upon them. A blind woman described how she "saw" each of them from their voices and touching their faces — and not as teenage stereotypes. She touched their faces with fingers so gentle, Robert later told me, that "it felt like a breeze on my cheek."

The Interview show aroused great hilarity, especially as some of the women described their first dates with their parents along, or going to a first dance *after* the age of eighteen. A man of eighty-seven urged them to stay in school and learn as much as they could; he had dropped out at the age of thirteen to earn money as a floor sweeper in a factory, and there he had remained for much of his life.

The following week when I called out, during the warm-up, "an elderly person," no two students used their bodies or their voices in the same manner. And one person who moved stiffly explained that his "arteries were hardening in the lower legs."

A visitor's report

One of a group of mid-western parochial teachers who had visited us during our "stereotype" work sent a note:

> Above all I remember entering the Creative Drama room. I was incredulous! A nun was "flying" about the room; a hippie approached me for a "joint," a bespectacled professor with tousled hair was lecturing in a loud pedantic voice, but no one was listening; a little girl was crying for her doll; an Irish accented

policeman was directing non-existent traffic; an athlete was flexing his muscles before an invisible mirror. The teacher was standing by the wall — a seemingly impartial observer.

You can imagine my relief, and amazement, to learn they were partaking of a class devoted to investigating the meaning of stereotypes. Shortly we were to see them change into human beings with feelings, needs, opinions and individuality. All through the intriguing techniques of Creative Drama. WHAT A RARE OPPORTUNITY FOR YOUNG PEOPLE TO DEVELOP INSIGHT!

CHALLENGES VII: CHARACTERIZATION

Name the stereotype

We have all been exposed to so many stereotypes that our minds produce immediate canned responses to almost any adjective or noun. Try these out with half or all the class participating simultaneously:

Priest, Nun, Saint	Jewish mother
Rich lady	Italian
Beggar	Vietnamese
Russian	Movie star
Newspaper reporter	Bored
Medic	Chauffeur
Banker	Teenager
Liberated woman	Sexy

Build your own class lists. You may find yourself a bit horrified to find the extent our world is categorized and straight-jacketed. Start to break through. Watch the TV programs your students watch for one week, and you'll understand better.

Interview

After a warm-up using 20-second reactions to a list like the one above, call out "Freeze!" Have several students approach others and ask them questions. Then, "Action!" for another 20 seconds, and again "Freeze!" and more questions. Compile a list of questions something like this:

- Where are you going?

- Why are you going there? What do you want?

- How old are you?

- Where do you live — farm, city, mountains, south, or what?

- Name four things you like.

- Where were you born? Have you ever moved from the place where you were born?

- Did you go to school?...for how long?

- What did you like or dislike in school?

- What people do you like? Why?

- Are you employed? What do you do?

- Is there something you dream of doing before you get old?

- Do you have children? Do you like them? Do you do anything with them?

- When you move around, are you slow or fast? Do you bump into things? Are you athletic and graceful? Do you stand straight?

- Do you speak loud, soft, fast, etc.?

The list can vary considerably. The interesting aspect of this is that, as the participants respond, certain changes will begin to happen unconsciously. Their physical presence changes, their voices, even their eyes. They are responding intuitively, and what they answer changes them inside. They've had many months in Creative Drama, and have overcome early self-consciousness and inhibition. Their imaginations are accessible.

They are also becoming aware when a response is simply another stereotype. They find new ways of urging each other past them, seeking cause and effect, once patterns and expectations are their own, not just imposed.

Extending the character through actions

- Try quick, small actions as the "deepening" characters. Wash as your character; write a letter; make a bed.

- Hold quick encounters with others — a mailman; a doctor; a grocer; a bus driver in a strange town.

- Make quick phone calls — to a relative; to a city agency; to a garage.

At each stage, allow time for evaluations. Do you feel different? Are you moving differently? Are you beginning to think differently than you would yourself? Etc. Where do you feel stereotyped?

THE AWARENESS IS SETTING IN; LIKEWISE AN IMPATIENCE WITH THE LIMITATIONS OF STEREOTYPES, WHICH AT FIRST AROUSED SO MUCH LAUGHTER. NEW CRITERIA ARE BEING INTERNALIZED FOR DRAMA WORK. ALSO, FOR LIFE.

AN ACTOR PREPARES. Constantin Stanislavaki. Theatre Arts, Inc., New York, 1939.
DEVELOPMENT THROUGH DRAMA. Brian Way. Longmans, Green & Co., Ltd., London. 1969.

EXPERIENCES VIII: CRITIQUING

Is there such a thing as audience responsibility? If so, to whom?

During a TV show, it matters not if the viewer talks, sleeps, eats, screams. He/she has no role to play for the performers. No responsibility for what they do. (And the opposite seems to be true as well.) Haven't you found an unquestioning acceptance of most TV fare? Some programs elicit greater enthusiasm than others, but little appraisal of what the program involves of ideas, values, characterizations, relationships or meaning. When I asked a group their opinions or thoughts at the end of a particular monster show many had seen the previous night, one boy candidly replied: "Oh, that's when I run for the pretzels . . .during commercials, before the next show starts."

Then we have auditorium programs. My students have toured improvised productions to auditoriums where teachers patrolled the aisles, threatening expulsion "if you make one sound." In one auditorium all students had to fold their hands on their laps and keep them folded. "And remember," exhorted the Discipline Counselor. "No laughing."

I understand the need which motivates this behavior from the adults. But I also fear that these young people may be stigmatized for life as members of a theatre audience: A major learning experience has been denied them.

What is the role of the audience?

In the Creative Drama space, we are concerned with introducing students to other ways of doing things, other capacities in themselves. We need more than an attentive audience. We need an audience of co-workers, responsible to each other. We need a perceptive, critical audience; an appreciative, identifying audience. Can we expect young people to just become this? The role of audience needs cultivation, based upon understanding and the new-found pleasures it can offer. Let's consider some approaches to four essentials in developing an audience, using Creative Drama techniques:

- Give-and-take

- Observing through the ear. . .and the eye

- Recognizing criticism as a positive

- Setting criteria

Give-and-take

We started one day by giving two students badminton racquets and a birdie. They batted the birdie back and forth several times. Then I whispered to Mary to miss the birdie because she wasn't looking. Her partner, Chris, became annoyed. "Hey, wake up!" he yelled. Then I whispered to Mary to start joking with someone across the room. "I can't play with her; she's not paying attention," Chris said in exasperation.

From this simple dramatization of the give-and-take needed between two players in a game, we were able to consider the kind of interaction needed — between players in an improvisation *and* between the players and the audience. They understood what we were talking about. We discussed the different kinds of audiences they've been part of. "Noisy." "Rude." "Silent. . .and bored." "Giggly." "Appreciative."

I asked three students to plan a simple improvisation. Meanwhile, a student director worked with the others on a series of signals for different kinds of audience behavior.

"Action!" The three began their improvisation. The audience, on signal, became restless, then noisy and vindictive. They turned serious and attentive, then they all went to sleep.

"Cut!"

"How did it feel, playing your scene to these different audiences?" I asked the players. The discussion was animated. They knew what was happening, yet they felt uncomfortable when the laughing was going on. They could hear the derogatory remarks being made about them. With all the noise, they felt like stopping and sitting down. . ."the audience made it impossible for us to hear each other." Then I asked, "Do you think a silent audience is the same as an appreciative audience?"

THIS IS AN EXERCISE WHICH SEEMS TO PAVE THE WAY TO AN EARLY AWARENESS THAT AUDIENCES HAVE SOME RESPONSIBILITY TO LIVE PERFORMERS. IT ALSO ILLUSTRATES THAT NO ONE IS INVULNERABLE. EACH ONE WILL BE A PLAYER AS WELL AS A MEMBER OF THE AUDIENCE.

Observing through the ears

"They just don't know how to listen!" adults so often exclaim — at home and in school. (Of course children say it about us too, and deservedly). Let's just agree that listening, and *hearing,* is an art which is undercultivated. So in the drama room we focus on the ear. . .with questions like these which lead into dramatic actions or improvisations: (I set a discreet rule that no person's names will be used in the responses):

- When has someone spoken to you, and you — purposely or not — didn't answer?

- When have you spoken to someone else who seems to ignore you? How does this make you feel?

- How does hearing affect our lives? For pleasure? For pain? For safety? For communication? For emergency?

- What sounds do you think you would miss most if you could no longer hear?
- When have you needed someone's ear, urgently, and they *did* sit down and listen to you?

Questions like these can draw upon real life and also upon literary or television situations, situations they've heard about. At this point, we try an improvisation where several people are doing something and not listening to each other. For example, a scene from the phrase, "Planning a Sunday outing," or "Getting the house ready for the moving van."

...and the eyes

"The sighted are so unseeing," said a sightless friend one day after she described the clouds to us as she "sees" them.

For several months a class of 6th graders had come to the Creative Drama space. Without warning one day I asked them to close their eyes. I was going to ask them questions, two students at a time. A murmur of anticipation swung around the room.

"Delira, on which wall is the fire extinguisher?" She thought and answered. I said, "You'll all check after you open your eyes." The squeezed-up faces indicated that others were trying to figure out where the fire extinguisher was, or if there was one in the room. "Gary, Robert next to you is wearing an interesting color combination. What are the colors?" Gary made a half-right guess. They opened their eyes as I moved on to two others. They grimaced at seeing the fire extinguisher facing them. "What has been changed in this room, something important, since you were here last, Janice?"

And on we went around the room, the previous set of two students helping with the next batch of questions. A simple activity with many possible variations.

"In our limited space, walk your route from school to home, describing to us as many details as you remember of what you see along the way. Include colors, things, arrangements, and people. On the way home tonight, take some paper and pencil with you, and make notes of what you remembered and what you left out."

IN THE ON-GOING TASK OF RELATING ALL THIS WORK ON SEEING AND HEARING TO THE RESPONSIBILITY OF AN AUDIENCE, THE STUDENTS WILL BEGIN TO PERCEIVE WHEN PLAYERS IN AN IMPROVISATION AREN'T REALLY LISTENING TO OR SEEING EACH OTHER. THIS IS AN EXTENSION OF THEIR OWN SHARPENED SENSITIVITIES.

Criticising as a positive

"Evaluation" is a word I like, yet I am using "critique" or "criticism" because it is so much a part of our language. Usually it implies negatives. Not so. Criticism, as your groups will learn, is also "the art or skill of making discerning judgments and evaluations, especially of artistic or literary works."

Initially we, the teachers, lead the perceptions of our students through our questions. Slowly, we are introducing guidelines. As each student begins to sense what to look for in an improvisation, he/she will get past the standard response, "That was okay."

The greatest value of being player one time, audience another, is that everyone knows the problems on each side. This leads to developing further expectations and standards. What's most exciting is when all this preparation jells. You hear an intense discussion interpreting an abstract improvisation. Yet you realize that, without any prodding, they are maintaining sensitivity for the feelings of the players.

Let me include an interne's written report of an improvisation based upon given language and, more importantly, the "Rap Time" critique afterward.

11 a.m. Monday. A class with 7th-8th graders

The Improvisation:

> The sand catches in his mouth and eyes as he drags his exhausted body across the desert. His face is distorted by the exertion. He stops; his head drops forward on the sand; his parched breathing stops. Then he coughs. He breathes again. As he peers through the raging sand storm for his friend, he calls out, in a voice thickened by grit and thirst,
>
> "Hi there!...How *are* you?"
>
> His friend struggles closer to him, battling the roaring winds:
>
> "Just...fine...thank you...And...you?"
>
> The first gasps out, his voice almost lost in the gale:
>
> "Fine...fine...will you...have...have a...lemon drop?"
>
> As though a mirage has flashed before him, the friend stretches out his hand, wheezing,
>
> "Don't mind...if...I...do..."
>
> But the mirage is gone. There is no lemon drop. He drops onto the sands, whispering, as his friend continues on alone,
>
> "See...you...again...sometime..."
>
> The whistling, hissing winds climax and subside.
>
> "CUT!" calls the assistant director.

The Evaluation:

> There is an outburst of laughter and appreciative applause. The two fellows and the girl who blew the winds take their seats.

The two dying men on the desert sit there on the floor waiting for the reactions of the class to their improvisation.

"I thought that was all riiiight!" says Jay.

"But why?" asks the teacher, as usual.

"Well, it was believable. You asked my group to watch their pantomime of things they touched or saw. . . .I *saw* that sand. I could almost *feel* it!"

"You could certainly *hear* it," grins Ea, looking at the sound effects crew. "We were wind, stupid, not sand," they answer.

Maria says, "I was supposed to watch for how well they planned. I think their planning was good. . .like they really knew where they were and what was happening. All the time."

"I don't know how you stayed so serious with that corny dialogue," giggles Aubrina. "When we do our improvisation, I'm afraid we're going to break up."

"Not if you really put your mind to what you're doing," says Joseph. He's done his scene already so he feels like an expert.

"Who'd you decide you both were on the desert?" asks Jill.

Dan answers. "We were two American guys, traveling for fun, who didn't know enough to stay off a desert in a sand storm. But I think. . .our characters were kind of general, weren't they? We didn't decide our ages, whether we were jocks or college guys or bums or what."

"Yeah," says Kenneth, "that's why I didn't really get any feeling that you wanted to get across the desert. But it was a great idea. Original, I mean."

I asked, "Did you decide why you wanted to get across?" and Joseph answered with his eyes large like he looks when he's pretending to be serious, "Wouldn't you want to get out of that sand storm. . .Man!"

Then the teacher asks Dan and Joseph how they felt about the Audience. Dan looks at Joseph. Then one starts talking and the other finishes: "To tell you the truth. . .with the sand and the wind. . .and pulling ourselves across the desert. . .and trying to remember the lines . . .I got to feeling so desperate and tired that. . .yeah, that I forgot there was an audience there."

THERE IS NOTHING TO COMPARE WITH BEING TOLD BY YOUR PEERS "GREAT IDEA" OR "I THINK YOUR PLANNING WAS GOOD BECAUSE. . ." WITH LOOKS OF ADMIRATION. THE AUDIENCE UNDERSTOOD WHAT WAS NEEDED TO STRETCH IMAGINATION TO A SITUATION SO FAR FROM LIFE EXPERIENCE.

A derisive member

Many times there is at least one student who uses the power of the critic to wreck vengeance like an axe-man. She/he yearns to cut — and hurt. If you wait long enough, peer group strengths will handle him/her. But meanwhile, the destruction...

Improvise scenes of criticizing. This may help. Cast your super-critic at the center of one scene. The topic: How many ways we can tell someone what we think of them, or of something they've done.

Or, work from a quote out of *Silas Marner* by George Eliot: "He'll never be hurt; he's made to hurt others."

Try questions along these lines:

- Do you know someone who acts as though nothing bothers him/her? Do you think it's true? How does this person walk, sit, talk, act in class or at home?

- Have you ever been hurt by someone, not physically but mentally? Was it intentional?

- How could you let that person know how you feel? How could you lead that person to change?

Divide the class into groups of two or four persons; each group will plan a scene which stems from the Eliot quote.

"Too cute for words"

I walked into Ms. Hopkins' class at her request. She was holding her second session of improvisation and was very excited about the students' enthusiasm. She had obviously set it up well, for they were involved and eager. After the third scene, Ms. Hopkins turned to me and exclaimed, loud and proud, "Wasn't that darling! Didn't I tell you! Wasn't she just too cute for words!?" The faces of the players went blank. Suddenly they became aware that they had been performing for an entertainment. By responding with a patronizing cliche, she blocked thoughtful, responsible interaction between performers and audiences. Is "cute" a useful measure?

Setting criteria

Before each scene, reiterate for the group exactly what is to be watched for: "Let's especially watch for the opening and closing of doors in this next improvisation; also, if they are aware of space in talking to each other from different rooms." Or, "Let's focus on their give-and-take. Do they listen to each other? Do they see what the other is doing?" Or, "Since we're working for what each character wants, without it being said aloud, watch for give-aways. What indications in their behavior suggest there's something on their minds?"

Conversely, with an advanced group, have the students tell what they are most interested in developing in their scene. One or two students can then lead the criticism as well.

ATTENTIVE? INTERESTED? FOCUSED? AUDIENCE MEMBERS ARE GROWING IN SELF-DISCIPLINE. THEY KNOW THEIR ROLE. THEY'LL BE ABLE TO SET THEIR OWN RULES OF BEHAVIOR IN THE AUDITORIUM OR ON A FIELD TRIP. THEY WILL NOT BE AMONG THE SPITBALL THROWERS WHEN THEY'RE BUSED TO LINCOLN CENTER OR THE SHAKESPEARE FESTIVAL. THEY WILL KNOW HOW IT SOUNDS TO PLAYERS TO RUSTLE CANDY WRAPPERS OR CHEW GUM NOISILY. MOST IMPORTANT, AFTER A WORKSHOP OR A PROFESSIONAL THEATRE EXPERIENCE, THEIR HEADS WILL BE WORKING — AND THEIR TONGUES. THEY WILL HAVE TASTES AND DISCERNMENT AND MAYBE, FOR THE FUTURE, THEY WILL DEMAND BETTER PRODUCTS OF TV AND SCREEN, PRODUCTS WHICH HAVE RESPECT FOR THEM AS THINKING PEOPLE.

CHALLENGES VIII: CRITIQUING

Listening activities

- Give the class a list of words, orally, and have them either write them down after hearing them all, or tell them.

- Give nonsensical directions, and have teams follow them about the room. Say three or four directions, and don't repeat them.

- Try "Mixed Numbers" from the FOCUS Challenges for this purpose.

- During Rap Time after each improvisation, ask questions like "Do you remember what he answered here? Were any words slurred or mispronounced? Where did her voice tell you more than the words?"

- Stimulate auditory perception of voices overheard while wearing blindfolds. . .telephone voices of strangers. . .voices in the halls.

Looking activities

Pantomime is useful for stimulating specific observation. Ask half the class to watch the other half do a pantomime, and then try to repeat exactly what was observed. (This differs from "Mirror" which is following another person simultaneously.)

Or, have three people describe a pantomime done by one person — every movement. It will remind you of Jose Marti's story of the seven blind men describing the elephant from seven different viewpoints.

Visual Scavenger Hunts: look out the window for 60 seconds; then write down everything you remember seeing.

Seeing Checks: On TV, watch who seems to really talk to each other, and listen in return.

People Watches: Observe people for what the face tells, what the feet tell, the walk, mannerisms, postures.

Supplement workshop criticism by outside assignments

- A critique of a television or radio show measured against certain given criteria.

- Collect critical articles and ferret out the author's criteria.

- Stage a debate on a featured movie or TV special.

WE CHOOSE PROJECTS

By my second and third year, I was better able to take more chances and explore deeper applications of Creative Drama. Recognizing it as a unifying process which can reach into many areas of learning, I tried combining it with theme ideas for projects. We had no blueprints. The students were developing their own patterns as they went along.

It was gratifying to have more faculty cooperation now. Some projects like "Human Beings in our World" encompassed a team of academic and arts teachers. We included other media more and more. People outside school, including parents, gave us assistance. We went out into the community to dramatize learning through actual experience. We even toured original improvised programs to other audiences, and led pre-school groups in dramatizing folk literature.

The foundations of our workshops of the first year provided a base of comfort and competence upon which we could build projects like these:

MODELS

A group of potential drop-outs got involved in learning through a program relevant to their dreams.

COURT

A way of dealing with discipline problems became a hook for introducing logical thinking and developing skill in validating evidence.

"SOUL BROTHERS AND SISTER LOU"

In my effort to get a class of non-readers excited about a book, we ended up with a ten-part radio serial.

HUMAN BEINGS IN OUR WORLD

We got a grant for a year-long interdisciplinary program (social studies, language arts, science, family living, art, music and drama) involving in-school sessions and extensive field work.

LET US BE FREE

Investigating the history of slavery turned into a two-and-a-half year project culminating in a film.

I describe these adventures to share the kind of projects which can grow out of Creative Drama. And to encourage you to develop similar or different drama-based original projects, tied into your own curriculum.

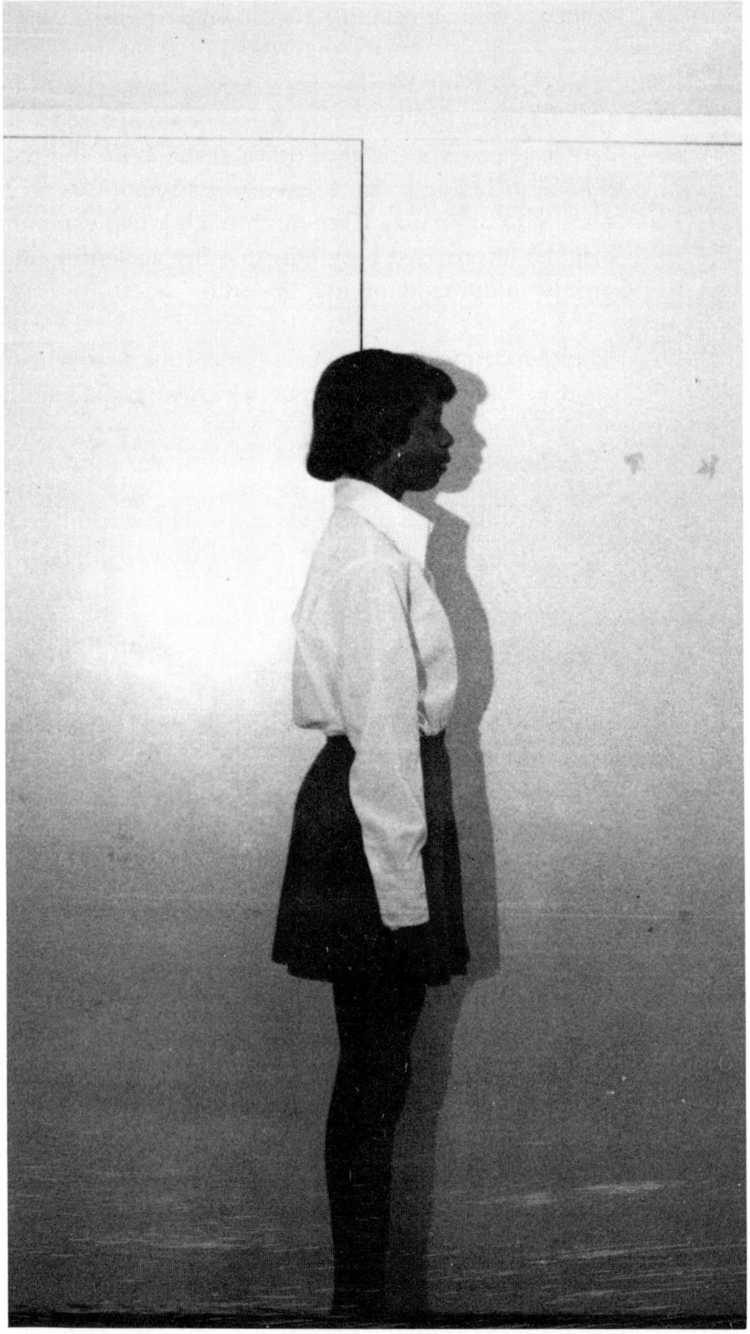

MODELS

There were about sixteen girls, 13 to 15 years old, who were interested, it seemed, in nothing. Patrols regularly found them crowded into the small basement girls' room — the air thick with cigarette smoke, although this was a reason for expulsion from school, combs busily re-styling hair-do's, perfume thick enough to gag on, animated conversation, outbursts of laughter and screams. In class, fights broke out within the clique. Then tears. Remorse.

Linda confronted me one day. "Why don't you teach us something *good* . . .like how to be models!"

Why not? In teacher's meeting, I broached the possibility. It set loose a stream of complaints. Most of these girls weren't fulfilling their "contract" work in their academics. They didn't concentrate. They disturbed others. . . .

The Guidance Counselor was with me. "They're all heavily into adolescence. They're concerned about their bodies, their appearance, AND the boys. As long as we have Creative Drama in our school, let's take advantage of it to deal with these girls where they are, and try to bring them *from* there. Better than constantly bucking them."

I defined my goals and got the go-ahead. Linda and her best friend Vanessa met with me to frame an invitation.

"Come and join a new group and become a MODEL!!!!
(Wear Skirts and Heels to the Meeting. No gum allowed.)"

Since the program was to be "by invitation," the selection was a problem, but by deciding on certain standards, it was possible to accept girls otherwise excluded.

1. Cannot be absent without written note.
   (From whom, was never defined)

2. Must be punctual.

3. Any giggling and out. We are serious.

4. Must go to all the classes she's supposed to.
   (This I somehow put through as the only way we could expect school cooperation with some of our special plans.)

5. Be neat and act interested.

6. Very polite.

7. One fight and she's out.

For the first session, sixteen "polite, interested, neat, serious" girls arrived. They walked in as to a grand ballroom, not my workshop space they'd worked in for two years. The chairs, for once, were set up in two straight rows. I sat in the back. Linda and Vanessa stood at an improvised podium, towering from the height of their platform heels.

We had planned the opening, even rehearsed part of it so Linda would be understood better..."cuz everyone ses I talk too fast." She waited until the room was in an extraordinary condition of absolute silence:

> "We welcome you to this new class in becoming models. With your invitation you got a list of our rules. The school is watching us. We got to be good to keep this special class. That means no smoking in the john too. If you are suspended from school, you are out of this group."

Vanessa continued, after losing her notes, dropping her pencil, and almost swallowing her larynx.

> "I will now take attendance. Do not answer silly things to make everyone laugh. Just say 'Present.' Stand as you say it. Then sit down quick. Since we are all going to learn to be models we should sit up straight in the chairs with our feet crossed and our hands in our laps."

Finally they turned the session over to me. Scarcely that. I was "invited" to meet the models group to help them learn about becoming models.

The John Robert Powers School of Modelling???

Now let me create no illusions. I know little about modeling. But I could easily empathize with these girls...see their basic discomfort with themselves, their self-consciousness, their pained attempts to be personable and attractive against the "going" styles of the day. Above all, their need to be appreciated by others.

I asked each girl to write or say onto the tape recorder what she thought a model is like, in order to get some idea of their expectations.

> "knows how to walk...how to talk good...looks sexy...makes clothes look good...knows how to talk on a TV show and not fidget...attract rich boys...everyone likes her..."

Amidst a flurry of synchronized hair combing, we set up a camera on a tripod, to take three Polaroid camera photos of each member. These were mounted on large sheets of paper, and carefully analyzed. "Let's look at ourselves. How do we hold our bodies? How do we present ourselves through our postures and expressions?"

They looked at all the pictures and wrote criticisms on each sheet. Everyone was equally vulnerable. This, plus fierce frowns from Linda, enforced the "serious constructive evaluation." Recognition of slouches, jutting bellies or rumps, forward thrust chins and heads, spine distortion, shoulder irregularity, led the way to group decision for movement training. So much better that they saw the need than that I imposed it. We set up ten sessions with a sensitive modern dance/Jazz/gymnastics teacher to start the following week.

What I hoped for

Susan, at that time, saw no purpose in learning Math or Science or even Reading. How would this stuff help her deal with her need for acceptance, her family brawls, her inner anger and hurt? Margo wanted to move out of her home to do something with her life. She was unsure, vulnerable, and measured herself against role models provided by television and cheap paperbacks. Dolores had been brought up by an indulgent father who went to college. He urged her to get grades, stand up and speak out. She wanted his approval. She also wanted to be accepted by her peers.

What I was looking for was a slow shift from the major concern for outward appearances to an awareness of the meaning of a person's inner existence. A recognition of what interests, involvements, enthusiasm, can do to make a person beautiful, more beautiful than the well-kept outer skin. A recognition of how un-beautiful a mere plastic doll is. The gradual realization of personal uniqueness, and the desire to enhance it.

This, I believe fervently, is a starting point preceding the quest for objective knowledge and skills.

Our first modeling event

After two months of our workshops, the group planned a "Last Minute Gift Ideas" presentation as part of the Christmas program for parents and friends. Eighteen merchants cooperated by lending or donating clothing and interesting accessories.

For weeks before the holidays, we improvised approaching the merchants and discussing our ideas for modeling and displaying gifts. I like playing opposites in order to make a choice, so I had the girls walk "a lazy person," "an uninterested person," "an uncertain person," and then a "pleasant person." We dealt with voices and articulation, growing through listening to each other. We imitated all kinds of dialects and speech patterns before making choices of personal manners of communication.

At lunch time, with three girls at a time, I'd set off to the main shopping center to visit shopkeepers with whom the girls had made telephone appointments. Most store owners were cordial and cooperative. The evening gowns — furnished by the Community Action Group — were the peak experience. Imagine seventeen teenage girls set loose in a shop to choose a gown from over one hundred tantalizing possibilities!

The shop visits had deeper meanings. Some of the girls were inveterate shop lifters — as are many young people in urban and suburban communities today..."for the fun of it," according to one social commentator. In dramatizing their approaches to shopkeepers, the girls had decided it would be interesting to find out what it was like to run a shop. They prepared questions — why had one lady opened a dress shop; what was it like running a pipe shop. They followed through their plans with consistency. In reporting back, after the actual shop visits, they expressed a kind of revelation. They had met shopkeepers as people. They detected the frightened, helpless looks on many concerned faces. They heard about shops which would have to close in January, because of theft and mugging and high costs of insurance.

EBONY invites us to visit

For over six weeks our Models group prepared for a visit to New York City. Over the phone, the Fashion Editor of Ebony magazine suggested a day's itinerary that included a stop at a wholesale clothing manufacturer to introduce the students to other fields related to modeling.

A day in the city would be costly. Four of us — three student co-signers and myself as faculty advisor — were elected to open a bank account and make weekly deposits of monies earned or donated. A surfeit of baby sitters descended on the neighborhood and faculty. One girl set hair for 25¢ a head. Another lined up special chores for a married sister.

Susan felt abandoned in this flurry of money-making. She had no resources at home. Who'd hire her to baby sit, with her reputation, she mumbled to me. For a week we didn't see her. Members of the faculty agreed to help. She could wash cars after school or walk the dogs. One teacher invited her to wash supper dishes. The day before the trip, an exultant Susan produced the needed amount in quarters and dimes and nickels.

Our drama work was primarily utilitarian. We role-played and projected ourselves into all kinds of situations for alternative behavior and purpose. How to give directions to a taxi driver; how to ask directions if we got separated; how to handle money without argument; how to eat at a fancy restaurant with a menu without hot dogs, French fries and hamburgers; how to introduce ourselves at a national magazine or in a modeling agency. Everyone had a preplanned responsibility. Everyone carried her own money. Every aspect of the day's trip which I could anticipate was dramatized, evaluated and re-improvised.

Can we open the door to the world a little wider?

Our first appointment was at 10:30 at a Models Agency. Our group sat, high and beautiful, on stiff plastic benches, only their eyes giving away their discomfort and awe. One majestic six-foot model after another swung through the lacquered double doors, miniature French poodle held as ornament beneath their arms. When one woman was preceded in by two Russian wolfhounds, I nearly lost my group out the nearest exit. As dignified as they tried to be during the long wait, it became increasingly difficult to maintain this role, faced by the stream of Junoesque goddesses. The agency head was polite and gratuitous. Smiling at no one in particular, she commented, "Of course, to be a fashion model today you must be five foot eight inches or over." No one of our group stood taller than five foot five. At that moment I realized how deep was each one's dream of being a model.

The Fashion Editor was as gracious and sensitive to the girls' feelings as the previous woman had been callous. A magnificent woman with black skin drawn tight over classic high bones, elegantly attired, she took all seventeen in hand with tact and good humor that captured the devotion and idolatry of each one. She led us about the magazine offices, introducing us — by name — to this editor and that secretary. Then we stalked through the streets, the girls trying to keep abreast of her long strides.

Knowing we were accustomed to dramatic improvisation, this keen woman had set up a drama experience at the garment house. We were seated on the buyers' chairs in the buyers' room; new clothes were displayed on racks by salespeople and models. Fabrics and style were described. The students were asked for comments and questions. She prodded their skeptical appraisals of price and fabric, designs and workmanship. With the owners' help, she taught the mathematics of pricing. There sat some of our math failures, catching on to "mark up" and "profit margin," filling out the pricing sheets with aplomb.

For lunch she led us to an oriental restaurant which did not serve chow mein or chop suey. She encouraged them to sample new tastes. Only a brief problem in figuring out the group bill for individual payment and the tip: "You mean we have to pay the waitresses too! What's the matter with the restaurant...we pay them enough already!"

A tired, foot-sore group of young women caught the interestate bus back to New Jersey, hastily compiling notes from the day. All the fine posture and glowing eyes of the day were dimmed by now. They'd played their roles well all day. What were the meanings which would be internalized within each mind and heart? This is part of the immeasurable of the dramatic process.

Had the door to the world been opened a little wider? Was the sense of self a little stronger? Had the Creative Drama preparation served to connect each student with possibilities in life?

> **Art lies at the wellspring of life itself. It is not tacked on to the periphery of living. It is a stirring of memories and visions. It opens up new worlds and new dimensions of awareness.**
> Elizabeth Fraser Williamson
> Canadian sculptor

COURT IS IN SESSION

How do you handle fist fights, name calling, gang attacks on a minority student, tattling, stealing, vandalism? So many school punishments have lost their effectiveness. The old solution — "you're expelled," or suspending a student for a week — did little or nothing to change a student's behavior or attitude.

One process I've had success with is "Court." Young people are exposed to courtrooms in heavy doses in television dramas. A number of my students have been in juvenile court for petty crimes or in relation to family problems. Court procedures are known to them in many ways.

For our purposes, Court is another form of dramatic improvisation, which may be based upon fact or fiction. As students begin to examine each other's behavior and feelings, rather than damning or ostracizing the individual, the peer group looks at anti-social acts with an eye toward change.

A spontaneous case

The ten o'clock Creative Drama class was just leaving. Guy came tearing through the door whispering urgently, "Hey, Ms. Wilder! Hide me. . . hide me!" He threw himself under my desk. Within seconds, David, Charles, Laretta and Fred came smashing through the door in pursuit. Fred looked furious; the others exuded a kind of delight in anticipation of something exciting. . .like a fight!

"Wait'll I get my hands on him. . .just wait. . .I'll choke every ounce of funky breath out of him!" Fred roared. The rest of the class straggled in, perking up when they sensed excitement.

"Is he here? Is he in your room?" Fred confronted me threateningly. In an instant, the entire class was standing about us.

"Fred," I said quietly. "You know I won't allow a fight in my room." I hoped I sounded convincing.

"Don't protect him from me. . .if you're hiding him, I'll. . .I'll. . ." His anger had been fanned by his friends to the explosion point. Fred is small for twelve, but he's skyrocket fast and he's strong, especially when he's angry. If anyone gets in his way he goes berserk. When he's calmer, I find him imaginative, perceptive and responsible in our Drama Workshops. But right now was no time for righteous indignation or "That's no way to talk to a teacher." I stalled for time. "Did Guy do something to you?"

"You're G--D--right he did!"

David sang out, "Yeah, Guy called Fred's mother a whore." I glared at David, so gleeful with his friend's misery. "What a thoughtless thing to say. . ." I began. I had learned that punching, spitting, slapping, pounding, scratching, kicking or lying are quite all right. . .but you cannot insult another student's mother!

"Call Court! Let's call Court!" yelled Laretta and Diane. David's face shifted gear. "I'll be Fred's lawyer. Okay, Fred? I'll be your lawyer?"

Fred hesitated. "You got Guy?"

"Yes, Fred," I answered.

"Where?"

"You won't touch him," I insisted, "you'll let the Court decide?" Fred raised his eyes. The peak of his anger was past. "Just bring the rat fink here," he muttered.

Sheepishly Guy crawled out from under my desk, whining, "He hit me first!" Without giving them a chance to tangle, volunteer legal aides quickly enveloped Guy, and David and Laretta whisked Fred off to prepare their brief. Others were already moving chairs to shape a "proper" courtroom.

Charlotte became judge. She'd handled this role before. Everyone else became witnesses and jurors except Ray who was standing over by the window, alone, as usual. I whispered to Charlotte and she took Ray aside to teach him, "Do you swear to tell the truth and nothing but. . ." making him the clerk.

From my trunk of fabrics, we formed a judge's cloak and a cover for the judge's bench. *Beginning Chemistry,* the fattest book in sight, was designated to serve as Bible.

Rules for today's trial

The Courtroom rules were the first order of procedure. Kristi wrote them down as they were suggested:

1. Be quiet in Court. Don't argue with Judge. Speak only when Judge recognizes you.

2. When on stand, tell what you saw, not what someone else told you.

3. No blowing bubbles. If you can't keep your gum in your mouth, get rid of it — give it to the clerk.

4. Keep your cool. If someone testifies something you don't like, do not get angry.

5. Be fair. Because someone's your friend or you're afraid you will be beaten up if you tell the truth, is no reason to not tell what you know.

6. Speak loud so we hear from the back.

She later returned to write "Obey these rules or the Sgt. of Arms will make you!"

Charlotte reminded everyone of the special court-like phrases we used: "You're out of order"; "I object, your honor"; "Call the next witness." Two sergeants-at-arms were appointed to make sure the rules were followed. Two "misdemeanors" and a person would be removed from court to sit alone by the wall.

The Judge called the prosecuting attorney to present his case and then called her first witness. The room became awesomely quiet. "Your Honor," began Fred's lawyer, David. "Your Honor, my customer. . ."

"Your client," corrected the Judge.

"My client, Fred Appleton, says he came to school today with five singles in his right pocket. He sat next to Guy in home base. Then he went to Math. Guy was sitting on his right side. He reached into his pocket. The money was gone. He looked at Guy and Guy was grinning, and he's sure that Guy took the money so he grabs Guy on the arm. . . and when Guy sassed him he grabbed his pencil and broke it and threw it back on Guy's desk and then Guy got real nasty and. . ."

"I object, Your Honor," interrupted Guy's lawyer, Janis. "The prosecuting attorney's talking so fast that I don't understand him."

"Will the Prosecuting Attorney kindly talk slower," said Charlotte.

The prosecuting attorney was in a huddle with his client and he simply nodded. When he continued, he spoke staccato, with exaggerated clarity. "Yeah. . .Fred / says / that Guy / ripped his test / paper / stamped on his foot / and said / out loud / you just kiss my. . .everybody knows your mother / is / a. . ."

The entire courtroom erupted. "You're out of order!" interrupted the Judge. "Stick to the facts!"

"But that is a fact," called out Fred, his eyes blazing.

"ORDER IN THE COURT," sang out Ray, the clerk.

"First witness. Charlie Green!" Charles was quickly sworn in. Charles is thin and slow moving. He doesn't look anyone in the eye. He chews gum on one side of his mouth, slow motion. When he gets up from a chair or sits down, he seems to unravel like a long piece of yarn. I've never heard him have an opinion of his own. As a witness he looked strained.

He answered David's questions with lots of "aaah's" and "yeahs." "I was sitting next to Fred. . .yeah. . .on his left side, I guess. . .and I heard Guy. . .aaah. . .cuss Fred and. . .well. . .he said. . .like. . . whatyouhitmefor. . .aaah. . ."

Guy was smirking. Fred was sitting forward in his seat, his face serious. This was real stuff.

"Your witness," the Judge called to Janis. She walked to the desk with professional disdain for the departing prosecutor. "Are you a close friend of the defendant, Mr. Appleton, or Fred, as you call him?"

"Aaah, yeah. . .I guess so," answered Charles.

"Do you ever think he does anything wrong?"

"I don't know. . .aaah."

"If you did know, would you tell him?"

"Aaah. . .nope."

"That's all, your Honor," said Janis.

Guy's sister, Darryl, was called next. "Darryl, how much money do you and your brother get every week?"

"Five dollars a week, for bus and lunch," answered Darryl.

"Did you get a dollar this morning?"

"Yep."

"Are you sure Guy got a dollar this morning?"

"Yep. My father ran after us to the bus stop 'cause we forgot it."

Facing the jury, Janis asked her final question, "Therefore, your brother did not need money today?" She then sat down, looking victorious. "Prosecution's witness."

The trial went on through a variety of witnesses. Some giggled. Most maintained their seriousness. Almost all these students have participated in Drama for six months or more and can give themselves fully to dramatic improvisation.

When Guy was finally called he asked to show the contents of his pockets as his proof of innocence. The judge labeled it "Exhibit A," and agreed to return the stuff to Guy when Court recessed. Guy produced several short pencils. Fred yelled, "Why'd you get so upset when I broke one pencil? You had others." After an endless array of elastic bands, bus stubs, candy wrappers, and a worn horseshoe, Guy found his crumbled-up dollar bill.

His lawyer looked at him thoughtfully as she asked if he had a mother. "Sure I do," Guy answered, as though that had nothing to do with the case.

"Do you like your mother?" Janis persisted.

"Yeah. What's that to you?"

"If I called her names right now in front of everyone, nasty insulting names, what would you do?"

"Whatdya mean, what'd I do? I'd slap you...and I mean hard."

"Okay," said Janis, with an "I've caught you" kind of look. "So even if you are my client I want to know why you said mean things about Fred's mother."

There was a pause that vibrated about the room. "Because I was mad. He had no right to accuse me of stealing his dough and then punching me around."

"Did you take the money out of his pocket? Remember, you're under oath."

Guy fixed his eye on Fred. "No," he said. "No, I did not take his money. (pause) And I'm...I'm sorry I said what I said about his mother. (pause) I take it back."

Fred's head was down. This began to seem an unsolvable theft but scarcely a wasted trial. Another witness said she thought she'd seen Guy's hand in Fred's pocket. The Judge quickly put that down as opinion, not fact. The clock's hands approached lunch time. The Judge briefed the jury and sent them out.

For five minutes everyone else talked quietly, in suspense. Then the jurors filed back to their seats. "The jury does not find Guy guilty of stealing the money but he did insult Fred's mother. We say Fred is guilty of saying Guy stole without proof and also he owes Guy a new pencil."

Fred pleaded, "He's got lots of other pencils in his pocket." The Judge said, "You've got lots more money at home but you still want your five dollars, don't you?"

It was then I noticed Charles standing among the seated witnesses. I suggested the Judge call on him.

Charles started, "...aaah...what's the...what's the...aaah...punishment...aaah...if he did take the money?"

No one knew. I stepped in here. "What's your point, Charles?"

"Well...aaah...what if someone...someone said he'd...he'd...aaah ...taken the money and...would give it back? Aaah...is there... aaah...a punishment?"

The judge looked nonplussed and turned to me for a suggestion. David spoke up. "That's never happened before. I think if somebody was honest enough to tell the truth, he shouldn't get any punishing."

The class agreed. "But," said Laretta, "who'd ever do such a thing? It's a stupid question. Nobody'd own up."

But there was Charles holding out five singles in his hand and offering them to Fred, saying "Aaah...you forgot which pocket...which pocket you put 'em in."

THIS IS ONE OF MANY COURT SESSIONS WE REALLY HELD IN MY DRAMA ROOM. ALMOST ALWAYS THERE HAS BEEN THIS KIND OF INVOLVEMENT AND CANDOR. UNDER THE ANGER AND HOSTILITY AND FRUSTRATION MANY STUDENTS EXPERIENCE, I'VE FOUND A DEEP SENSE OF FAIRNESS. AND A SENSE OF HUMOR AND RESPONSIVENESS TO CHALLENGE WHICH ENCOURAGES THIS WAY OF HANDLING FIGHTS AND OTHER DIFFERENCES.

"Order in the Courtroom — that means you!"

The first time a fist fight broke out in my classroom, without thinking twice, I called out "We'll decide this in Court!" For my Court experiences go back a long time to the intimate moments around the family dinner table, after a kicking-hitting-screaming argument between my brother and me. My parents, always resourceful and imaginative, would call "Court!" As soon as the meal was finished, Dad would don a moustache (I still don't know why he thought a judge needed a moustache) and a dish towel to indicate a robe; mother would put on her most serious expression. We had an opening chant, taken from some long-forgotten camp play. You might like to make use of it sometime:

> Order in the Courtroom
> That means you.
> It's getting pretty late
> And we gotta get through.
> Now then, Court clerk
> What's the next case?
> Bring it forward
> And none of your sase.

I never did know what "sase" meant, if it meant anything. It was just part of the ritual. Each of us would have a turn to explain our side of the story. No interruption was tolerated. By bedtime we'd be talking to each other again.

A training program for Court

I decided to try the same thing at school. From our spontaneous beginning, our schoolroom Court expanded into a major program involving about twenty-five trainees from 6th, 7th and 8th grades. We started with weeks of developmental exercises to sharpen perception and skills. With the cooperation of a father who worked in the County Parole Offices, we were permitted to spend days in various courts, meeting with lawyers, judges, police, civil rights representatives. We got enthusiastic assistance from the Law School of Rutgers University. Law students brought us legal issues to dramatize — issues which had implications for our students such as "No Knock" laws and problems of search and seizure. We actually participated in a Mock Court trial at the University concerning a real tenants' rent strike. The tenants were present as the defendents. Our students were briefed to enable them to prepare questions which they asked of the defendents. When we rode home that night, I was sure all twenty-five students were determined to enter the legal profession.

But the values of court go beyond handling discipline problems or learning legal procedures. We explore the options people have in handling the frantic moments of their lives. First we enact the conflict between two or more people which can erupt into a battle. Then we dissect the issues involved — and the inner feelings. We divide into groups of four or five for planning other ways the basic situation might have developed. Each group finally presents their dramatized version for others to evaluate.

By introducing the court procedures, we introduce objective reasoning and logic; try to discriminate between prejudices, opinion and fact, and develop skill in validating evidence. Here are some of the exercises we have used for sharpening sensory perception and using deductive/inductive reasoning.

You are a detective

- Two people leave the room. While they are out, everyone else rearranges important aspects of the room. They also change their own seats. The two people return. They are asked to detect what has been changed.

- This time, two people are blindfolded. Silently, everyone else changes seats. They take turns giving the two blindfolded students verbal directions of moves about the room — moves which test their memories and sound perception. For example, "Walk to the wall where the fire extinguisher is," or "Get a record from the cabinet." Or, "Can you identify the voice you will hear next?"

- Here's another game to test your detectives' hearing. Divide the class in two groups. Each group takes a portable recorder or cassette and tapes ordinary sounds inside or outside the room. Simple sounds like rubbing, hitting, scratching, breathing, blowing, gurgling sounds. The same sound at different time intervals can sound totally different.

After a period of time, both groups return to the room. They play their tape for the group to identify each sound, *or* what else it sounds like.

Scavenger hunts

Do you remember old fashioned scavenger hunts? Remember how teams were given lists of nearly impossible items to find and bring back at a designated time? Teams would sometimes be gone for hours and then arrive back, exhausted but triumphant, with an ostrich feather, a bagel, or a silvered baby shoe. Here are two variations of the old scavenger hunt.

- INVESTIGATION. The class is divided into teams of two. Each team is given a list of items. The object is to find where each item can be located, purchased, or where services can be rendered. NOTHING IS BROUGHT BACK BUT THE INFORMATION. Imagination and ingenuity are most useful in this. A sample list, which would vary a great deal depending upon where you live, might include

>   A candlemaker
>   A foreign coin exchange
>   A diagnostic center for tree and plant diseases
>   A farm that raises Guernsey cows
>   A translator of Oriental languages
>   Repair service for umbrellas
>   An artist who designs "coats-of-arms"

- COLLECT THE EVIDENCE. Teams of three or four persons go outside and walk along a designated block or two. They search for items which have been dropped, collect them, and bring them back.

Next, the group is asked to draw deductions: the age of each item, who might have dropped it, in which direction the person was going, at what time, any indications of person's age or sex or purpose. They try to put together a "snooper's" story using deduction, imagination, and — always — humor. The entire group shares in the relating, illustrating the story with actions of how the person might have been proceeding, etc.

Separating evidence from opinion

There are so many possibilities we accept as fact, without questioning. Often someone says something is so in a voice of great authority, and we just accept it. For this activity, neither guessing, hearsay, nor possibility are accepted. It's proof that is required!

In groups of two, give lists to each group with several problems to be solved. They must find proof and return with it. Then everyone finds an original way of sharing their evidence, perhaps as scientists in a lab; as city tax collectors; as lecturers; radio or TV commentators, etc. (You'll find designing these problems is quite a challenge for you too!)

- Prove that a person by your name really exists as a member of your family at a particular address.

- Prove that earliest man lived in a particular location two million years ago.

- Prove that oil and water don't mix and why.

- Prove that a plant is not an animal.

- Prove that a complex math problem really has no solution.

- Prove that some prominent musical group are still alive (and not by saying "I saw them last night.")

- *PERSUASION.* In groups of three or four, plan a situation in which one person is trying to persuade the others to do something important. For example, one person must convince the others to turn the car around because he or she thinks they're driving in the wrong direction for Kalamazoo.

- *IN DEFENSE OF.* One person at a time, addressing the full group, presents arguments defending
    him or herself against pretended criticism
    an idea
    a civil right (it might be good to re-read the Bill of Rights for this, to provide some strong possibilities)
    a personal right
  The Persuasion activities are good preparation for this.

- *WITNESSES.* A group of six, seven or eight people plan a situation which will gradually erupt into an argument and then into an actual fight. The fight should not involve all members. It is important, for this improvisation, to pre-set the details leading up to the actual fight.

TO SAVE FLESH AND BONE FOR THE NEXT CREATIVE DRAMA SESSIONS, USE "SHADOW BOXING" TECHNIQUES FOR THE FIGHT. NO PUNCH OR STAB CONNECTS. IT JUST LOOKS LIKE IT DOES. THIS REQUIRES PRACTICE, EXCELLENT TIMING, AND SKILLFUL "GIVE AND TAKE" BETWEEN FIGHTERS.

Present the improvisation. Then give each spectator a piece of paper and ask them to write their answers to questions you will ask, such as "Who started the fight? For what reason?" "Who was involved in the fighting?" Who was "just arguing"? Who felled whom, and how? What was the argument about?

Finally, have the answers read aloud. Rarely will you find that everyone has seen the same details or the same persons doing something. Students will recognize how personal prejudices can play a role in what one sees.

- *VOIRE DIRE.* The dictionary definition is "to say the truth." In our legal system this pertains to questioning prospective jurors in the jury selection process, in order to discover biases which may prevent them from making objective determination from the facts in a given case.

Initially, I used this process in the classroom while a jury was being chosen in California to try a young black woman — a case which the students were watching with great interest in Social Studies. Our "lawyers" decided that prospective jurors should be examined for their personal prejudice toward black people and toward women.

Some handled this indirectly by discovering where the juror lived; did they or had they ever worked together with black women on a job; did any black people live in their neighborhood. Other students added questions: "Where would you sit if you got on a bus and only three seats were vacant — next to a Puerto Rican, a white man, and a black woman?" Or "Would you swim in an integrated swimming pool?"

The students divided into prospective jurors and lawyers. The jurors were allowed to play characters of their invention, not themselves. Questions were planned by teams of three lawyers while the jurors were off planning a short biography of their character's life.

EVALUATION AFTER EACH QUESTIONING IS VITAL TO THIS EXERCISE. WERE THE QUESTIONS INCISIVE AND TO THE POINT? DID THEY BUILD, ONE ON THE OTHER? DID THE JURORS FEEL THAT THE QUESTIONS WERE SO WORDED AS TO PULL PERTINENT INFORMATION FROM THEM WITHOUT THEIR BEING AWARE?

Dramatizing a story in literature or in the news

You may want to take your first trial from literature. One I've used successfully, "The Silver Box," by John Galsworthy, will give you an idea of how to proceed.

We dissect the story first according to who, where, when, what happened.

WHO: Mr. Hutchins, a man in his thirties. He's been out of work six months.
        Mrs. Hutchins, his wife, similar age. She works all day as a cleaning maid for a wealthy family.
        The landlady, elderly and suspicious of people.
        Two policemen.

WHERE: A humble but clean flat in an old tenement house.

WHEN: Early in this century, when many people are out of work. Unemployment compensation and welfare payments do not exist. People are hungry and desperate.

WHAT: When the landlady comes for the rent, she is surprised that Mr. Hutchins pulls out enough money for two months' rent. So is Mrs. Hutchins. We proceed with the skeletal events of the story, and later breathe many details into it, such as the relationships between people, identities of other people related to the story, etc. Then we are ready to outline a trial.

DEFINE THE CHARGES:

    Mrs. Hutchins: theft of a silver box containing coins and bills totalling $500.00
    Mr. Hutchins: Assault against an officer of the law

CAST THE PARTS:

    The Judge
    Clerk
    Guards
    Lawyers for the Prosecution; for the Defense
    The Accused: Mr. & Mrs. Hutchins
    Witnesses???

Before you hold the trial

- Each character prepares his identity and his story in relation to this case. Some questions for each character: "What is your relationship to the accused? What do you know about the theft? Does your character feel bold or timid on the stand? Why? Is your character concerned with justice or making an impression (as on an employer)?"

- Lawyers meet with their clients in order to organize their briefs. They may need to be reminded that their main desire is to impress the Judge and jury on behalf of their clients.

- The Judge jots down a plan for the trial to keep it moving — limiting the question and answer time for each witness; acquainting the clerk and the guards with their responsibilities for swearing in witnesses, maintaining order in the court, etc.

- Everyone should agree on basic courtroom procedures which the class thinks should be observed (as the Courtroom group did for Fred and Guy's trial).

- Allow enough time for the jury to meet, the verdict, and sentencing.

I like to begin with, "And now, the Court will please rise until Judge _____ assumes the bench."

Some suggestions for material for your next trials

- Situations from life in school or in the neighborhood

- A shop-lifting case

- A child negligence case

- A land dispute between an Indian group vs. a large manufacturing company

- The witches of Salem, Mass.

- The trial in *The Devil and Daniel Webster* or *Alice in Wonderland*

- The front pages of your newspaper. That's where I found my favorite news clipping —

    Amos Meier reported his African parrot missing, but said it could easily be identified because it spoke only German. Police found a parrot in the home of one of Meier's neighbors. The neighbors denied the parrot was a fugitive and said that it spoke no known language.

    The case of Meier vs. Bartlett was brought into court. The bird remained mute while Meier argued his ownership and the cost of training and feeding the bird. Suddenly the bird burst into song. "Ach, du lieber Augustine," it sang. Meier and his bird went home together. The Judge did not say what his opinion against the neighbors, the Bartletts, would be.

U.P.I.

ADVENTURES IN READING: FROM BOOK TO RADIO SERIAL

If learning to speak happens quite naturally for most children exposed to spoken language whose ears (and minds) are functioning normally, then reading should be as natural for healthy eyes.

Both reading and speaking involve the recognition of symbols through our senses. Our social environment depends upon these language symbols, printed and spoken, for communication.

The average kid listens, speaks, and READS innumberable times in a given day. Yes, reads! Road signs, store signs, billboards, names and designations on buses and trucks, and labels. . .all kinds of labels from gum and candy wrappers to sneakers, t-shirts and food. True, color, logos and design help — but aren't these also language symbols?

What I recognize is that children, most children, learn to speak and to read when they have to, when they want to. There's no great mystique about learning to read. The mystique is about NOT learning to read. Is there some missing enzyme in our educational approach to reading? Do you think if we were to teach walking in school we would produce non-walkers?

I found myself confronting the reading problem with a class of sixth graders who wanted to dramatize a new book, but they balked at reading it. This translated to me that they BELIEVED in their ability to LISTEN to the story, understand it, become the characters, invent language and movement, and bring the plot situations and feelings alive within our drama space.

How could they be led to believe they could also read?

Can Drama help reinforce the reading program?

Once again Mrs. Richard of the Instructional Media Center had turned up an exciting book for us, *Soul Brothers and Sister Lou,* by Kristin Hunter. She gave it to three girls. Briefly, she outlined the story and caught their interest. They tore into a Drama workshop. "But how can we act the story before you've read the book?" I asked. "You read it to us!" came back to me, in unison.

Briefly, the book is set in the south side of a city where the inhabitants wage daily struggle for survival. Lou lives with Momma and seven brothers and sisters in a small five-room house. She and her friends, a teenage neighborhood gang, turn an emptied storefront church with an old upright piano "too old to stand moving" into a clubhouse. It becomes an important symbol to the teenagers. They plan a neighborhood dance to finance the rent. Someone tells the cops there's going to be a fight, and they raid the dance, shoot Jethro, and close the house. The story deals with the frustration and bitterness at the unwarranted shooting and the options the gang members find — other than homemade bombs and revenge — to salvage their dream after Jethro dies. As a reviewer wrote, "It is much more than a lucid picture of life in a Northern ghetto. It is also a young girl's growing awareness of her own worth and pride in her black heritage."

I read the first chapter. With the swiftest teamwork ever, the class apportioned the roles, structured the scenes, and improvised the chapter. At the end of the hour, they were deeply involved with Louretta Hawkins, or "Sister Lou," and Ulysses, Jethro, David and Fess. Being chased out of the back alley by Officer Lafferty was an affront to *their* rights.

Seeing the interest generated by this book, I promised to get copies for all to read. Unblinkingly, everyone said okay. A week later the books were distributed in time for the class to read Chapter III.

DON'T LOOK SO AMAZED. WE DIDN'T GO THROUGH PURCHASING PROCEDURES ANY MORE THAN YOU DO WHEN YOU ARE RESPONDING SPONTANEOUSLY TO STUDENT INTEREST WHICH WAS NOT APPARENT AT SCHOOL ORDERING TIME A YEAR BEFORE! SCHOOL BUDGETS DON'T ENCOURAGE CREATIVE TEACHING, DO THEY!

Time to start reading. . . ?

The following week. . .everyone came. Only three students had read the ten and a half pages of the chapter. Four days later, still the same three students. The following week, when the same three answered, I said, "Let's pass the book around today. Everybody read a few lines." You see, I still hadn't caught on.

Dutifully, the first, then second, then third person opened his/her mouth and tortuously, defenselessly, stumbled over a word, a syllable; groped through the sounds of a meaningless sentence. The three good readers impatiently corrected a pronunciation or provided a muttered word.

I STILL FEEL ANGER AT MYSELF. I FORCED THEM TO EXPOSE THEIR SECRET FAILURES TO EACH OTHER, TO ME. I KNOW IT WASN'T THE FIRST TIME, BUT IT WAS ANOTHER TIME, AFTER THREE, FOUR, FIVE YEARS OF SUCH FAILURE. IF ONLY ONE HAD DARED REFUSE. . .IF ONE HAD SAID DEFIANTLY, "NO, I WON'T! I CAN'T! YOU CAN'T MAKE ME!" BUT THESE VIVACIOUS, ARTICULATE YOUNGSTERS SAT THERE LIKE ACCUSED PRISONERS RECEIVING SENTENCES.

Finally I said, "Look, we don't have to read this book. . .not yet. I'm going to go on feeding it to your ears. Anyone want to help me, say so. You can do the acting." I felt eyes come off the floor.

I resolved to remove the stigma of visual reading, to try to bring them the excitement of the printed word through their ears, to try to reassure them that the combined words could add up to something other than frustration. I wanted to help them believe they could read. More than read, understand and feel the meanings behind the words. . .that, wonder of wonders, the words were there as friends, ready to reveal every aspect of human experience.

I didn't really *know* what I was doing at that time. . .but it seemed right. At the next workshop I explained they *were* reading. Didn't they realize, they were reading through their ears!

We met twice a week. I'd read a section, drawn on by their attentiveness. Such an attentive audience! I'm sure they pulled forth my best performances, past, present, or future. Together we'd analyze each section of the story — look for the intent of each character, scrutinize inner and outer actions, see points of conflict. Then they'd set an outline and improvise within it, playing different parts each time. After our "rap time" we'd often redo the scene with others playing each role, to see how else it could be played. They took full liberty in "fleshing out" a scene which was delicious to them, like an argument between Lou and her spoiled older sister, Arneatha, or the dance.

Distancing from the story for sharper insights

Sometimes I'd introduce abstract exercises or parallel situations with other types of characters. When I do this, I look for material that is incisive, with direct dramatic impact.

The character of Jethro was presenting some problems. He was easy to play in his cheerful joking and sparring with Sister Lou. But when he became epileptic at the clubhouse dance, neither the boys nor the girls playing Jethro could deal with his helplessness. He was acted as a funny caricature — someone who shook.

I departed from the book to introduce Ray Bradbury's tale, "The Dwarf." In it a dwarf comes nightly to the House of Mirrors at a carnival to parade himself before a magnifying mirror when no one is watching. One night the man in charge calls others to watch when the dwarf arrives. Within seconds, they see him tear out of the house and run wildly into the night. As a joke, the man had substituted a shrinking mirror for the magnifying one.

Gilbert wanted to play the dwarf. At fifteen, he was often abused for his small frame. He compensated by being fast, tough, and aggressive. His improvisation affected everyone, myself included. I can visualize him posing before the imagined mirror like a weight lifter admiring his magnified muscles, dreaming himself six feet tall.

Most of the students understood why I'd chosen this story to shed more understanding on Jethro's feelings. Soberly Duane commented, "Jethro tries to be funny all the time to hide that he feels different inside, like everyone must be looking at him wondering when he'll go into a fit."

At the next session we went back to the clubhouse dance. The entire class played teenagers, parents, relatives, police. The dance was in full swing when the police broke in, guns drawn. They lined everyone up against the wall. Jethro, crossing the room, started to shake. A shot rang out. He fell. Frantically Cara, playing his Aunt, cried out, "My boy has epileptic fits. How come you couldn't see that! Oh the Lord will judge you if you've killed him!" The cop said, "I had to shoot him; he was reaching for his gun." "He / has / no / gun!" wailed his Aunt.

When we cut the scene Lolly ran over to me. "Read the book again. What words did *she* use?" I opened the book and handed it to her quickly. "Here," I said, "Read it with me." Caught up by the power of the scene, her eyes looked at the page. Her mouth spoke the lines. Fervently, the meanings already alive in her body, she read. No one said anything. But the next week Lolly came in confiding, "I read the next chapter. I couldn't wait to find out what happened next."

Lolly had given me a much hoped-for cue as to how I should proceed. I started asking for one or two volunteers to re-read a page or two after we'd improvised a section. Or, a little of the next section — as a preview. By term's end, almost everyone was volunteering, even for a few sentences.

"Why do you think you read so well AFTER we've improvised part of the story," I asked one day. "Doesn't that tell you something?" A few just squeezed up their faces, not accepting that they'd done well. Mark answered that he knew what it was about — now.

Into a radio serial

In September, "Soul Brothers and Sister Lou" continued as promised. Almost the entire group returned. Plus a few. Where should we take OUR book next? A few suggested a play. "Seventeen chapters in a play! What audience'll stay that long?" said Lenore.

A radio serial was agreed upon. The Upsala College radio station liked the idea of presenting a school program to the community. We could perform at 2 p.m. each Thursday, for ten weeks.

We taped our improvisations of Chapter One and Two. Over the weekend I wrote it up as a script for our next rehearsal. Yes, I'd make a few changes, tighten a few sections, but essentially it was theirs. They listened carefully for lines they'd invented.

Gilbert was missing for the second reading. And again the next day, casting day. I sought him in the halls. He was angry, betrayed. I'd turned against him just like everyone else, he accused. I'd taken his part of Jethro away from him. He wouldn't do any other part because HE'D LEARNED ALL THE LINES. "But Gilbert, no one was promised a part before today's casting...and you weren't there."

After school I learned he could barely read. When the story "Soul Brother and Sister Lou" changed from something to act into a reading for radio, Gilbert took the script to his Remedial Reading teacher for secret help. He was determined to be Jethro! At home he memorized whole pages — Jethro's lines and every other line.

HAD THE EXCITEMENT OF A RADIO SERIAL SWEPT ME BEYOND MY CONSIDERATION OF THE STUDENTS? I HAD LET GO OF THE PROCESS WHICH PLACED THEM FIRST; WERE THEY READY TO BE PRESSURED BY THE NEEDS OF THE PERFORMANCE?

I'D HOPED THE SPECTACULAR CHALLENGE OF BROADCASTING WOULD CARRY THEM PAST THEIR APPREHENSION OF READING...THAT THEIR CLOSE ACQUAINTANCE WITH THE FEELINGS AND PEOPLE OF THE STORY WOULD MAKE THEM COMFORTABLE IN THE EXPERIENCE. I WAS SURE, GIVEN TEN BROADCASTS, THEY'D DO WELL AND GAIN AN UNUSUAL REINFORCEMENT OF WHAT THEY *COULD* DO — READ.

BUT WAS IT JUSTIFIED IF ONE STUDENT, LIKE GILBERT, WAS HURT? WHAT WERE MY PRIORITIES NOW?

The faculty urged me on. And Gilbert came the next day, mumbling that he'd read a small part if he could try Jethro "maybe, next time?"

Two days prior to our "opening," we had an on-mike rehearsal...a chance to become acquainted with the microphones, broadcast signals, volume levels and timing. The studio technicians were friendly and encouraging. Perry, whose visual perception problems denied him a reading role, took his seat in the control booth. His unusual manual abilities equipped him to learn the technical aspects of all kinds of media.

The first broadcast was anything but dramatic. Ulysses and David read easily though unexpressively for a page; than others would continue, racing to the finish line. There were tech problems. We were too many people in the studio space. It's an understatement to say no one felt ecstatic afterward. But no one said we should quit.

In class, we played back the tape of the rehearsal. Everyone listened, frowning. "What do you think?" I got a glossary of negative adjectives.

"I sounded like a retard," said Marie. (This seems to be the most disgraceful humanity they can dream of, despite anything one can say.)

"You don't become radio actors just wham poof! C'mon, let's analyze what needs improving."

"Everything," muttered Jeff. Gilbert sat snarling in a corner, ready to spring if his best friend waved at him.

"With the numbers 1 to 500, tell me how miserable you feel at this moment."

THEY HAD TO GET PAST THEIR DISAPPOINTMENT, BUT ONLY BY ALLOWING ROOM FOR IT. THEN PERHAPS WE COULD START LAUGHING AT IT...WHEN THEY SAW THAT IMPROVEMENT WAS POSSIBLE.

Each faced another two or three. Simultaneously, everyone started with a number. Some started by mumbling with disgust.

"Forty. . .forty. . .forty. . .three hundred and ninety-nine!"

With intensity rising, "Ten. . .ten. . .sixteen, fifteen, four hundred." I could hear some voices beginning to enjoy the possibilities of the exercise, screaming at each other in a surge of sound and fury.

Next they did individual words and spoke them as they "felt." Love, long for, run, hurry, breathlessly, laughed out loud, whew! We tried saying "love" meaning "hate," "beautiful" meaning "ugly," "no" meaning "yes," "hurry" meaning "slow down," just to further unlock our ears and voices.

Then, back to the script to paraphrase what each character was saying. We'd done a lot of this weeks ago when the script was introduced. But meanings had grown stale from repetition. Finally we re-taped Installment One. And listened to it. It sparkled.

. . .with less and less rehearsal

Installment Two was a little smoother except when, in his haste to pick up a cue marked "with excitement," Darin knocked over a mike and lost his place. We brought the wrong record for our theme music at the beginning, and Merele almost wasn't allowed to come with us because of a make-up test.

The third broadcast hit an all-time low. Tech problems. We had to repeat the program three times, finally getting on the air too late for our audiences in the schools to hear it. One parent phoned in at 2:30 to demand, "My radio isn't playing *Soul Brothers and Sister Lou.* What's happened to those kids?"

Yet the dynamics of this struggle with a time schedule were beginning to work. The "having-to-produce" at 2 p.m. on Thursday was a corset into which we had to fit. Our actors, far from being repressed by the experience, were expanding to meet it. They were rising to the situation.

My notes read: "Fourth broadcast. . .dramatically valid. . .and are these kids pleased with themselves! And am I relieved."

By the fourth week, Gilbert had made a qualitative leap ahead. If success breeds success, he was building on his reading like one too long hungry at last given a CARE package. At rehearsals he read his parts and everyone else's too. His body taut and erect, script in hand, his voice raised with excitement, he'd strain after each sentence.

Merele had always read mechanically perfect. Now she was reading with feeling for the character, her voice mellow and urgent.

Almost all of them were beginning to merge the expressiveness of their improvisations with their reading; they talked thoughts, picked up cues, and helped each other by picking up missed words — in character.

THEY WERE BECOMING A COOPERATIVE WORKING TEAM. THEY FELT SPECIAL. GETTING OUT OF SCHOOL TO BROADCAST WAS SPECIAL. GETTING FAN MAIL FROM OTHER SCHOOLS WAS SPECIAL. THE SERIALIZED PLAY THEY'D CREATED THEMSELVES WAS SPECIAL.

WHEN THIS PROJECT IS OVER, WILL THEY REACH FOR MORE BOOKS TO READ?

WILL THEY SIT BACK ON "THE TIME I WAS ON RADIO" OR WILL THEY SEEK OTHER CHALLENGES TO STRETCH THEIR LIVES?

IF SOMEONE SOMEWHERE SNEERS AT A MISPRONUNCIATION OR A HESITATION, WILL THEY REVERT BACK TO THEIR OLD FEARS OF READING, OR WILL THEY SMILE AND SAIL ON?

The answers to these questions we can't know. We can only offer experiences...and hope. But I do know that at our tenth and final broadcast, our group of boys and girls picked up their script and read it without any rehearsal until we got into the studio. With competence and casualness, they passed the scripts and gathered around the mike for a run-through. They knew the characters. They knew the thrust of the scenes. They understood the conflict and the feelings. A few cues were slow. So what? A lot of speech was slurred. Again, so what? Like pros they stood around the mikes, dropping each completed page silently to the carpet.

They knew the feeling of pulling together. They knew the feeling of creating in an art media, a feeling which bursts the seams of ordinary living. They knew they'd grown, and could evaluate it. Maybe they strutted for a few days afterward. But that's not too bad, is it?

SOUL BROTHER AND SISTER LOU. Kirstin Hunter. Avon Books, New York. 1968.
READING, HOW TO. Herbert Kohl. A Bantam Book. New York. 1973.

HUMAN BEINGS IN OUR WORLD

Our grant proposal read, in part:

A project for inner-city intermediate school students in original investigation and experience based on the theme: "Human Beings of Our World"

> What are our essential similarities?
> What are our essential differences?
> How can we learn to accept both?

To be led by an inter-disciplinary team of teachers representing academic and arts disciplines.

Educational Rationale:

We recognize that we have not been uniformly successful in teaching academic skills as an end unto themselves. We have chosen our theme "Human Beings in Our World" in order to observe how a learning problem which requires an organic or creative approach can challenge each student to seek out skills as he needs them. We predict that he will be more successful in less time when he acquires skills for a purpose.

Further, we aim to avoid imposing preconceived ideas and values of our adult world in favor of allowing our students to bring all of themselves to a learning problem in order to seek new answers as if they have never been found in the world before. Debate and disagreement will be considered essential for this kind of learning adventure, as well as inquiry, social encounter, research, trial and error, human and intellectual experience, evaluations, responses, deductions, feelings, sharing.

Leadership Teams

Our planning team represents Language Arts, Social Studies, Family Living, Art, Mental Health and Creative Drama. This is the first time we are combining our disciplines in this way. Other teachers who have agreed to work with us as resource leaders represent the Instructional Media Center, Mathematics, Music, Science and Industrial Arts. Parents and other adults of the community will serve as resource people working with the students when requested.

Student Group:

30 to 50 students from grades 5, 6, 7 and 8 will be accepted for this 9-month project. All aptitude levels will be represented.

Procedure:

- First it is essential that we, teacher-leaders, have full opportunity to exchange ideas, objectives, understandings — that we become a team. Toward this end we have begun, in August, informal discussions.
- Next, we will prepare a joint sheet of general questions for the students as our "launching point." These questions will project guide-lines. Other questions will be added as raised by the students.
- Now we will be ready to meet with the students. All further planning, thinking, doing should occur in student-leader teams.

Schedule:

Sept. and Oct.	Preliminary planning for overall project, culminating in United Nations "People Day" on October 31.
Nov-Jan	Small group work on first area of concentration to terminate in a project designed to communicate all findings.
End of Jan-March	Small group work on second area of concentration. Groups will be rearranged for each concentration area.
End of March-early May	Small group work on third area of concentration.
May-June	Planning for a large event in which the total theme results will be portrayed, as in a giant mural.

Outcome:

- Student groups shall be required to submit weekly reports of efforts, skills and resources used, evidence found and a projected plan for their next steps.
- Each group shall interpret their discoveries in a group project. They will be asked to explain and communicate to the total group.
- The total project at the season's end shall sum up feelings and discoveries about the "Human Beings in Our World."

We hope to see children

- probing and working in areas where previously they were reluctant and learning skills long resisted
- working through peer group problems in order to achieve the objectives of our project
- involved, happy, and expressing themselves through all the media at hand, even those who have rarely contributed an original or independent idea
- the growth of understanding of different problems of human relations in our community and in the world.

Budget:

Instructional Materials	Film rentals, film and tape, supplies	$225.00
Instruction	Overtime Salaries	200.00
Food Services	International buffet for school and guests	175.00
Student Body Activities	Special Events and admission fees	200.00
Community Services	Contact and transportation of international guests from Metropolitan area	100.00
Equipment	10 cameras at $10.00 each	100.00
		$1000.00

WE GOT THE GRANT!

I went out and bought the Instamatic cameras, a tripod, twelve dozen film cartridges, a reel-to-reel tape recorder (reel-to-reel because it allows for easier editing) and four dozen 30-minute tapes in boxes for easy classifying and storing. And four dozen film cartridges for the school Polaroid camera; developing equipment and chemicals for black and white film, and film for the school's movie camera.

Why all this film and camera? Some of us are most adept with words to express ourselves. Some speak more easily through movement. Still others, I've found, can say much through the use of a camera. Camera skill even breaks down to those who work best with moving images and those who can select and express with one still photo or slide more than can be said with words.

I also bought a clipboard for each student. This was a bit like putting on the costume of a dignitary. How authoritative even the smallest fifth-grader looked, poised with clipboard, pen and paper, interviewing an airport controller or an arts council director. Sometimes we can each feel differently about ourselves by handling one item which "permits" us to see ourselves differently.

Using cameras related easily to my first year sequence I described in *FOCUS*. Everyone now understood the concept. We did a lot of filmless shooting at first in order to begin selecting the image we wanted, framing it, adjusting to eliminate extraneous items from view.

Developing and printing film is a useful skill. Some students were launched into a life-long hobby. Some first tries, though, almost discouraged photographers for life. There was the day Paul and Eric tore around looking for a darkroom to process their film immediately. The maintenance supervisor offered his toilet-closet. In their haste, and in the dark, they almost flushed the film away!

Setting up a weekly schedule

> 1 hour, Tuesday afternoon, for planning; with five student representatives and three or more teachers
>
> 2 hours, Wednesday morning, for full group workshops in the drama room
>
> All day Friday, for field trips; half the group one Friday, the other half the next, except for special occasions for the full group

Memberwhip was voluntary, from grades five to eight. We were eager to discover if the stimulation of creative experiences could dissolve the arbitrary grade and age barriers. Our "process of organic inquiry" would not encourage competition, we felt; it should not put younger students at a disadvantage since individuals could participate at their own level and in their own time/space patterns. Also, we on the faculty agreed that grading would be based only on growth in cooperation and responsible commitment; meaning regular attendance, participation, effort to follow through on self-appointed tasks.

We knew we were getting concessions from the school just because we'd been awarded the state grant. Certain teachers were bound to resent the project as it cut into their time with students. Would these teachers encourage their students to attend regularly? Would there be pulls on the students' involvement with us?

"They feel left out," speculated one teammate. "It wasn't their idea. They're going to be critical of everything we do. Just watch...they'll even talk us down to the students."

From the start we stressed to the student participants that to be part of the exciting new experience, they would have to keep up their "contract" work in Math, Science, Social Studies and Language Arts. And most of the school *was* supportive.

Enticing students into the project

We needed to spark enthusiasm to tempt volunteers for our project. How could they envision the possibilities of such an amorphous program? We decided to start in the style we intended to pursue.....an experience...a challenge...room for input by each person...the excitement of approaching an unknown and making it familiar through dramatic preparation.

On a September Monday, I issued a notice to each home base:

VOLUNTEER! PICK STRAWS! APPOINT!
TWO STUDENTS.

The famous Kabuki Theatre of Japan is in New York City... first state visit in nine years...in magnificent costumes...with oriental instruments. They will enact a traditional Japanese play from hundreds of years ago.

There are forty-six tickets only. Representatives from each home base will meet in the Art-Drama room to "try out" gestures and characters of Kabuki Theatre.

A separate note to all teachers asked for any assistance they cared to offer for the orientation. We also explained that we wanted a heterogeneous group, and they should encourage *any* student who expressed interest to participate.

From the start, the students felt special. In the middle of the school day they were urged, over the intercom, to report to the Drama room for "ORIENTATION!" The word itself was impressive! As one student said, "You only get s'cused for ball practice or if the doctor's examining in school. Whoever heard of getting out of stuff to go to drama?"

All the students who came, except the fifth graders, had at least one year of Creative Drama and Creative Art and were ready for an ongoing project of this scope. It would be a challenge to integrate the fifth-graders in with these advanced students.

By Friday, a Social Studies teacher issued a special packet she'd written and mimeoed on the history of the Kabuki Theatre and Japanese culture. She included open-ended questions which the students could answer only after doing some research. There were map questions and spaces for drawing specified musical instruments. Finally she gave them a special vocabulary to check out.

Next step: Calligraphy. . .with ink stones and brushes. How better to perceive the exquisite flowing line of the actors' positions and gestures than to try to make it on rice paper and recognize it in art prints. We did sample Kabuki make-up on several students. And finally Paul's father, Professor Faris of Upsala College, shared his love and knowledge of Japanese theatre with us. He brought diagrams of the stage; he explained and led us in symbolic gesture. He explained plot line and characterization and the meaning of tradition in theatre.

I played selections of Kabuki music. Initially, the unaccustomed tonal qualities and intoned recitation tickled the ears of our group. A few started moving to the sounds of the flute and samisen with stereotyped caricatures conditioned by TV and the comics. Others objected to this.

At the Kabuki theatre

Our students were an alert audience. . .even if they weren't exactly enraptured. The slow pace was difficult, so foreign to the pulse of twentieth century kids. The droning tones of recitation. . .the endless, strange subtleties. And yet, they had just enough moments of recognition, thanks to our preparation, to glean what was happening. They maintained (impatiently) patience throughout.

Afterward, we visited backstage. The Japanese mother of two students interpreted for us. Our students had enough background to be able to raise questions. They were speechless, though, as the Japanese gentlemen deferred to her with deep bows. For the first time we learned that her speech identified her as a member of the Japanese elite. She'd come to the United States as the war bride of an American corporal. "Discovering" her in this way was an important bonus of the trip.

Another bonus was the "surprise" ice cream treat on the way home. Through the year, we ferreted out the best ice cream parlors in the state, and even had we done nothing else we did learn what good ice cream tastes like. (As you see, we believed in the values of sense stimuli!)

Each trip had follow-up time. We never limited responses to writing about or telling about. Some wrote because they wanted to. Others taped reports. Some few responded in poetry. Or painted pictures, cartoons, murals, photographs.

"Will you join us?"

After that initial trip we held a second meeting and asked for a personal statement — on paper — of interest and commitment. We explained that the program's evolution depended upon them — their attendance, imaginations, interests and research. Each person was vital to the achievement of this program

Most of this group did join. . .except those who were behind in their academic work. Some lasted through out International People's Day at the end of October and then couldn't quite deal with the lull that followed the high of that event.

Follow-through is not an easy quality to find in oneself. Especially if you can't imagine the eventual rewards to be reaped. Everything else beckons with such immediacy. Palates are conditioned by the apparent, the recognizable. Yet something encouraged more than half the original group to stay with it through the full year. They worked their ways through obscure, undefined problems. They dealt with discouraging times as well as fulfilling times. They built ties with each other, ties of mutual effort and sharing which were out of the way of ordinary learning experiences.

Our first Drama session sparks many lines of inquiry

"What situations or problems do you think we have in common with most people of the world?"

David thought everyone must have to teach children what was right. "Right?" The word itself stimulated all kinds of dramatic improvisations, each student seeking to convince the others what was RIGHT, what was WRONG. A Social Studies teacher used this cue to introduce research into social structures other than the nuclear family. Several advanced readers went into books by Margaret Mead and other anthropologists.

We had several slow readers, who, under the stimulation of the group's enthusiasm, offered to do research on an assignment. The librarian led them to the right books. They found the right pages and then xeroxed them in the office. That Xerox machine contained its own special powers: the students brought the Xeroxed sheets in and read them to the class! They ran the machine; they read the results. Xerox in a school was fairly new at that time and the wonder of it was still fresh. We exploited this new reading method with other students.

Those who didn't choose to read found other ways to do research. Some even through comic books. The research led us back to the drama room and art room for more improvisation and activity.

One group dramatized this problem: a little boy steals something from the head of his family, tribe, or clan. Somebody will discipline him.

How will this vary from one familial situation to another? From one period of history to another?

There was strong disagreement during "Rap Time" after a scene where the elders of a tribe of Northwest Indians publicly rebuked a boy. Our student played the boy like a "wise guy." "An Indian boy just wouldn't act that way."

"All right, prove it." The usual response. Back to books or experts for evidence. The scene was replayed with a proud, defiant boy, properly respectful of his elders, accepting his punishment because he had "sinned against his people" and "disgraced his parents."

Sharon helped us gain a new insight into parents. We got into how a father feels about being out of work. How he acts worried and more impatient. "He's worried about money," said Rona. Ralph played a father, first at work in a factory, then coming home at the day's end. Receiving his layoff note; and trying to hide it when he came home, two weeks before Christmas. The group began to realize, through enactment, that parents have needs and existences apart from their children. We ranged from anthropology to sociology to psychology to history to literature. We even looked into some theatre scripts of Ibsen and Miller.

Growing into a team of teachers

By having at least two of the teacher team present at each workshop, we maintained an alertness to each new direction the students were routing the project. We tried to take our leads from them.

As teachers, we were seeing each other in action for the first time. We knew we weren't there to judge each other. Yet we felt vulnerable to each other's evaluations. Two teachers worried me for a while. They raised questions which called for specific answers in line with their thinking. This would stop our students short: I had been working for a climate in which many answers could be seriously considered.

How could we reconcile our approaches? One teacher seemed so quiet. I sometimes felt indecent with my bursts of enthusiasm. I didn't know what to do to make her more relaxed. Her eyes sometimes shone, but she said little for weeks. Team teaching takes time. We had to learn to trust each other.

The development of a scientific investigation

Aaron reported on the three major racial skin pigmentations. He'd discovered that his skin was "full of melanin." Everybody was interested. I pointed out the freckles on my nose and arms. "Melanin," I said. The white kids searched for their traces, while the black kids looked a little disbelieving. We began to examine coloring and its relationship to heredity and geographic origins.

The improvisations took off in all directions. Americans and Europeans froze in Alaska because they couldn't adjust to the cold due to skin pigmentation. On the desert a sixth-grader offered to conduct a rescue mission because his dark skin would be able to take the intense sunlight better than the rest. One group of six depicted a world just started in which people can be any color they want to, to match their clothes or their houses or whatever.

Certainly not unusual scenes. I mention them because they were indicative of the growing openness of the group. More and more, almost anything could be dealt with in improvisation and in discussion.

Later that week I learned that the science teacher upstairs was being pestered for more information. "You mean the blood isn't different?" Someone revealed that sickle-celled anemia was prevalent in dark-skinned people. Suddenly the investigation veered again.

Most of the dramatic improvisation was intensely serious and guilelessly candid. In one scene the participants decided to change social roles by wearing masks designating sex and color. They were immediately relegated to certain jobs and treated in certain ways until they tore off their masks to reveal their true identities.

During this time I found people beginning to look more discerningly at each other. Little comments overheard: "Go on, you're not really white." "Well, you're not black, more like brown." One day I suggested a stage makeup class.

I taught a standard first makeup class, using Steins' bases ranging from very pale to very dark, and including a yellow. As I was applying samples of the bases, I commented that no skin is a solid color. "Examine the skin of your partner. Try to name all the tones of different colors you see."

They responded with enthusiasm. In dark brown they found tones of blue and red and yellow. In a "white face" they found yellow and brown and pink and orange and blue.

In our proposal, we had mentioned looking at other people. We hadn't realized how vital it was to start with looking at each other and at ourselves.

They made each other up, in two's. Many white students chose dark brown bases. Many dark-skinned students chose a blanched white. Some tried for the carotene pigment of Alaskans, and a few tried to equal the skin coloring of Northwest Indians. They laughed. They collaborated. Barriers toppled that day as we looked at the meaning of "only skin deep."

International day

We were already planning for our costumed international celebration on October 31. This started as a simple enough possibility, but it grew into a mammoth festival as everyone responded with ideas and more ideas.

We sent a preliminary sheet home to parents inviting participation. Another sheet to faculty and staff. Students investigated possible guests representing nations and cultures of the world. They did almost everything. . .letter writing, phone calls, personal contacts. We were beside them to guide, encourage, and rehearse procedures.

In workshop we improvised functional ideas: meeting new people, phoning someone you couldn't understand. (Have I mentioned the phone company loaned us about ten phones?) Afterward, they critiqued each other. "Hey, man, just because they speak another language doesn't mean they can't see." "You're treating them like they're stupid. . .like they're in kindergarten because they talk different. . ."

WAS THIS CREATIVE DRAMA? YES, IF YOU'LL ACCEPT MY EXTENDED DEFINITION THAT "ANY WAY OF DRAMATIZING LEARNING THROUGH ORGANIC EXPERIENCES WHICH ARE PLANNED, ENACTED, EVALUATED AND OFTEN RE-ENACTED, ARE VALID ASPECTS OF CREATIVE DRAMA IN EDUCATION."

October 31st came. From 7:45 that morning the foods started arriving for the Food Tasting Buffet, cooked by the Family Living classes; by parents and grandparents; by students in their home kitchens.

The World Bank was set up on the second floor with dittoed copies of monetary units representing the major nations of the world. Posters explained how to change money.

A professional leader conducted international Folk Dancing in our multi-purpose room. A Tower of Babel Language Center was situated in another section, where foreign guests helped students and parents pronounce, from prepared sheets, household words in about twenty-five languages.

There was international folk singing; international games; a Japanese Tea Ceremony with authentic materials; a World Pen Pals Center led by a representative from Experiment in International Living in Vermont. (Many students established pen pals that day which continued for years.) There was a UNICEF Health center with films, an international film room running Canadian and other films all day.

AND, most special, there were over eighteeen countries represented by guests. Almost all of them wore national costumes — of African nations, Israel, South American countries, England, Germany, France, Italy, Scotland, Iran. Buzz sessions were held in designated corners of the building where five to eight students met with a foreign guest to discuss cultural/societal matters. I recall passing an eighth grader, who had done his preparation well, in intense discussion about socialized medicine with a Scandinavian visitor.

We heard that every costume book in the city was loaned to someone from our school. The students and teachers, most of them, wore costumes they'd made or borrowed. I wish I could show you photos of Mrs. Leach in her kimono and obi, or Mrs. Rabb as a sheik.

You've held festive days like this, I'm sure, so you will indulge me my superlative recollections of it. It was a day long remembered.

The week afterward

Such a great production was bound to leave a void afterward. Workshop size shrank. At the next planning meeting, Paul, Ellen, and Gary said *they* were still interested, but they thought others weren't. "They don't think there's going to be anything else that's as good," said Ellen. What did they suggest? How about an emergency meeting — "with refreshments"?

Over the intercom the next few days the principal reminded everyone about the emergency meeting. At the appointed hour the room filled up. A little formally. As though we hadn't had all those class experiences together for two months.

As teachers we all have our special "lectures" for rough moments. Years of directing plays has shown me the regular points at which a group loses heart. At such times we can use reason; we can scold and insult; we can rely upon "duty and responsibility...you promised" kind of stuff; we can penalize or bribe; we can threaten to throw it all over.

At first I felt a bit rejected. All of us teachers had put so much into this project. The state of New Jersey was looking at us. They'd entrusted us with all this money because they approved of our idea. We'd made such an incredible beginning. Why, look at this International People's Day...what an extraordinary event...and they'd done it.

Out of the corner of my eye I saw Mr. Garah cover his mouth. That meant his laughter was near the explosion point. Suddenly I relaxed, regained my perspective.

"Look," I started over. "We've said from the beginning we're in this together. If I lose interest, if you or you do, if Mrs. Varetoni does... well then, we take a vote about going on. What do you think?"

That was where I should have started. The restrained faces opened. Everyone started talking. "I was just behind in my work and hadda catch up, tha's all." "I didn't know there was anything else to do here." "I got a letter from that pen pal...she wrote me from Ceylon." "My mother cut out the newspaper article on us. She says she's so glad I'm in this school so I can do things like this group."

We teachers didn't resell them on continuing the project. They re-enthused themselves. At last someone said, "So what do we do next? What's our next trip?"

And the planning went on for the next block of time, into Phase II, which became "Reaching out in our State — to People."

Some teachers were as let down after Phase I as the students were. The project's results were not tangible enough. Was it any more than just a grand purposeless entertainment? One teacher who had difficulty with process learning said this out loud. She needed regular tests and measurements. "I just do not have time for this kind of thing!" And she closed the door.

Several other teachers agreed with her, but those that remained with us deepened their commitment.

PHASE II: Reaching out to people

We centered our investigations on life styles — qualities of city living, rural living, factory living.

Our Friday trips in a van that seated fifteen took us all over the state. Everyone had maps and helped chart our general route. We visited a large farm with animals and basic crops run by three generations of the same family. Another week took us to the waterfront at Port Newark; the hiring hall of the Longshoremen's Union; then from pier to pier with a union guide on board our van explaining what we were looking at, what the products were, where they were from, where they were going. We went to a foundry, a country bakery, an artists' studio in an old barn.

The students behaved more and more like a group of visiting professors, increasingly adept at holding conversations, wording their opinions, and asking thoughtful, provocative questions. And always the workshop experiences provided the preparatory warm-up and the follow-up to sharpen meanings.

PHASE III: Investigating each other

What do we know about each other? By now we were ready to focus attention on our own lives. We improvised simple routines of daily life: meal time; early morning at my house; family outings; arguments with my brother or sister; who walks the dog?

During this phase we set up overnights at each other's homes. Very few white students had ever stayed in the home of a black student, and vice versa. We were treading close to the "delicate balance" line here, and we knew it. Some faculty members were against this activity; more were supportive. Not everyone wanted to participate, but that was all right.

The overnight came. At the last moment a few more students pulled out. The air was full of nervous tension. Those who were house guests brought their clothing to school. They came dressed up and shining clean.

Two other teachers and I had scheduled students to stay at our homes. A boy and girl drove home with me that night. Two fifth graders I usually had lots of fun with. They barely talked. Supper was incredibly stiff. I could see them making mental notes of everything we said or did. . . how our daughter behaved. . .how we talked to each other. . .how we

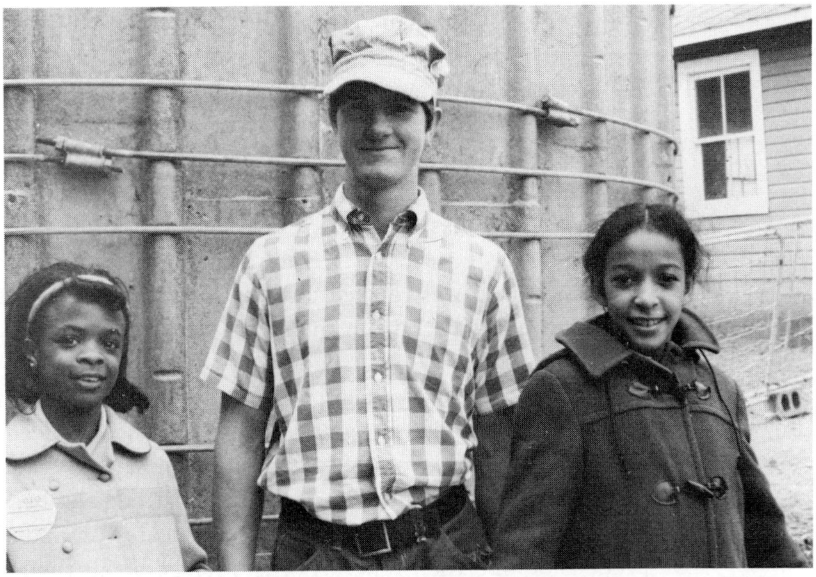

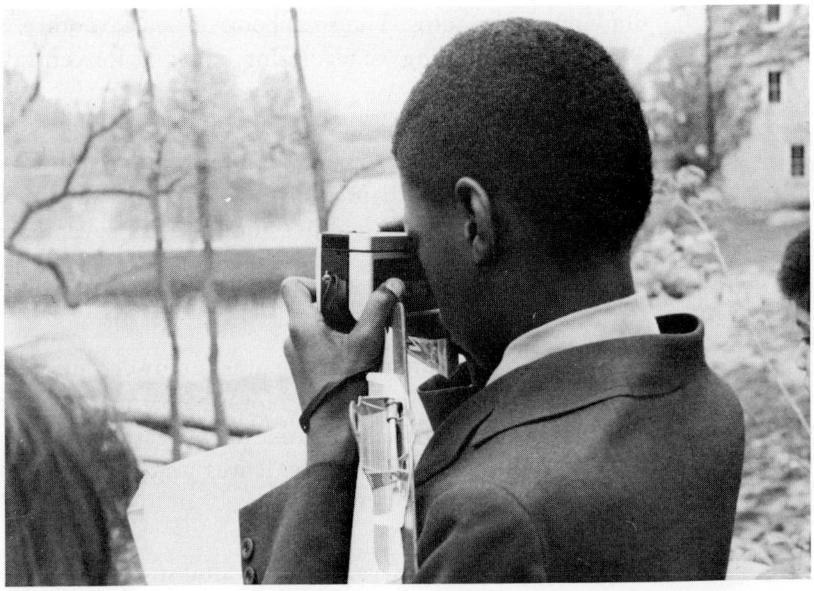

answered the phone during dinner. Everything came under surveillance. I was suddenly conscious of our walls and our food tastes and our informality as though we were on a stage. I felt the exchange of looks when my husband helped clear the dishes.

The breakthrough came when he offered to do some magic for them. They became kids again. And it all became fun.

I was embarrassed by the gift their parents had sent. And appreciative. In class we had never discussed house gifts. Later it was hard for Robbi to tell me she was afraid of sleeping in a strange house without a light on. I finally guessed it. We had story telling and said goodnights at least a dozen times.

By breakfast all was relaxed. And back at school they were as casual as world travellers back from their ninetieth trip.

The reports, afterward, before the entire group, were full of details and pleasures. I watched the faces of those who had avoided this experience as Cal, a white boy, told of being taken to play basketball by a black father, and another girl described the great bed she had slept in. I watched, too, the faces of the hosts and hostesses, and shared their apprehension and then relief as others talked about their visits to our homes.

FINAL PHASE: Summing up feelings and discoveries about the year's efforts

During May and June we pulled the many fragments together. All the taped discussions, interviews, evaluations, notes and diaries. All the drawings and photos. The scrapbook of our adventure. Sorting through. Reliving. Assembling. Categorizing. Looking for central meanings to pull through like threads.

Slowly a form evolved for our final program: a multi-media presentation with a script largely chanted in choral reading, with movement and pantomime, with taped and live sounds, with several screens showing slides and film as well as shadow play against an arrangement of sheets hung like banners.

On a stifling June night all the parents crowded into our multi-purpose room to share this final event. Not a performance, but a reflection of a fruitful year of teamwork, creative investigation, individual and group growth, self-expression and joy. It was gratifying to see how many parents understood that meaning.

The script outline was very simple, almost contrived, designed to include reference to the many things we'd done. In it, a group of young people make contact, accidentally, with an outer space figure who can't decide whether to land on earth or not. They offer to be its guide, and introduce their lives. The figure finds the conflict and violence on earth idiotic. It doesn't understand many earth concepts, like the whole mechanism for making wishes.

1st student: But you see, there are so many, many things we wish for in the future. Some wishes are just for our own lives...some wishes are for everyone. You too, if you wish.

2nd: I wish...I wish for everybody to agree to make peace.

CHORUS: Peace! What really is Peace?

1st: I don't know what peace is, not really. I haven't experienced it.

2nd: Our lives are always full of headlines and pictures of war.

3rd: Yes, war in city streets, war in people's hearts, war in other lands.

4th: And even when there's no war, it just seems like a rest period before another one begins.

CHORUS: Will there ever be peace?

2nd: Peace when all children are free to laugh and sing and play without fear?

3rd: Peace when nobody has to be afraid of the bomb, or of napalm, or of a missile.

1st: Peace when we can begin to trust each other as friends, not by the color of our skin...

5th: ...or the language we speak.

2nd & 4th: Will there ever be peace, our worried world cries...

CHORUS: Peace is a chorus...waiting for voices.
Will you add your voice to ours?

But the figure from outer space doesn't want to chance staying on earth...it's too risky a place. Better to return to a civilization where they'd solved a lot of these problems and don't have to just wish.

ART FOR PREADOLESCENTS. Angiola R. Churchill. McGraw-Hill, New York. 1971.
TAKING PART: A WORKSHOP APPROACH TO COLLECTIVE CREATIVITY. Lawrence Halprin and Jim Burns. The M.I.T. Press, Cambridge, Mass. 1974.

LET US BE FREE

If there's one project that stands out in my mind for its meaning to the students — not to mention me — it's "Let us be Free," a film which took over two and a half years to create.

This super-8 three-reel film dealt with slavery in the world, its causes and effects upon people. It also documented the rich heritage of Black peoples before, during and after slavery. The film toured many schools, arts programs and educational conferences. Our students were interviewed on radio and educational TV. A student panel always accompanied the film, to answer questions and explain how they made it in Creative Drama. The students received letters and commendations from local government leaders, educators, and filmmakers.

However, behind the successful film lies a more important story. It concerns a class of sixth graders, most of them Black, who stumbled into a search related to their personal identities. It didn't start that way. But the impetus of their will to know about their past carried them as a cohesive group through years of work. And that's the story I want to share.

We didn't start with a film in mind.

We started in September, 1967. Months before Dr. Martin Luther King was shot. Before the riots in our cities erupted. Before a July 8, 1968 headline in the New York Times urged educators, "Turn to a Balanced Teaching of Negroes' Role in American History." But the times already lent a readiness. The growing Civil Rights movement effected an emerging self-awareness for Black Americans, a need to identify with their heritage before slavery.

I was leading the class to dramatize many of Aesop's Fables, and then parallel them with contemporary situations. I mentioned Aesop was a slave, captured from Thrace by the Athenians in the sixth century, B.C. "Was he Black?" asked Kathy. "How'd he get to Greece?" "You mean there were slaves everywhere. . .not just in America?" Then Robert asked, "How'd slavery start, anyway? People weren't born slaves, were they?"

Everyone had an idea. Some ideas were pretty wild. Jacqueline, who rarely showed much interest, said, "Maybe one man didn't want to take care of his farm hisself and he din't want to pay no one to work, so he stole his neighbor's daughter and made her do all the work. . .for free."

We acted her idea, tried it for credibility. Then volunteers agreed to check the library for facts.

Several weeks later, an eighth grade student, Rhoda, stopped me after her class. "I want to know why we don't study more. . .about us." She spoke intently, angrily. "And I want to know why. . .why. . .that substitute teacher said. . .my people never did anything. I want to know about what my ancestors *did*!"

I suggested she work with the sixth graders as my assistant. Together we all would find out why people became slaves and how people lost touch with their ancestry.

We had no plan to follow. We'd flow-chart some ideas, improvise them, discuss what we'd done, do research, and then improvise again using our new knowledge. A new question set us off in another direction. Helter-skelter, we moved across the continuum of history and people enslaved at different times in different places — white, yellow, black or red. We gathered reams of information and ideas. Historical figures, imaginary characters, events and fantasies shaped the time and space of our workshops.

Finally Keith urged, "A movie! Why don't we make a movie? And my father'll help us. He knows all about movie cameras."

Some weeks before, Keith's father, Mr. Harris, had attended an evening's Creative Drama workshop for parents. He'd expressed amazement that Drama was not the "fluff" he'd anticipated. Now he came over after his work shift to talk about our projected film. Keith stood by proudly, listening.

And so a film came about as a natural development for a group of twentieth century students for whom film is as much a part of their environment as instant food and television.

Learning the techniques of film

As a non-movie maker at the time, I depended heavily upon experts like Mr. Harris. I told the students we'd be learning together as our research and filming progressed. What liberation it is not to pretend we teachers know everything. Have you discovered how students take on more responsibility and exercise more initiative when we step back a little?

Eight students became the Script Writing Committee. They met with me regularly. Page by page the scenario evolved as they sifted through all our ideas and research. They took notes during improvisations. They outlined sequences. They wrote lines for group chants. They chose poems by great poets like Paul Laurence Dunbar, Langston Hughes, Countee Cullen and George Moses Horton. Tempers flared occasionally over what to include and what to leave out.

We started actual filming as soon as we had several pages of scenario ready. Planning film images to animate each sequence posed unique problems requiring creative solutions. It took time to recognize — to perceive how the eye of the camera differed from the eye of an audience watching a stage play.

The first reels came back from Kodak. My diary notes read:

> In the darkness of my room, Keith and Michael S. projected the first two reels. Laughter, shrieks and exclamations of disbelief:

"That's me!" "Do I look silly!" "You don't look so bad, look at me." Sam, Robert and Michael A. are rolling on the floor. Rhoda sits sedately as befits the assistant director. Gradually they get quieter, more intent. Then, "Hey Ira. You really look good as Aesop." Silence. From Karen, "I don't like how I did that." Serious critical appraisal has begun.

The lights come on. A few want to shoot it over. It was too much the same...not enough variety of shots. The camera stayed too long on one picture. Kara and Robin have ideas for other visuals.

The medium was right for the message

The film served as a strong adhesive in sustaining group interest. More so than class study and discussion. The challenges were vast. But what it meant to see oneself on newly returned film every two weeks...in many noble and diverse roles. Actually looking at one's face against the stretch of history! Invariably, after projecting the latest footage, I'd notice Michael (any one of them — we had four) walking out of the room standing ten feet taller, or Linette chuckling to herself remembering how great she looked on film.

Part of my job was to be sure they did look great. Lighting, costume touches, film angles — these were part of it. Enthusiasm and understanding of a particular role, adequate improvisation time and discussion time — these were an even more essential part.

We began to understand that filming a story is like organizing a collage, requiring an assemblage of different images, angles, contrast and variation in tempo and mood. We started listing all the possibilities for visuals to enhance the scenario. Then we found, made, or borrowed the desired materials. For one section we used hastily-made foam puppets. For another we filmed sections of old cement walls in town. Someone found an abacus for a five-second shot; someone else found photographs and pictures in library magazines, especially old National Geographics.

Mr. Harris explained certain concepts of optics. It takes a viewer time to recognize a film image, he said. The camera can't move willy-nilly about an image. Serious thoughts about light, shadow and angle became part of our planning. And ways to animate the static image — a prop, a picture, or a sculpture.

> Nov. 15. Dr. Thelma Newman, sculptor, writer and art collector, invited some students to her studios to borrow a group of her authentic African sculptures as visuals for a section of our scenario. Magnificent pieces. I leave school each night with apprehension until we safely return them to her.
>
> We wonder how to animate them visually. Michael C. suggests that the camera keep moving around them, the way we move about a piece in a museum. Terry wants to have the sculptures moving too. He places them on turntables, and turns on the turntables at different speeds. Fredericka is helping Doug and Keith set the lights so that shadows highlight different features of a sculpture as it rotates.

Sound. . .lighting. . .costumes. . .

Meanwhile we were working on our sound material. . .recorded background music, line readings, choral reading and chanting, sound effects and songs. We brought in a guest to teach the group several old African songs. To accompany other scenes, we enlisted several bongo players.

We lacked equipment or money to put the sound script on the film, so we tried synchronizing sound and film with an ordinary tape recorder. Excruciating.

Help came from a nearby university with professional sound studios. Our principal excused us all from school for two afternoons — he saw the desperation on our faces. The university staff worked with us in producing a tape which, with some adjustment, lined up with the film. We reran the film reels so often to synchronize the sound that the film sprockets began to split.

Three students handled lighting for indoor shooting. They became very competent at cutting shadows, lighting only a face, a hand, mouths, eyes. We used fresnels on standards, and borrowed photographic spotlights. Sometimes we used strong flashlights or headlights. Back lighting for silhouettes posed an interesting problem, different than for the stage.

We used costumes as soon as we started shooting. But the word is an overstatement. What we did was "suggestion." By carefully selecting camera angles we created an *illusion* of authentic costuming, using all the fabrics from my costume trunk, plus an assortment of old drapes and spreads. A specialist in African studies helped us with headdresses and draped robes. Dashikis were beginning to appear as contemporary dress; several mothers had already made them for students, and we practically begged them off their backs to use for the film.

When strangers viewed our film and commented, "How'd you ever get all those costumes? You must have had some budget," my students and I exchanged a smile-behind-the-eyes look, and said nothing.

The research involves us all

Our script became a compilation of thinking about the social and economic roots of slavery, and about the uncrushable human spirit. Books have proliferated since we started, but in 1967 there were few in the libraries, and I had to purchase many.

When we dug into the history of ancient Africa, we found civilizations that were impressively advanced. We enacted the Ashantis working in copper and the Ishongo people using an abacus eight thousand years ago. We found respect for learning and for the scholar prevalent throughout our research. Sam played the seventeenth king of the great kingdom of Songhay, a thousand years ago, who built many schools so his people could learn. We dramatized African codes of law and ethics, and proverbs like

Not to know is bad; not to *wish* to know is worse.

A slave is he who cannot speak his thoughts.

An uneducated man is only half a person.

The material we unearthed was important to the white students as well as the black. All of us discovered that slavery is a recurrent theme of history. Most white students did not realize that many of their ancestors were also enslaved at some time. The project took us into considerations that surpassed color lines, that dealt with basic human struggles, helping us gain more respect for each other's heritage.

Perhaps that was what motivated each individual far beyond his/her usual energies and commitment. Mr. Harris, who knew many of the students outside school, commented that Sam, who was usually in the office for punishment, became consistently productive with "Let us be Free," and there were introverts who became expressive in contributing to the program, and extroverts realizing the rights of others more and more.

Jacqueline, who ventured the first guess on causes of slavery, went on to become our stage manager, efficient and demanding. Anita, small, unsure, who cried the first time she was filmed because she thought she spoiled the scene, appears again and again in the completed film, as she volunteered for all kinds of roles.

Designing a beginning for the film

Everyone felt that the first scene should show that people are born free, as members of the human race.

> Wednesday. Kathy and Fredericka ran in today. "We've been practicing outside. We've got it...we've got the opening scene..." Dark eyes shining in each face. Bodies pushing against me from all sides. I ask to see the "it" they've got. They laugh and pile onto the floor in a huddle.
>
> Sam and Robert have followed them with a written sheet. They begin reading; alternately:
>
> I am born! I am born!
> Look at me! Look at me! Look at me!
> I listen to the world around me.
> I can see. I can touch everything.
> Deep inside,
> I feel so many different feelings.
> I crawl...
>   I kneel...
>   I climb...I STAND...LOOK AT ME!
>
> Meanwhile from the human mound on the floor comes an arm reaching up, another, another. Like young sprouts pushing through the soil. Now a leg, a head raised, a torso winding up. With eager looks on their faces. Unmasked. Guilelessly beautiful. This will be Scene I.

There were stalemate points in the development of our film, of course. Sometimes I didn't know what direction to steer the thinking next. One time, in the early days, I realized that a question I raised touched such sensitive tissues that the entire group closed shut. At that moment I felt an insurmountable barrier between us. . .and I felt alone, inept, and very white.

> Dec. 8. I learned something important today. By sharing my own cultural heritage as a Jewish woman, I've overcome some of the remaining self-consciousness in the students. We all suddenly feel closer. I talked about Hitler and the concentration camps, the millions who died, and people I know today who wear their camp number burned into their arms — but proudly, openly. Many of the students did not know who Hitler was, what country he dominated, nor of the Nazi atrocities. . .sixth graders!

> After I described the cattle cars used to transport people, Michael related it to the slave ships from Africa. There was silence. Somberly Kathy's soft voice asked, "But weren't there any bathrooms?" Her face remained wistful, but the class broke up. The tension of the class relaxed.

Preparation for a day's shooting

Michael reported from his research on the slave ships that were rowed to America. . .about the thousands of men, women and children crowded below deck on voyages that took three months or longer. . .about the different tribes of Africa represented, speaking many languages. . .about those who died from hunger, thirst or overwork, and those who jumped overboard rather than live as slaves. He wanted to combine all these points in a scene for the next Saturday's filming in Branch Brook Park.

> It's the first time we're getting into the real tragedy of our material. I wonder. . .will they be able to handle it.

> Ten students volunteer. He briefs them. They are to be rowing under a vicious master, to be played by polite, amiable John S. They start, giggling. Michael cuts the scene. "Too corny, and you're not focusing." They accept the criticism and start again. Two Social Studies teachers have joined us and ask to row in the scene, "to experience Creative Drama." Maintenance loans us broom handles for oars, which helps focus the action.

> John cracks the whip. "Row faster!" Doug beats the drum, low and regular. The "slaves" are pulling together and getting faster and faster. Suddenly two girls throw down their oars and scream.

> When Michael cuts the scene, we learn the screaming wasn't planned. "It just happened," explained Karen, jubilantly. "I felt like I just had to scream or burst, with that drum beating and John yelling. . .I'll bet that's just how these people felt."

> They feel elated. . .magnified. They know a moment of emotional freedom and of empathy with the past. We evaluate the scene. The Social Studies teachers look impressed.

Red-haired Cindy stops me as we go. "I feel so bad," she says. "Why, Cindy?" "Well...because I just realized slave owners were white...like me...and well, won't everyone feel different toward me after this?" Inside myself I groan. It's hard to assure her that differences no longer matter.

By summer, the script was almost completed. We had moved from ancient Greece through seventeenth century America to twentieth century freedom fighters. But how to end this epic?

During a hot July, Robin created some scenes which caught everyone's imagination. Starting with the question, "Is slavery over..." she asked for everyone to add one sentence:

> Is slavery over if I can't get an education of my choice?
> Is slavery over if I can't live where I choose?
> Is slavery over if I can't vote in my home town?

The camera started with close-ups of faces of our students and people of different ages on the street, and then ranged about the city, picking up different people doing different jobs at different locations. On our first sound track was Sly and the Family Stone's version of "Stand Up!" On the second, starting faintly, was the voice of Dr. Martin Luther King's "I Have a Dream." On the third track one student's voice began, gradually joined by more:

> History is pushing
> Pushing hard
> History is made up of people
> What will be our future, America?
> What will be the future of our world?
> For our children, Black, Yellow, Red or White?

I visualize one more scene, which was not part of the film. It is at a large state meeting of teachers, principals, supervisors and superintendents. "Let us be Free" has just been shown. And now the adults are closely questioning our student panel. Finally a woman from the Department of Education stands up.

> I want to say that the meaning of this project in drama is represented by the poise and articulateness of these young students. They have expressed themselves so well. It's obvious they have learned to pull together through their long months on this film, each carrying out his and her responsibility in a most competent manner. They have reason to be proud of themselves. I hope they will carry this with them for the rest of their lives — the meanings behind the creation of this film.

If young people, any young people, gain an intimate sense of the greatness from which they come, won't it help them see themselves and their potential in more positive ways? I don't know what may be the ancestral background of your students. But I will guess that an examination of history in terms of their "roots" may help them get involved in learning too. For a richer sense of themselves...for a truer understanding of each other. Isn't this the real reason for studying history?

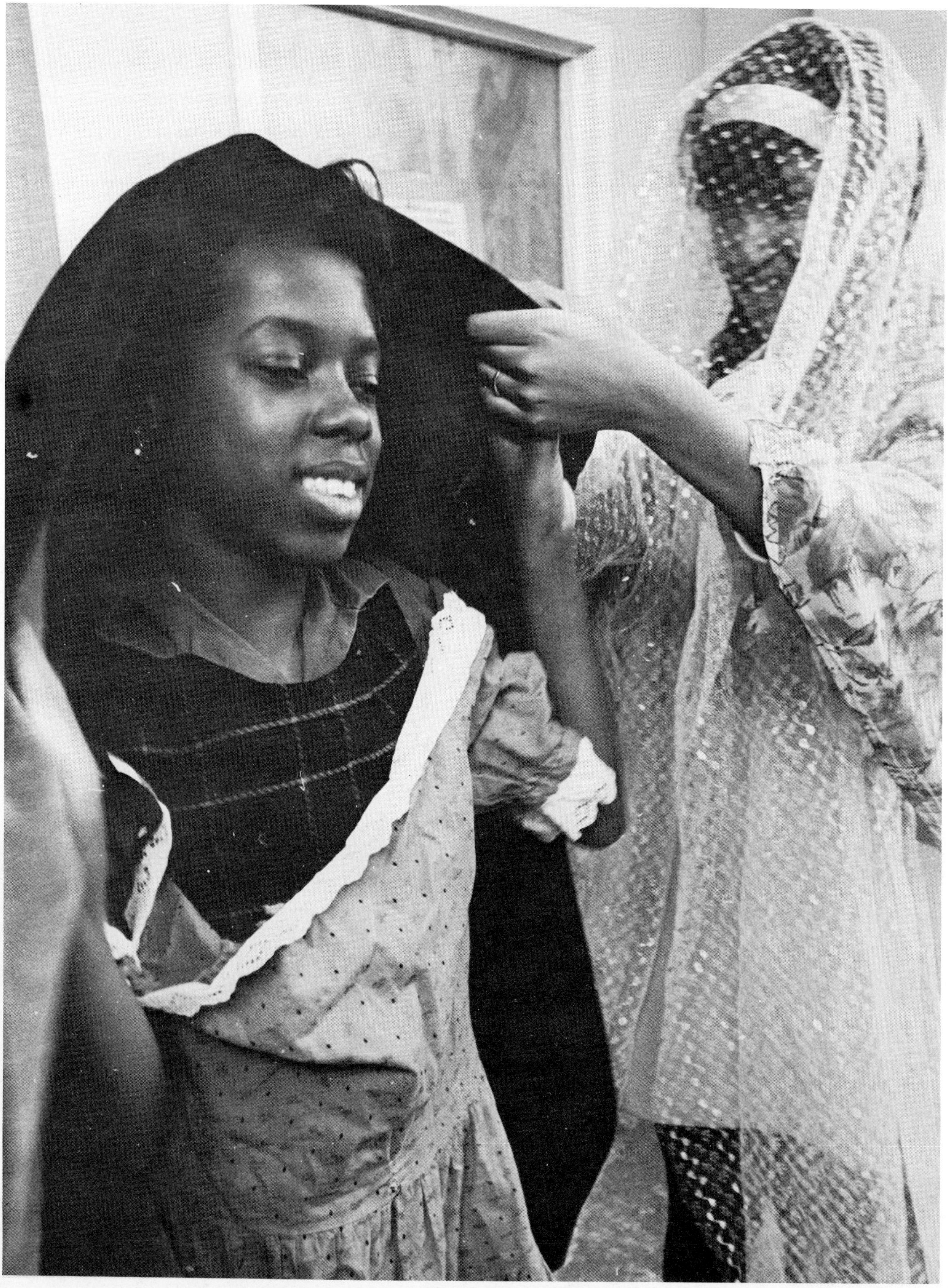

MY CARPET BAG

I picture a carpet bag, its sides bulging with assorted shapes, filled with a random mixture of special stuff.

This section is that kind of mixed bag. I'm expanding some of the shapes and dimensions, some recurring themes you've found throughout this book. And dealing with some specific apprehensions which keep coming up: "This is all very nice, but at my school..."

BUILDING AN ENVIRONMENT

What you bring to the space you're working in

PERSONAL SPACE; PERSONAL RHYTHMS

Making use of much-overlooked aspects of individuality

ENCOURAGING THE INDIVIDUAL WITHIN THE GROUP

Getting past the dominant personalities

WHY START WITHOUT WORDS?

Recognizing inner language, and a way to reach it through movement.

WHY USE THE QUESTION

How we can pull forth ideas, opinions, experiences, feelings

GRADING

So you've got to give grades!!

WHAT, NO DISCIPLINE PROBLEMS?

You don't have to be scared about losing control in the Drama room. The structure can grow from the students, as they learn to set their own controls.

BUILDING AN ENVIRONMENT

What part does the environment play in encouraging the creative involvement of the individual? How do we build such an environment?

We've all heard people who, from the first word, are saying "You gotta do this" and "You gotta do that." And, even as adults, you and I feel ourselves responding "I don't *gotta* do anything!"

At a school I visited in England, when I mentioned that I taught Creative Drama I was ushered into a classroom where, I was told, I'd be able to see a splendid session of Creative Poetry Writing. The teacher's finger pointed me quickly into a far corner as she addressed the class seated in military line-up. "And now class, we are going to write cree-a-tive-ly. You understand me?" Her voice penetrated like a tea kettle whistle. "Cree-a-tive-ly...Straighten your backs now. Pencils up. I want you to show me your best cree-a-tive wrii-ting. Are you ready, get set, go!" (I wish you could hear my imitation of this.)

IN THAT ROOM I COULD FEEL THE AIR SIZZLE WITH TENSION. THE STUDENTS SAT RULER STRAIGHT AND DIDN'T DARE TAKE THEIR EYES OFF HER FACE, EVEN TO REGISTER THE ARRIVAL OF GUESTS. AS I LEFT SHE COMMENTED, "AREN'T THEY DARLING CHILDREN...SO BRIGHT YOU KNOW!"

On another day I visited another classroom. There were thirty-two students. As they arrived the teacher had a special word, a quip, a question of interest for each one. He was relaxed. By his physical attitude he communicated that he knew they'd all behave well and do their best. The students anticipated being in his room. They were already conditioned by the pleasures they had enjoyed with him. They were comfortable enough to reach out to me, a stranger in the room, offering me a chair or an explanation of what they'd done at their previous class. They reached out to each other with camaraderie. The room itself was an ordinary square space. The windows were dirty; the furniture was old and used. But I left there feeling warmed by the human exchange between a teacher and his students.

YOU'VE READ ABOUT MY USE OF CONTEMPORARY RECORDS AND LIGHTS. YOU'VE READ ABOUT THE INTERESTING FABRIC TRUNK AND ASSORTED PROPS. THOSE ARE CERTAINLY PLEASANT ATTRIBUTES, BUT FAR FROM ESSENTIAL. THE ATMOSPHERE OF THE SPACE EMERGES FROM YOU.

Your Manner

You look at your students as though they're people and you like them. You aren't afraid to smile, or to groan if it's 90 degrees and you're as uncomfortable as you know they must be. You notice a new pair of eyeglasses or a new hair-do that you know a teenager is dying to have noticed. You welcome them into your space.

A student-teacher I observed lost her group the moment she opened her mouth. She had planned well. She knew the process of drama. She was anxious for everything to work just right. And in her zeal her voice came on with a suffocating "rah-rah-come-on-team!" attack.

I looked at the students. They had tuned her out. There was no responding look of eagerness or willingness to be part of her game. She had left them out of her planning.

YOUR VOICE CAN BE SO IMPORTANT. BEING SUPER-ENTHUSIASTIC CAN BE JUST AS OPPRESSIVE AS LACKING ENTHUSIASM ALTOGETHER. THE PACE AT WHICH YOU SPEAK AND HOW MUCH YOU TALK ARE IMPORTANT AS WELL.

Jane, another student teacher, sat perched on the edge of her desk. She started easily. "What'd you think of the game last night?" The students were eager to share their opinions with her. She wasn't in such a rush to get to work that she couldn't deal with matters she knew were bursting inside them.

A few minutes later she jumped to her feet. "Okay, whatdoyousay we get into action." "Can I call action?" yelled one girl. "No! Let me do it this time; I never get to call it," from another. "You can call cut," said Jane easily, averting disaster.

The words and the style were hers. We each have our own style. The respect is what we must all offer in order to set the tone of a supportive environment.

Keep your senses alert. See the student who is afraid to try. See the one who is trying to please you and needs to be encouraged to please him/herself. Hear that small voice which doesn't dare call attention to itself.

THE CREATIVE ENVIRONMENT STARTS WITH BEING REALLY INTERESTED AND WANTING TO HEAR FROM YOUR STUDENTS. IT TAKES SELF-AWARENESS, A CONSCIOUSNESS OF WHAT YOU'RE DOING, WHY AND HOW. IT DEMANDS CONSTANT SELF-CRITICISM...NOT THE KIND THAT SAYS "OH IT'S HOPELESS," BUT THE KIND THAT SAYS, "WELL, THIS DIDN'T WORK TODAY FOR THIS AND THIS REASON; TOMORROW I'LL HAVE TO TRY IT ANOTHER WAY."

THIS FLEXIBILITY WITHIN OURSELVES CHARGES THE ENVIRONMENT AND RE-CHARGES IT, KEEPING IT SUPPORTIVE FOR OUR STUDENTS AND GRATIFYING FOR OURSELVES.

PERSONAL SPACE; PERSONAL RHYTHMS

Are you aware of your own sensitivities to different spaces? How spaces affect you...where you feel comfortable and whole, where you feel less natural. Look around the space you're sitting in at this moment...do you like it? I'm not talking about fancy furnishings or elaborate decor. There is an intangible something which affects us.

We feel different sitting in straight rows for a lecture or a course than we do sitting about a table with colleagues. We feel different packed into a tight elevator than we do climbing an open staircase with several friends.

In what kind of spatial environment are you most comfortable working, reading, thinking? You, yourself.

All I'm asking for is an awareness that you do flourish in certain environments more easily than in others. That some spaces give you claustrophobia...some spaces expand your verve and expressiveness.

Some teachers feel smothered by students hanging all over them. How about the students? I remember a boy who'd go beserk if an adult invaded his personal space.

I've said it...Personal Space. Which is what this page has been leading to. Each of us has a personal space need. It's as much part of our individuality as our handwriting or our mannerisms. If we crave space and instead we're packed into a narrow bedroom with three siblings, it will affect us. Similarly, if we're packed in straight rows in airless, poorly-lit classrooms.

Schools and space

Today we're more aware of this and many, many schools have done away with the rigid rows of desks and chairs in favor of casual, movable seating about the room. Many teachers have moved out from behind the barrier of the desk. When furnishings are not placed with geometric exactness, there is an easier movement flow within the room.

You've heard me speak of seating students in the Drama space in circles — on chairs or on the rug. This means that everyone is equal, everyone is visible, everyone deserves being heard and seen. Be alert to those who seek to hide behind another person, or those who push their chairs back so they have more space on all sides.

When groups do improvisations, they can set up anywhere in the room, and they are able to build their dramatic environments to allow themselves maximum comfort, acting in space. This is one way of giving recognition to the need for personal space.

Recognize personal time as well

Of all the aspects of individuality — psychological, sociological, intellectual, physical, and so forth — one aspect I want to touch on is too often neglected. It's an aspect I find very important in Creative Drama: the tempo at which an individual thinks, plans and acts.

The perking point of human beings varies. Despite all the tests which say "To be completed in 18 minutes," or 12 minutes. Despite all the pressures put upon each of us to perform in some time-controlled slot or accept failure. People just don't work that way.

Jeannette, aged thirteen, had limitless inner visions. I sensed them as I watched her staring out the window. Everyone in class became awed by the original and fanciful ideas she could dream of. But we had to respect her slow, drawn-out pace, as she pulled her words from off the air waves. This was her timing.

Steve would always become impatient. He was quick, wiry, in constant motion. I'd no sooner utter a suggestion than he had a vast array of ideas ready to spew forth...a supply which often made it difficult for others who hadn't yet thought of anything. I had to hold him down without squelching him. For this was his timing.

The fast people often put the slower people down, make them feel like they have less to offer. And then we, and they, miss out on all the special ideas they have...given time.

Sacho was very methodical. He was secure when he could organize every detail to the point of others' exasperation. He could not walk away from reading a story until he'd finished the chapter, put in the book mark, placed the book in its proper place, shoved the chair under the desk. The boys would be yelling for him after class. He was folding up all the materials left lying around.

Of course there had to be many reasons why he was like this. But they don't matter. The fact is, he behaves this way. His personal rhythm must be respected, not changed to adapt to mine.

How to enhance awareness of different rhythms.

In working on characterization, we can isolate this human ingredient... take a look at why two people with different time clocks sometimes get in each other's way. In developing a character, we can focus attention on the timing of the person. Between fast and slow there are so many variations.

One of my favorite ways of dramatizing this is to set up a basic action ...changing a tire or playing a card game. In advance, I select a set of records. Each record has music which stresses a different tempo — waltz, country blues, minuet, Flight of the Bumble Bee, and so on. We do the scene once through, and then repeat it to one disc. Midway we change the music to an opposite rhythmic pattern. We repeat the scene to two or three more discs. The participants respond to the music and the scene changes completely. Isn't farce based upon a different timing than melodrama? Tragedy different from an old silent movie?

ENCOURAGE THE INDIVIDUAL WITHIN THE GROUP

Sarah, John and Dodie were assigned to plan an improvisation. It required only one look their way to recognize Sarah had taken over; she was intently explaining her idea, appointing them their roles and even what each should say. Dodie was nodding in agreement relieved that no ideas were required of her. John looked reluctant but in the face of Sarah's enthusiasm he remained quiescent.

To appoint small groups and tell them to "go plan" is a sure way of perpetuating the leadership of a few and the passivity or frustration of others. You've seen it regularly: those who have easy access to their ideas and the self-confidence to urge them upon others; those who have ideas but hesitate to suggest them for fear of rejection; and still others who don't yet know they have ideas at all.

Our problem, then, is to seek ways of involving all the students in cooperative planning for an improvisation. This planning, in the early weeks of Creative Drama, is really more important than the shared improvisation.

"But Dodie never says anything," one impatient student complained when I suggested pooling ideas.

"Maybe," I commented wryly, "because no one takes time to listen to her." (And I sneaked a look at Dodie's face to see how she feels about this.)

I am trying to set a tone, a new consideration — that everyone has the capacity to conceive ideas; that everyone requires different ways and timing in which to do this; that each person deserves the respect of being heard.

How Can We Involve the Thinking of Each Member of a Group?

I ask the class for suggestions. Someone may say, "Let's work in teams of two. Each person will ask the other for an idea."

"But," observes a quick thinker, "what if we have two different ideas?" "Aw, that's simple," quips the class gambler, "you just flip for it." I may then suggest, "Maybe you can find ways of combining both ideas." During planning time my role becomes just that: helping twosomes integrate their separate ideas into one, or combine for a third possibility.

In larger groups, students can choose one member to serve as "interviewer." The interviewer's responsibility is to ask each member for a suggestion, offer his/her own ideas, seek ways of combining several ideas and, if necessary, take a vote.

The dynamics of the planning time will contribute richly toward the group spirit of spontaneity and sharing in the actual improvisation and add to the ambience of the Creative Drama room.

One other suggestion: encourage a group of four or five students to dramatize how they plan an improvisation. They will not tell the audience what they're doing beforehand. Slowly the audience will catch on as the improvisors try all possibilities to reach agreement on a plan — through discussion, argument, defense of an idea, joking, reaching an impasse or reaching a group decision for a scene. It is useful for everyone to look at the problems others encounter in planning. And the humor of it can relieve the tensions and competitiveness which often prevents real sharing.

Again, it takes time. The shyest and the most aggressive members will, in time, learn how to encourage each other, deal with each other, and accept each other. Individuality does not preclude collaboration, does it?

WHY START WITHOUT WORDS? RECOGNIZING THE INNER LANGUAGE

If we eliminate the stress of spoken language for a while we will, ultimately, free the expressive abilities of each student which leads to language flow. We are seeking the involvement of the whole person.

In Creative Drama we can start with the sources of language, often called "inner language," deep within the child's muscles, perceptions, and fantasies. We have the opportunity to lead him/her to re-find what he or she thinks and feels, and to express meanings in many other ways.

First it's necessary to free the body to be an expressive instrument without inhibition and self-consciousness. A difficult task in our society. "I don't like my body," Joanna pouted to me. "But why?" I asked in candor. "I think you're beautiful." "Oh," she responded, "in gym no one wants me on the team because I don't run fast and the teacher says I'm knock-kneed." What appalling measurements!

To the class I say, "Let's discover what our bodies can do; how wonderful they are. Do any of you know why animals, before man, couldn't hold a tool in their hands and therefore didn't invent them?" Hand examination begins. One, then a second student recognizes it has to do with the thumb.

After holding pencils with and without use of the thumb, we go on to try out actions the hands and the fingers can do. We wave, we saw, we pull, lift, drag, clench, pound, shape, push away, repair, design. Abstractly we move the fingers, hands, and wrists to music. We mold air into cloud shapes, symbols, objects. With "just our hands" we express anger, fear, joy, questioning, refusal.

We try out other body parts. We "laugh" with our knees, with our spines. We are straight, crooked, bent over, undulated. We are wishy-washy; we are regimented. And then the feet, which are so rarely considered at all. We wiggle them; we twist them, we arch them. We express rejection, alertness, excitement-to-boredom. Then we hold conversations between feet: an argument, a romance. I remember the great hilarity of a group of feet gossiping, the students lying on their backs with feet alone showing above a table.

Why shouldn't we allow speech too soon in improvisations?

Because it becomes the main or only means of communication. This is conditioned academic behavior: "from the neck up," with some hand gestures controlled from the elbow. However, when the body is freed first, the natural addition of language flows easily, extending the expressiveness.

"Why should we move in order to learn?" I asked. Some of the kids' thoughts:

- We've got bodies. We're supposed to use them not just sit on them.

- Sometimes I wish we could just send our heads to school and let our bodies go out and play.

- I hate to just sit. I get all fidgety. Pretty soon I don't even hear what the teacher is saying.

- When I'm moving around in drama I don't worry so much about the words. They just come by themselves.

There's a plethora of movement-in-education books today. It doesn't matter if you yourself haven't danced or if you aren't too comfortable moving about with your students. If you are just willing to accept and challenge the potential expressiveness of their bodies as well as the minds of your group, you can provide the necessary atmosphere.

Encourage observation of animal movements and postures; observations of people and what their posture, tempo, movement-language indicates about them.

Pantomime is another non-verbal activity which can serve in so many ways. They can be people doing many different things; they can also be birds and fish and animals; tangled wires, short-tempered doors, yeast rising, beach balls, bowling bowls and wilting gladiolas.

Even when you're well into spoken language, start each session with stretching and bending, shaping and twisting. Then use some movement problem for warm-up. With the blood circulating, the lungs breathing, and the muscles relaxed, the imagination will be so much more accessible to challenge.

GIVING FORM TO FEELING. Nancy King. Drama Book Specialists, New York. 1975.
CHILDREN DANCE IN THE CLASSROOM. Geraldine Dimondstein. The Macmillan Co., New York. 1971.

WHY USE THE QUESTION?

I have tried to develop the use of the question as an essential tool in the Creative Drama process. Each child has a world of experience and perception inside, too little drawn upon in the course of curriculum teaching. The question is a way of bringing it forth. By the questions I ask I stress "I am interested in what you think and value and what your life experiences have been."

It's so important that the atmosphere of the Creative Drama space constantly reinforces respect for individual differences. Only than will children be ready to consider a question, relieved of the paralysis of "Am I giving the right answer?"

A word of caution to all of us adults: we must guard against the manipulative question. How easy it is to smirk at a parent overheard saying, "Now aren't you going to kiss your Great-Uncle-Theobold hello?" That question is wielded with the lever of control. How many children will feel safe in answering "No!"

Don't we all box ourselves in with "What word would you use to describe this?" With the implication of right or wrong, how many young people will risk an answer? The question should be raised when we can deal with a variety of answers other than our own; acknowledging each answer, seriously given, as having some merit.

But our own answers have a place too

I will not always remain neutral and Socratic as I raise objective questions. Indeed no. If I feel strongly about something I will comment on it. However, I will guard against this until I am fairly sure that the atmosphere of the room assures each class member that they can question me, disagree with me, even smile at me. "There goes Ms. Wilder. She's hot again," is a comment which I enjoy for its candor and acceptance of me, a person too.

There are many ways to question

- DIRECT QUESTIONS. What are you doing? Where else could that be? How do you think this could be done differently? The "five w's and the h," as suggested in the section on "Imagination," serve well as the basic guide for building early improvisations. The direct question is also useful as a guideline in approaching evaluation of scenes and activities.

- IMPLIED QUESTIONS. Sometimes you can ruminate on a question, as though talking to yourself. "I saw a large hole in the garden. I wonder what might have caused it since last night." "I was thinking about David dropping out of school so suddenly. I've been wondering what happened here or at home to prompt such a sudden decision."

THE "IF" CLAUSE. I first discovered this useful lead-in in the writings of the Russian director, Stanislavski. "If I were evacuated from my country at 10 years old, flown on my first plane to a strange land where people talked, ate and lived differently, how would I feel?"

"If I were that wasp flying into this room full of gigantic, animated things all making noises at the same time, what would my instincts cause me to do?"

"If." It's fun to have a group build a list of "If" questions for occasional use. "If my parents were roosters. . ." "It I lived on a saucer. . ." Whimsical, silly, imaginative "If" thoughts.

If you're getting no response to a line of questioning, students probably lack a body of knowledge from which to respond. Many questions must wait until they have some sphere of reference.

TEACHING AS A SUBVERSIVE ACTIVITY. Neil Postman and Charles Weingartner. A Delta Book. New York. 1969. Especially note Chapter II: "The Inquiry Method."

GRADING...OR EVALUATING THE PROGRESS OF A PROCESS

At the Canadian World's Fair some years ago there was a detailed miniature village carved of wood. Two men had worked on this for fifteen years. I recall marvelling that they had worked patiently all those years, never rushing to complete the final product. Along the way their skills must have grown, their perceptions sharpened. They must have changed in many ways through this process.

Fifteen years is more than the span of time many young people devote to schooling. "Devote" is scarcely the word. For too many, it's "time served." Yet those years are part of their growing. At no point along the way can we say with certainty what the result will be, what kind of person will emerge. Attempts to qualify, classify, test and measure the passing stages — "she was in the lower percentile as a reader but the upper tenth in Math and just average in Geography" — is empty posturing about what? We can hurt as we can help, but we are merely contributors to an immeasurable...the life process.

Drama is a process, too

Throughout this book, whatever the precise wording or example, I'm talking about using Drama as a route, a way to self discovery, another *process*. I've resisted arbitrary time tables as much as possible.

My concern is how to stimulate and encourage each student's thinking and expressiveness. Value judgments, absolute assessments and grades can cut off candid responsiveness instantly. How tenuous the creative voice, the original inventor, within the growing person. Will I be able to hear it when it first speaks? This concerns me more than measuring it.

Yet I sense the furrow deepening on your brow, and I can guess why.

School requirements say "You must give each student a grade"

Grading troubled me. It still does. I've watched young people — outside public education — participate happily and freely in Creative Drama for years. They've never asked for a grade. Every workshop group does its own critiquing. Rarely has anyone even asked me, 'How did I do?"

But within a school system other needs exist. To put it simplistically, a school uses tests and measurements as a way of accounting to the community that teaching and learning *are* going on. Grading is also designed to track a student's development. A school such as ours had to validate its existence.

However, we *were* given some options. The faculty was asked how we wanted to recognize students' progress. We didn't have to use grades as such. But many teachers were bound, at first, by old conventions which they accepted without question.

I explained that Creative Drama, concerned with an intangible process of individual growth, cannot grade against any "norms." Each student contributes according to his/her capacities. We deal with no objective facts or end products. I never predict any point of development at which any or all of the students should arrive by a given time.

Together with other Creative Arts teachers I argued for subjective evaluation. Behavioral changes *can* be recognized. . .increased enthusiasm, growing motivation, social interaction, initiative, and responsibility. These can be observed. Creativity is harder.

Can we measure diversity?

What grades would we have given Galileo if he'd been in our classroom uttering blasphemous contradictions of our teaching? Or Stravinsky, who heard dissonances in his head when we were grading him for not carrying a given tune?

Creative giants may not walk through our classrooms (although we're not really part of our students' lives long enough to know). Yet can't we say to each student, "You have something of your own to say. . .in your own way. Try it out. The result doesn't matter. . .not now."

If I grade that creative venture with a 95% or a 55%, won't I halt the free flow of its development by measuring a mere moment as though it were a final result? Rather than encouraging original effort, won't I be asserting, with that grade, "This is what I like. This is what I don't like."

Our school's decision

Gradually, gradually, thinking changed at our meetings. The entire faculty agreed to avoid grades, except for classroom tests in academic subjects. We chose to use evaluation reports and personal conferences with parents and students, meeting twice a year. These reports were to present our individual aims and reflect our awareness of each students' efforts and needs. By February each teacher issued an independent report page. Some designed two pages. We collated them into a book on each student.

My first evaluation page read:

THE CREATIVE DRAMA PROGRAM AIMS TO HELP EACH STUDENT

- Strengthen his/her ability to concentrate and to think through an idea or a problem;

- Organize and communicate ideas, questions, and feelings through speech, attitude and physical expression;

- Gain positive awareness of his/her abilities while gaining sensitivity to the feelings and abilities of classmates.

Then I listed the activities students had done, such as interviewing, pantomime, spontaneous speaking and acting (the way I described improvisation to parents). I checked improvement in areas such as

- Willingness to participate
- Cooperation with classmates
- Initiative and follow-through on projects
- Courage to express an original idea
- Leadership within an activity, a group, or a chosen responsibility.

After we started projects, I added personal comments, such as

> Jane is a member of EVERYDAY LIVING THEATRE — a workshop exploring various communication techniques, *i.e.*, gesture and pantomime, script writing, radio announcing. With three others, Jane is writing a script. She read many scripts to analyze how the form differs from story writing. (Her idea!) Next week her team will pick a theme and plan their characters.

For another report I issued certificates decorated with Greek theatre masks painted gold. Specific involvements were still listed for each student, and at the bottom there was space for comments about that previously shy boy who "dared to portray" certain vigorous characters, or a previously uncooperative girl who "handled some major responsibilities for her group."

The report sheets kept changing in terms of design or wording, but the basic form and purpose remained constant.

For 250 students, writing them was a lengthy job, but we were well rewarded by the responses of students and parents. As Ruthy commented when she graduated, "I knew you all cared enough to think about *me* when you'd write comments."

Presenting reports to the parents

Twice a year we met with the parents. You probably do the same. At that time we'd present the report sheets and discuss them at length. If necessary we'd go to homes, or even places of employment. I spoke with some parents who had never been part of a conference before. They anticipated that I was there to complain.

"I want my girl to be good," I heard often. "I want you to beat on her if she's bad, so she'll learn."

"No," I'd hear myself saying. "We don't really think that'll help her. We'd like your ideas on what she can do after school, to keep her happy and busy. How about the 'Y?' Then she won't roam the streets until you get home. What do you think?"

How much I learned from these conferences of the realities of a student's life and of the parent's life. How much these meetings helped me in my relationship with the student.

Students evaluate themselves too

I believed then, and I do still, that one of the strongest ways to reinforce awareness is to have the students reflect on and evaluate a program they've been part of. Before the end of our first year of Creative Drama, I asked each class to decide if this program belonged in public education, and why. A few wrote they didn't think it belonged in school because some boys made too much noise and then everybody didn't get a chance to do their scenes. Many wrote what they liked and what they didn't like. Several didn't like pantomime because it made them feel silly to be so quiet. (That told me how uncomfortable they felt having their bodies stared at. I learned that I needed to introduce pantomime in other ways.)

Sometimes I asked, "If you were an outsider, maybe a guest from abroad, what questions might you ask to understand what Creative Drama is?" Or, "Looking back over these months, what experiences in workshop or on field trips are you able to recall?" At first faces might be blank. Then one person's memory would spark another's. Finally, everyone would be ready to write their recollections.

Student evaluations of this kind were often shared with parents as a way of underscoring the interests of their children.

Finally

Hughes Mearns, in his timeless odyssey, *Creative Power,* describes a visit by a professor of Teaching Methodology who wanted a demonstration of creative activity — on the spot. Mearns lowered his voice so as not to disturb the intense concentration of the students engaged in creative writing. "I have a good stop-watch in my desk," he whispered, pointing to a nearby park. "Take it and go out...sit down on the grass for an hour, and time the growth...of the dandelions."

Of course, within an hour, dandelion growth is as immeasurable as a child's growth is within a limited time span. But dandelions also grow best in a fertile environment, warmed by the sun.

We are, each of us, limited in our perception of what is going on within another human being. But these methods of evaluation, simple as they were, opened one more level of trust between the students, parents and faculty. We became collaborators, intent on keeping the learning process vital and rewarding — for all of us.

WAD-JA-GET. Howard Kirschenbaum, Sidney B. Simon, Rodney W. Napier. Hart Publishing Co., New York, 1971.
THE HALLS OF YEARNING. Don Robertson and Marion Steele. Andrews Printing Co., Lakewood, California. 1969. See "To Grade Is To Degrade," pp. 41-67.

WHAT, NO DISCIPLINE PROBLEMS?

> Nothing exists without structure. Every atom, every identity, every action has structure. . .every performance, every presentation has structure. There is no such thing as structureless creativity. There are only people who are not aware of perceiving structure.
>
> Michael Kirby, *Drama Review*

One of the stumbling blocks, I find, which discourages teachers from trying Creative Drama in their classes is fear that they won't be able to control their kids. Usually called "discipline problems."

Our conditioning still equates an orderly, controlled class with good teaching. . .the way a clean kid is supposed to reflect a good home.

After a workshop series I led for teachers, in which most seemed to agree with the philosophy and approaches I advocate, the major questions that emerged were:

- Will I be able to maintain control?

- Will they become silly, unmanageable?

- Will I know the difference between noise and the sound of involvement? How will I explain either to my supervisor?

- It's all valuable, but is it worth the struggle?

My own experience is that some classes will move naturally into Creative Drama because they are already dealing with their own ideas and with each other. Others will have difficulty making the transition from outer-directed to self-directed.

Still others will resist becoming part of a cooperative group program. Once they make the transition, though, they'll work enthusiastically and discipline themselves. And there may be problems, but discipline? No, rarely.

Let's examine several classroom situations.

We don't want to be in school

Most of you can remember an unruly class you met for the first time. The chaos had nothing to do with you or your program, but you did have to get their attention. I remember a class of twenty-three boys and two girls. Eighth grade. They resented being in school at all. They formed a tight peer group — against one white teacher who spoke "fawncee" — saying "drahma" instead of "draama." They'd come into the room and start their own games of tag, hit-and-shove, drum-and-stamp. My voice felt itself retreating into my stomach. No one could hear me.

I'd prepare as many as five, six, seven different workshop ideas, and they remained inside my own head. One day, in my brightest voice, I asked a riddle. Then I set up a magic trick my husband had rehearsed with me all weekend. (Magic is his hobby, and I'd overlooked its value till now.) First six, then ten, then all were intrigued. No one could figure the trick out. I took one boy into my confidence so he could help me. We were allies. I changed to a second trick with three pennies. Now, my ally and I were a force. Others begged in. We initiated two.

I only knew five stunts. But they worked. The class became a solid group, stumped and fascinated by the mystery of magic. The concentration sounded loud and strange in my ears. All that week I was stopped in the halls. "How'd that last one work? C'mon tell me. . .I won't tell." (And all that week I crammed to be able to top my performance in the next workshop with them.)

An unusual way in? Yes, but it worked. By term's end (don't groan; it didn't take that long) the vigor and imagination inherent in that group was finding active outlet in our improvisations. By year's end they wrote invitations to the administrative staff to see a project they had developed, "so they'll know we're good for something."

An established, orderly class

With this class, they know how to work well with you, you with them. The situation is comfortable. Why rock it by introducing new techniques? Is Creative Drama worth the upheaval?

A third grade teacher, in one of my workshops for teachers, commented that because Creative Drama worked for me I thought it could work anywhere. I just didn't understand her situation, she said; her kids were spoiled, suburban children, emotionally immature. They didn't know how to do anything for themselves, and they'd absolutely fall apart if she gave them an inch to make decisions.

Another teacher spoke up. And another. We'd been meeting for four weeks. . .they had been a responsive, enthusiastic group, participating fully. But now their scepticism surfaced.

"I tried 'mirror.' It worked fine. . .as long as I led the whole class. When I put them in two's, they became silly. . .absolutely unmanageable."

"I know just what she means," said another teacher. "I told my students to dramatize a story. Now you can show me your ideas, I said. But when they got up they just giggled and mumbled and no one could understand them. It was just wasted time. They couldn't handle the freedom."

Finally a teacher who'd sat there listening and smiling spoke up. "I didn't try any activities until last week. I started with some "focus" exercises. If someone got silly, I urged them to use their "focus" better. It took a little while, but it went well, except for two boys and a girl who made jokes and were very self-conscious. I felt encouraged and started some full group activities. Non-verbal, as you suggested. Bedlam!

They got so excited, working all together. We rarely work together any more since we changed to open classroom. Well, I didn't know what to do."

"So what *did* you do?"

"I sat them all down and I said, 'Now, look, I can't do any of this if you fall apart. So let's shelve it.' 'Oh no, no, we want to do more.' 'All right,' I answered. So I asked them how we could work it out so that we didn't disturb all the other classes near us."

"Everybody had suggestions. Even the silly boys. 'We'll be good. We'll be good!' I asked what we'd do with those who couldn't cooperate. 'Let them go do their own work at the tables.' I agreed. But I put the project aside for that day to show I meant business."

"Did you show them you were angry?"

"No, because I wasn't angry. From our discussions here I really expected it would take some patience. Well, the next day I told them we'd do some pantomime at 11:00 for fifteen minutes. After fifteen minutes I stopped and told them they were working so well that maybe tomorrow we would continue. The next day they reminded me what I'd promised from the moment they arrived."

THIS TEACHER HAD FOUND HER WAY AND WAS GRATIFIED BY IT. SHE WAS WILLING TO BE THE PATIENT ADULT, TO NURTURE THE TRANSITION FROM CONTROLLED, INDIVIDUALIZED STUDIES TO CREATIVE GROUP WORK BECAUSE SHE UNDERSTOOD THE POTENTIAL ADVANTAGES FOR THE STUDENTS.

Traditional takes time, too

When you begin teaching in a traditional manner, generally you start by establishing *your* controls. But learning doesn't happen all at once. You still have to be patient. You have order, but what else? What have you done to build an environment where you meet the needs of growing human beings to become self-motivated, responsible individuals?

Teaching through drama, you start from a personal commitment to the child and his/her capacity to think and work out problems with others. It must be a commitment, or there's little reason to try these approaches.

But, you don't let out the reins all at once. Creative teaching requires a structure. Freedom to think creatively requires the comfort of limits. We know that gradually the students will begin to set controls on their own behavior because they understand what they're doing.

Try to recall in your own life times when you've been absolutely bewildered at being confronted by new choices. Or, maybe you can remember a time in elementary school when you fell apart because there was a new substitute teacher who "taught differently." Can you relate this to your students' radical changes in behavior when you introduce a new way of working?

Two new teachers

One of my graduated college students visited me. He was now teaching. Anthony started speaking bitterly of how much he had to give to education. He'd come into his school with so many new, relevant ideas for creative teaching...but the students were not ready for him. The teachers were unsupportive of anything different. His administrator kept telling him he needed more control — as though control was all that education was about.

We sat down and tried to analyze how he proceeded with the students. Gradually he saw that he was placing his standards and expectations on them without finding out where they were. He was angry with the whole teaching situation and brought his anger into the classroom. He was thwarting anything that might happen between him and his students. The environment of trust and respect, of good humor and magical expectation, was missing.

Another time, I walked into the classroom of a teacher who'd taken five training workshops with me earlier. Defensively she explained that I shouldn't expect to see any creative activities going on. In a loud voice for the students' ears she added, "I've tried, Ms. Wilder. But these students don't know how to accept any responsibility. They just go haywire." One child started to protest this judgment. She cut in, "You're the last one to say that, Julia. You got so excited in planning with Mattie that nobody else could hear themselves think."

After school we talked further. "Catherine, exactly what are you saying didn't work? How did you measure?"

"Well, the noise level, for one thing. And then, everything that happened made them laugh."

"Do you remember how much you and the other teachers laughed in our first three workshops?"

"Oh...yes..."

"Don't you think children might also feel a kind of delight and yet strangeness at first, and giggle a lot too?"

For a moment her face brightened. Then, "But what if the principal had walked in and heard everybody in such an uproar?"

"Are you measuring by old standards of a good class being a quiet class? Were the noises related to the assignment you had given them?"

She thought a while. "Yes," she said finally.

"I don't think you had a failure at all. I think you must have warmed them up well for them to find so much pleasure..."

In six weeks, she greeted me at the door of her room, "Ms Wilder, the children were hoping you'd come today. They have a surprise for you. We're studying Greece, and they've prepared their own improvisations of Greek myths. Some groups have chosen to turn them into short plays which they've written out in dialogue. Others will just make them up as they go along."

The children raced about the room with naturalness and enthusiasm, assuming full responsibility for their preparations. Greek music was playing on a phonograph. And several regal Greek gods and goddesses stood proudly by, adorned, Grecian-style, in bed sheets.

WHAT WE SEE AS DISCIPLINE PROBLEMS OFTEN NEEDS CAREFUL SCRUTINY. IS IT REALLY THE STUDENT BEING "BAD" OR IS IT A DISPARITY BETWEEN OUR EXPECTATIONS AND THE STUDENT'S LEVEL OF MATURITY WHICH IS BEING ACTED OUT? IN OTHER WORDS, WHEN IS IT OUR PROBLEM?

Share yourself

A teacher joined one of my workshops. She explained her school was encouraging her to do Creative Drama with the students because she had minored in drama at college. She'd bought all the books on CD; she knew all the exercises. But, she said, it wasn't really working. Her students had no ideas. They just stared at her when she made suggestions. Or else a few of the bigger kids would turn it into a play period and scream taunts and jokes at each other. Then she'd have to send them to the office which was no good because it was the principal who wanted Creative Drama in the first place. What should she do?

Her tone and manner suggested a very orderly person. Further discussion revealed her high expectations of herself. Anything she did had to be done well. I started by asking, "What goals have you set for yourself in leading Creative Drama?"

"Well, I want them to be creative people."

"What does that mean, to you?"

She quoted to me from Brian Way, Nellie McCaslin, Richardson, Spolin. . .

". . .to you," I repeated.

"What I've just said, creative people are useful people."

"But this is all the theory of others. Let's start with just one simple, small goal. You want them to begin to realize that they have ideas — their own ideas — and that no one will laugh at them for telling one of these ideas. How can we do just that?"

We talked for a long time, analyzing the growth of rapport between a well-intentioned teacher and a group of bewildered students. They didn't know what she wanted of them. They might even have sensed she wanted them to be a successful experiment. And she didn't really know what she wanted from them, or of herself.

She was considerate in writing me weeks later: "I started trying to share myself more. I told them I felt good one day. I briefly explained why. It was just a little thing. Then I asked what made them feel good. At first only one or two people offered anything. I commented appreciatively on each experience. Others began. Soon I couldn't hold back the sharing of little things that were pleasant. One boy even shared that he felt good when his brother was scolded because it meant things would be better for him that day at home. What happened was that we began to talk to each other. Nobody had to prove himself a big shot. We were just people. I really have enjoyed the change, starting from that day."

How about you?

- IF YOU WILL DARE TRY THIS APPROACH AND THESE ACTIVITIES...

- IF YOU ARE WILLING TO NURTURE INDIVIDUAL GROWTH INTO SELF-CONTROL...

- IF YOU CAN BE FLEXIBLE IN YOUR PLANNING, SUBSTITUTING ONE ACTIVITY FOR ANOTHER WHILE MAINTAINING YOUR OBJECTIVES...

- IF YOU ARE CONSISTENT IN YOUR EXPECTATIONS OF EACH INDIVIDUAL...

- IF YOU CAN HOLD ON TO YOUR DIGESTION DURING THE PROCESS OF CHANGE IN A CLASSROOM AND NOT FEEL YOURSELF A FAILURE THAT CREATIVE DRAMA DOESN'T WORK IMMEDIATELY...

- IF YOU CAN ACCEPT THAT NOISE — RELATED TO THE ACTIVITY — IS NOT A DISCIPLINE PROBLEM...

- IF YOU'VE GIVEN THE GROUP A CHANCE TO UNDERSTAND WHAT THEY'RE DOING, AND WHY...

...the rest of the year will work because normally, it's true...we don't have discipline problems.

EASY MAGIC. Roy Holmes. Harper and Row, New York, 1974. Magic tricks I've used successfully with limited equipment.
EDUCATION AND ECSTASY. George B. Leonard. A Delta Book, New York, 1969. I recommend Chapter II, "The Human Potential."

OTHER PEOPLE WHO CAN HELP

A long time ago, as a young actress, I became aware of the vast world of people beyond my own existence...and of my need to know more of them. Once I was cast as an impoverished Russian girl in Maxim Gorki's *The Lower Depths.*

How could I, reared within a small middle-class New Jersey town, identify with the hopeless yearnings of Natasha? I set out to seek her in the streets of New York City's East Side. I talked with her in the open markets, observed her on the tenement stoops in the faces of young-old women surrounded by ragged, energetic kids, absorbed her through my perceptions, my imagination, and an awareness of my own feelings. I was finally able to create her within the scripted play.

Intuitively I drew upon this awareness when I entered public education. After months of "circular" improvisations — circular in that the same situations and characters were repeated despite the workshop's design — I realized that these young people were also constricted by the limits of their environment and their human encounters..Their imaginations were walled in.

I began to invite guests into workshop — to work with a group or talk with them. Just casually. To bring their lives to us. Soon I started taking groups outside...it might have started when the Language Arts Department asked me to help the seventh and eighth graders learn interviewing skills. I felt that the workshop training needed to be implemented with strangers. With permission from a supermarket manager, we went to interview shoppers outside the store. Back in school, each student, using notes and tapes, evaluated his/her interview. They were proud of them. I encouraged their comments about the people they interviewed...what they felt about them, their physicality, their voice and speech, their manner and responses, to try to deepen their awareness of the total experience.

Soon fragments of these encounters began to flavor characterizations in improvisations, like "that tall lady who talked through her teeth," or "the man who couldn't look me in the eyes, like he was afraid of *me.*"

Obviously the outside experiences had validity. So I continued. Inside the preparation through drama activities...outside the experience. Over and over again I realized that the preparatory activities in the drama room helped them see, hear, and respond with insight to their new encounters. It was exhilarating to me too. Soon I was consciously trying to expose these young investigators of humanity to as many new encounters as possible...hoping that at least one experience might challenge, agitate, stimulate a vaster dream for their own lives.

Guests we brought into the drama workshop

- A city maintenance inspector specializing in ecology.
- An African dancer and his drummer.

- A blind organist.

- A guru from a NYC Yoga Center.

- A university professor to explain Kabuki Theatre to us.

- Two law enforcement officers, who found it was as valuable for them as it was for the students to try to understand each other's point of view.

- Foreign guests from eighteen countries.

- A representative of the Experiment in International Living Institute.

- Lawyers and faculty of a law school.

- A TV cameraman of a favorite soap opera.

- An international mime and a modern dancer.

- Faculty members of our own school: one played his guitar for us; another told us about her travels.

Trips outside school

For a time another teacher and I were permitted the use of the Board of Education van. We'd pack in fourteen students and set out to re-awaken and maintain their youthful curiosity and sense of fun. Often it was a "Mystery Ride." "Phyllis, which direction should we start in and for how many blocks?" "Twelve blocks to the right," she'd say. As we approached the twelfth block: "Ralph, where shall we turn now?"

It was understood that whoever noticed something we should explore would call out. Instantly we'd stop the van and pile out to inspect the area as though we'd never seen anything like it before. We had cameras with us, and tape recorders. Everyone had name identification cards. One time we explored windows and their reflections; another time we talked with an Italian window washer who'd been two months in America; another time we indulged in double ice cream cones while chatting with a dairy owner. Once we photographed a mail box from every possible angle; another time we just poured into a private school to get out of the rain, and the Mother Superior was so taken with the group that she ushered us into their private dining room for cookies and milk.

You don't have a van? A station wagon will do. Bring a parent or two with you so they can help you interpret what's going on. In addition to standard destinations like art centers, theatres, radio and TV studios, farms, and government agencies, some of the trips we made might stimulate new possibilities.

- We interviewed postal workers on the first postal picket line.

- We took part in a discussion group with ex-addicts at Drug Addiction Rehabilitation Enterprises, a residence center.

- We photographed representative aspects of a large city; then a rural area.

- We led improvised folklore with residents of a county shelter.

- We participated in a college drama workshop.
- We visited a county court room; the Judge stopped a trial to ask for questions from "our young guests from East Orange."
- We boarded an ocean liner in New York harbor.
- We met with the head engineers at an international airport.
- We talked with vendors at a farmers' market.
- We interviewed arrivees and departees at an airport, a bus terminal, and a train station.

But where do you find all those people?

Gradually it became known that "Wilder's always looking for interesting people." Members of the faculty, the staff, and parents started sending me suggestions: someone they knew, heard was in town, read about. They knew I'd pursue their suggestions and the entire school might benefit through a visit by a special person. . .like the Japanese mime, Yass Hakashima, who led workshops and finally gave a performance for the school.

But in the beginning, it was just chance. I'd recognize a drift of thought as a result of a particular improvisation, or a question would come up in a workshop which indicated a readiness for a particular kind of encounter.

For example, a street of trees was about to be felled by the city to bring through a new road. The Art teacher and I sensed an inarticulate concern from the students, expressed in some drawings and several improvisations. We grabbed at this, stimulated further investigation by the students, and used the implications of this for drama and art. I remember students playing animals dismayed to find the trees gone; people in their homes arguing whether the trees which protected their air were more important than roads for cars.

This seemed a good time to invite in an environmental expert. Next we took the students out to join a picket line of community adults, university professors, and college students marching around the trees.

Are you surprised? Do you feel this goes beyond the realm of education? We thought about this and decided that the strongest support we could give these kids for constructive behavior was an awareness of other ways to effect change — together with others.

This collective action forestalled the destruction of the ancient line of sycamores for more than a month. We didn't win, but we had taken a position. The students felt part of a community of concerned people they never knew existed. And our drama work reflected, for weeks after, new levels of compassion and collective spirit.

Let me explain that I'm not naturally a pushy person. I procrastinate into oblivion approaching someone to help ME with a personal need.

But once I saw what it meant to the students to meet exciting people, as equals, and to communicate with them, I propelled myself forth with determination. Yes, risk was involved. I was refused once in a while. Sometimes someone else would turn up. Sometimes I'd have to accept no for an answer. This rarely happened, though. We seemed to offer an interesting challenge to our guests and hosts. . .an experience they hadn't encountered in quite the same way before.

Criteria for choosing guests and hosts

Whenever possible, I tried for people who represented potential role models. Interesting people aren't necessarily good at sharing themselves with young people. When there was a choice, let's say between one ecologist or another, I'd choose the one who evidenced a warm understanding of the needs of young people and the capacity to "talk with" them, not lecture at them.

I feel strongly that young girls need to meet capable, professional women — women who are doing exciting, fulfilling things with their lives in addition to being wives and mothers. In this way we can encourage girls to think beyond house cleaning, baby-sitting, waitressing and nursing. They may take a keener interest in education when they see its relevance to their own lives.

And similarly, I see the need for boys to meet positive, involved men who are contributing of their brains and their creative imaginations. Sports heroes are fine. But what else can a young man aspire to, besides a supersleuth or a masked wonder?

Do you prepare a guest or a host for the visit?

Definitely. It's important to give a person a context. If they're coming in to school, they should know what we're dealing with in the drama room which made us contact them; how the students will be prepared; and how the visit will be conducted. Often they have suggestions and perhaps advance material to send us to include in our orientation.

It was clear that no one was invited to lecture. Never. There was always dialogue and, as often as possible, a dramatic experience. With the representative of the Yoga center, we talked, asked questions, and then participated on the floor with him for an hour session. Yass Hakashima, the Japanese mime I mentioned, met with groups of twenty-five students in 30-minute workshops throughout the morning. In the afternoon we all joined him in the Upsala College theatre for an outstanding performance. The visiting lawyers and law students brought us legal problems which they explained, and we proceeded to improvise them in many situations.

I involved students in contacting guests and hosts. After my initial contact they wrote confirming letters, made follow-up phone calls, and arranged necessary details. Often a student would invite a guest to come home for lunch, or a parent would send in a special luncheon package. The student also met guests at the door and toured them about the building, if time allowed.

When we went out of school, our hosts were prepared for the size of the group, the major area of student interest and, again, that this would be a dialogue. I tried to be sensitive about people or situations which might be negative to the minority members of our groups. Above all, I found it important to explain that our students were coming to visit as dignified young men and women with questions and opinions.

Some starting places for finding people

- LIBRARY. It's nothing new to you to make use of your school library and your town library, I'm sure. Our Instructional Media Center designed and operated by Mrs. Ethel Richard, lured student and teacher alike by the imaginative materials she selected. Her clippings were up to date even if they weren't filed yet, and from these we drew the names of many guests.

- PARENTS. Once again I recommend you to your parents. Get to know them and let them get to know you and your plans. Keep an open ear in class when students refer to their parent(s). (I avoid direct questions so no one feels his/her parents aren't interesting.) Sometimes just a casual remark about needing someone who can do such-and-so will cause a student to go home and ask a parent. Sometimes I've sent notes home, asking if anyone can lead us to a particular kind of person. Thanks to such a note, one mother stepped forward to serve with our Court group; a father who worked for the Parole Board got permission from judges for our Court visits.

- NEWSPAPERS. Our needs became an excellent stimulus for students to read the newspaper regularly. "Who's New in Town" became collector's items in our room. Also the entertainment pages, the social, and the church pages, where a special speaker was often referred to.

- CIVIC GROUPS. Resource people may not serve as guests, but they might help with advice, indirect assistance, a steer in the right direction. We were invited to a Chamber of Commerce luncheon with several students. The men and one woman present were impressed with the poise of the students who explained our procedure in filming "Let us be Free." After that, many members were helpful in leading us to sources we needed. They introduced us to town merchants in connection with our "Models" interviews, and paved the way for us to approach many other civic leaders.

The Mayor's office got news of the interviews students were conducting door-to-door in their neighborhoods about how people felt about town services and keeping the town clean through civic responsibility. He invited fifty students to his chambers to present them with a special award.

- CHURCH LEADERS, MUSEUM DIRECTORS, RECREATIONAL AND CULTURAL ORGANIZATIONS. Y'S AND COMMUNITY

CENTERS. All these directors and leaders are in touch with many sections of the community and can be a rich source for ideas and cooperation. For our International Day they all helped us find the large cast of foreign guests who participated with us at school.

- AND, OF COURSE, FRIENDS AND ACQUAINTANCES.

The rewards go even beyond what you see on the faces of your students, and the reflections in their next improvisations, discussions, written stories in Language Arts, or words of approval from parents attesting to their child's enthusiasm.

The rewards are also personal. It becomes a great challenge. You have moved learning outside the confines of the curriculum to encompass the unexpected discovery. For yourself as well as for your students. What I've gained from talking to all these guests is immeasurable. I've glimpsed points of view and life styles I might have missed by remaining insulated within the school's walls. To see more and more possibilities for drama. To reaffirm how relevant drama training is for life. . . out there in the world. To reaffirm that that world is the stuff of drama!

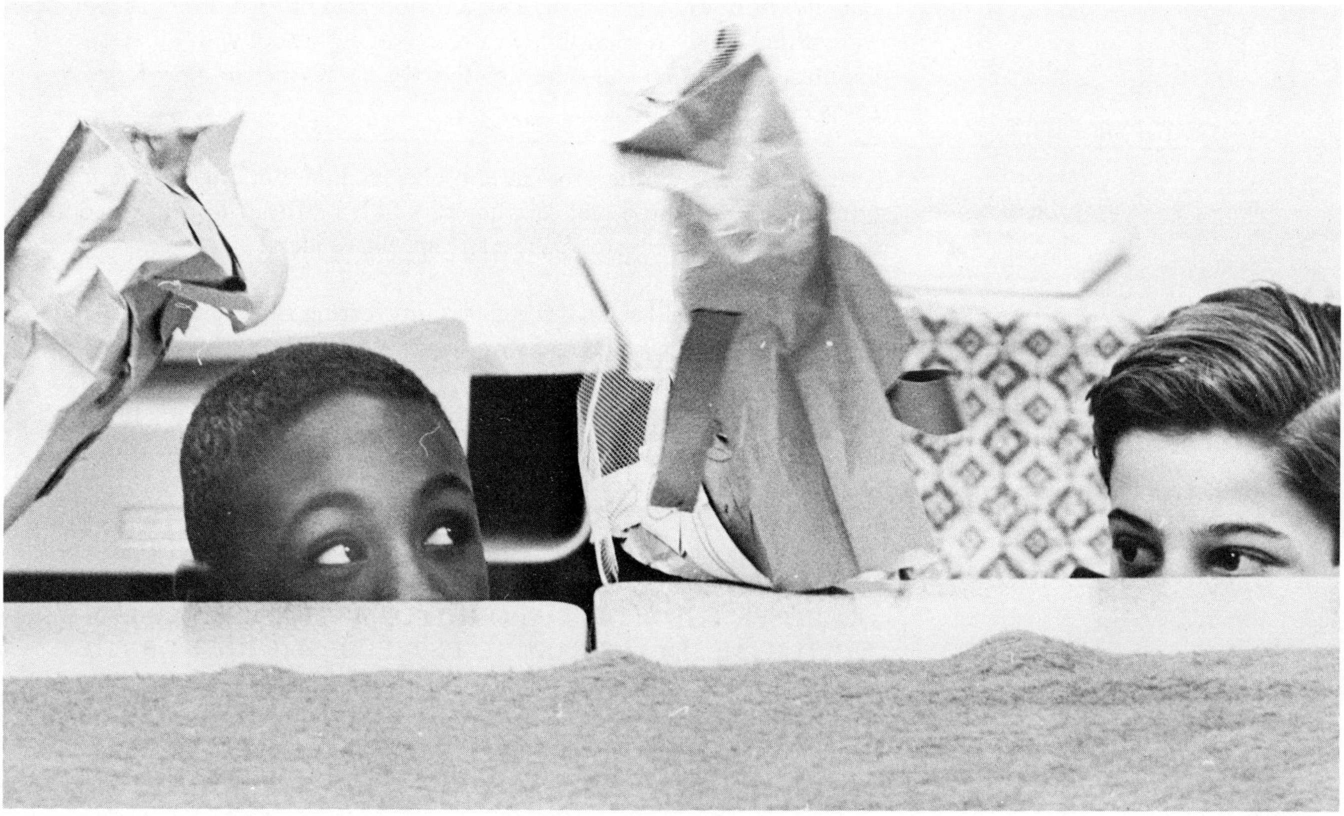

SURVIVING WITHIN THE SCHOOL SYSTEM

I suppose that anyone entering education will feel bewildered and unsure...alone...in need of a friend, an ally. I suppose anyone will find it taxing until he/she learns the rules, expressed and implicit. But that insecurity can be compounded if you're coming in to start a new program — a program which has no precedent in the school systems of the state, and for which no one is prepared, not even you yourself.

I had so much to learn.

"You were so damn sure of yourself, or at least that's how you appeared to us. When you spoke, your voice sounded so confident," explained a colleague years later.

"You seemed fairly unapproachable yourself," I returned.

But the truth was that we were all a little afraid of each other, as we were afraid of the responsibility of being a new school with all eyes upon us. As the first full-time Creative Drama teacher in New Jersey, I was especially vulnerable.

Team planning was the procedure in our building. But a team meeting often meant very little real communication. It's difficult to throw people together and say, "Presto! You're a team. Share ideas!"

In retrospect I feel I wasted too much time eating my yogurt alone in my room, telling myself I had work to do. Or avoiding the teacher's room early in the morning because I'd been stung by a caustic comment at a faculty meeting the day before. It took months, even years, to learn from others that where I felt sensitive, I often threatened the sensitivity of others by seeming so sure of myself.

WE IN THE CREATIVE ARTS ARE OFTEN SO INVOLVED IN WHAT WE'RE DOING AND WHAT WE BELIEVE IN THAT WE DON'T SEE THE PEOPLE AROUND US AS FRIENDS...AS POTENTIAL ALLIES. IT'S EASY TO PERCEIVE THE REST OF THE SCHOOL SYSTEM AS A STUMBLING BLOCK INSTEAD OF A RESOURCE. I OFFER HERE SOME EXPERIENCES ALONG THE WAY OF MAKING A PLACE FOR MY PROGRAM (AND MYSELF) WITHIN THE SCHOOL COMMUNITY.

The maintenance man

On my first day in the building, another teacher and I offered to help Lou Watts, the maintenance man, unload some boxes of books. Afterward, we had coffee with him and the matron in his closet room on the ground floor. This was the first of many such coffee clotches.

Within that small room, there was a genuine feeling of mutual acceptance. Lou was often the person I'd turn to when the frustrations threatened to squeeze out my perspective. He became a fount of helpful suggestions, producing a cabinet — and a lock! — when I despaired of holding onto my records, repairing or making things for the drama program. His help was generous through the years, and I knew that without it my program could easily have faltered. Imagine if he had protested the stuff we dragged into the drama room to "change the set" — the refrigerator boxes, the screens, the what-nots with signs painted on them: "Please don't move. . .this is our set for the movie tomorrow morning." Imagine if he had complained to the principal that he couldn't vacuum in the mess of the drama room.

On my end, I tried to cooperate in every way possible by assuming responsibility for the care of our room. The students pitched in too, "to help Mr. Watts." We also kept him posted on what we were doing. He was an integral part of my planning, and I made sure the communication line between us was always open.

I'VE ACTUALLY KNOWN DRAMA PROGRAMS THAT FAILED BECAUSE THE MAINTENANCE PEOPLE WOULDN'T PUT UP WITH THEM. HAVING THEM ON YOUR SIDE CAN MAKE SURVIVAL MUCH EASIER WITHIN THE SCHOOL. IF YOU'RE LUCKY ENOUGH TO FIND KIND, RESPONSIVE PEOPLE, THEN THE REWARDS ARE DOUBLED.

The office secretary

Another person I gravitated to from the start — and how I wish she were alive today to laugh over some of these memories — was the office secretary, Shirley Paterson. She had rich humor and unimpeachable candor: "Play no games with me, honey," her direct gaze demanded. "Either be straight or keep out of my way." I believe she enjoyed many of the zany things I did with the kids. She attended everything she could.

Shirley knew I was ignorant of many of the implicit ground rules of the school. She helped me learn them to protect myself, while she encouraged me to ignore complaints where they might strip my program of its excitement.

Shirley alerted me to the fact that several teachers were bringing complaints against the noise of my room to the principal. I wasn't doing things they understood, "and they don't ever dare do anything different," she commented. "Why don't they come talk to me directly?" I asked. "For a lot of people that's too long a distance," she answered.

THE OFFICE STAFF ARE ALSO PEOPLE. I'VE SEEN TEACHERS TRY TO INTIMIDATE THEM BY PULLING RANK, OR BE INTIMIDATED BY THEM BECAUSE THEY DO HAVE ACCESS TO OFFICIAL EARS. GRADUALLY I BEGAN TO REALIZE, FROM SHIRLEY AND FROM MR. WATTS, THAT IT WASN'T ENOUGH TO BE DEVELOPING A PROGRAM WHICH THE STUDENTS ENJOYED AND WHICH I FELT HAD MEANINGS FOR THEM. I HAD TO LET OTHERS IN ON WHAT I WAS DOING AND WHY IT BELONGED IN A SCHOOL SYSTEM AT ALL. I HAD TO MAKE MY PEACE WITH THE REST OF THE FACULTY.

The teacher's meeting

From the early months I had my own personal heckler. His guffaw bellowed wall-to-wall when I made even the most innocent comment. He shook up my equilibrium and curdled my nerve endings. Sometimes I felt my throat tighten just anticipating his response. If he wasn't at the meeting yet, I'd ask to be called upon early in the agenda, and speak as fast as possible. He puffed a large cigar, which provided him another source of amusement when he learned that smoke made me hoarse.

I think what toughened me was to recognize my feelings in others who talked less and less. Suddenly I was *not* intimidated; I was angered that we let him do this to us.

Incidentally, the guffawing stopped as I became strong enough to josh with him. As a missionary, I was over-zealous and tense. Humor is so often the key to relieving a situation. Over the years, he and I developed an arm's length kind of respect for each other.

DEAR TEACHERS: WHOEVER YOU MAY BE. YOU MUST SPEAK UP...AT TEACHER'S MEETINGS...IN THE OFFICE...WHEREVER. IT'S NOT ENOUGH TO BE HAPPY BEHIND YOUR CLOSED DOORS WITH YOUR STUDENTS. YOU CAN'T BUILD A SPECIAL PROGRAM AND PRESERVE YOUR OWN SANITY UNLESS YOU ARE A RECOGNIZED PART OF YOUR SCHOOL SYSTEM. NEITHER CAN YOU LIVE IN FEAR OF THE TYRANNY OF OTHERS. SPEAKING UP MAY BE PAINFUL AT FIRST, BUT IT'S LESS PAINFUL THAN REMAINING QUIET AND HIDING. HOW MANY TIMES THE TEACHERS WHO SIT SILENTLY AT MEETINGS WHILE OTHERS FORMULATE POLICIES ARE HARBORING VALUABLE IDEAS.

Often, at meetings, the focus would be a "can you top this?" attack on a particular student. For example, one teacher would start telling about the malicious, psychotic behavior of Robert. Another would top the story.

A few of us knew the boy in a totally different light. We heard each other and began to gravitate toward each other. Gradually, we formed an unspoken, unnamed caucus. We gained courage from each other and began to speak up more easily. We all realized that causes are more successful when advanced by more than one.

A new ally

Let me tell you about the new art teacher. I suspect that he inadvertently gave me some relief because *he* was more threatening at meetings than I had been. Dressed in sandals and dungarees, with a full beard and an absolute surety of his erudite opinions and decisions, he formed a new union with me at meetings. Not that we ever preplanned our positions. Not at first. He and I shared adjoining rooms divided only by an L-shaped construction of 10-foot-high cabinets. Initially we talked *at* each other about our ideas. It was an amazing discovery when we realized we thought essentially the same things.

We joined forces one day. A group of thirty students were to work with us for several hours. Our theme: exploring city spaces and country spaces. We preplanned rather tentatively, starting with group discussion to explore possible ideas. We went on to quick individual drawings based on some of the ideas; creating sounds of both spaces, then rhythms; shapes, and patterns. We developed group murals; group chants, group movement collages of activities typical of each area. We improvised the city as it looks to a pigeon, a fire hydrant, a stop sign; the country as it looks to an earthworm, a fish hawk.

It was an exhilarating session for the students. Us, too, to find we could work together so well. After that, our voices were even stronger at meetings. Several teachers told us, years later, "You and Jim, you both seemed as if you were on a crusade." I mentioned this to our principal. He said it was what he had hoped for — teachers with strong opinions — so there'd be dialogue to effect change.

THAT COMMENT BY THE PRINCIPAL STARTLED ME. WHY HADN'T WE RECOGNIZED THAT EARLIER? INSTEAD, TEACHERS HAD COMPLAINED THAT HE GAVE US TOO MUCH REIN, NOT ENOUGH ABSOLUTE DIRECTION, AND TOO LITTLE PRAISE TO LET US KNOW WE WERE DOING SOMETHING RIGHT. IS IT THAT TEACHERS ARE UNPREPARED TO BE INNOVATORS? IS IT THAT WE DON'T ADEQUATELY RESPECT OUR ABILITY TO INITIATE, OUR RIGHTS TO BE STRONG FORCES IN BEHALF OF THE CHILDREN WE TEACH?

Learning to respect different styles of teaching

A social studies teacher boasted of her stringent demands on her students. She emphasized work and discipline. Her caustic tongue often dropped tart remarks about the drama program. For a long time I backed off from her.

One day she offered to come on a field trip to New York City with me and a bus of students. Her behavior that day belied all her words. Under a starched, efficient manner, she enjoyed the students. We had a delightful day. Back in school, I learned to respect her teaching. In her way she reached children as I, in my way, reached children. We were both right to teach in our own ways.

A teacher who'd flamed at me for daring to have the children reading scripts in my room since Reading was her discipline, agreed to lunch with me one day. We met as two women with families we loved. We discovered other common interests. She invited me to help with a Spring all-day program she was designing. It was much easier to pass each other in the school after that. She told me, "We didn't think you'd last it here — not with these kids."

But we need friends

How important it was to find friends on that faculty. And it did happen. I began to listen hard to the teacher next door. She was making a transition from teaching traditional Home Economics to an experimental program called Family Living. As different as our programs were, we recognized a mutuality in our efforts on behalf of our students. It was important for me to realize that she was battling too. She and a Language Arts teacher helped me understand some of the forces going on within the teaching teams.

"You stay after school to work with students and parents," they said one day. "Do you think that makes others who go home at a regular hour feel you're trying to show them up?"

Or, another time, "You come on too strong. Hold back a little. People who don't have strong opinions are jealous. Make waves, but with less fanfare. Don't appeal to everyone to get in the act. Not everybody's going to join. . .they see it as *your* project."

I learned the importance of reaching out to individual teachers privately — over lunch, or during a tea/coffee break. Of joining a group stopping at a luncheonette after school. (If I had those years to repeat, I might even have joined a bowling team.)

IN THE DRAMA ROOM WE ENCOURAGE COMMUNICATION BETWEEN HUMAN BEINGS. WE SET UP AN ENVIRONMENT IN WHICH IT CAN HAPPEN. WE NEED THE SAME COMMUNICATION SKILLS ALL OVER THE SCHOOL, BETWEEN US AND OTHERS.

Nurturing your own psyche

But, to be an innovator is to take risks that everyone isn't going to love us. . .not all at once. . .maybe not ever. We spend many hours of the day in that school building. It takes tremendous physical energies. It also requires psychological and emotional strength.

Not only do you need one staunch friend in school to groan with once in a while — you need to design your life to allow enough diversion for renewal. When my family started complaining that I approached the supper table like a dyspeptic, I joined a health spa. I'd often drag myself there — but I'd go. Even a half hour of vigorous exercise and three minutes in the sauna, and I'd go home a revitalized person. Sometimes I'd go during lunch and another teacher would join me. Otherwise I'd have been on an ulcer course — and without energy.

A school is such an insulated small world. Without knowing it, I found my conversation, my dreams, my Sundays completely engulfed by the plans, the problems, the interactions, the hurts, the children. It's urgent to break out, to separate oneself in order to rejoin with renewed perspective each day.

We renewed expired theatre subscriptions. . .dropped in on a neighborhood movie occasionally (usually dismal, but a change!) A Sunday hike in the mountains. A lecture on a topic not related to education. Whatever it is, it's needed and to the good. As with any problem, we can handle it better if we walk away from it once in a while.

A public relations program can help too

I've been talking about attitudes and people who helped me survive that first year — beyond personal commitment and energy. But my program needed help to survive too.

With regular budget and program cuts, some kind of public relations program for administrators becomes increasingly vital. As I write today, Art and Music supervisors have been eliminated, some arts programs are in jeopardy — but there are *three* Creative Drama programs still flourishing in the new Middle School.

The principal needs inside information

Some important guests were touring our building. They walked into my area just as Peter was delivering a baby on the floor. The "mother," played by Jake, was dressed in a skirt and shawl. The baby was "delivered" through his mouth.

The guests stayed for one minute and were hurried out before they could hear the evaluation of the improvisation by the class.

Should I have walked over immediately to explain what was taking place, and why? Should I have helped the guests and the principal understand the context of this improvisation? Yes! But I didn't think quickly enough that day. The next day, it was far harder.

When I finally got to see the principal he said, wryly, that he had difficulty in telling the guests this was not a class in sex education, A.D. 174.

That was when I began, consciously, to build my own public relations campaign. I had to substantiate my approaches and uses of Creative Drama in terms compatible with educational goals.

From then on, when an administrator, a colleague or a guest came into my space, instead of just acknowledging them with a smile, I grabbed the opportunity to explain what they were looking at; why I'd chosen this activity with this group; some quick insights into the growth of several of the students through Creative Drama.

In order to do this, I began to collect, clip, write for all kinds of supportive material — articles, books, interviews, commendations for Developmental Drama in Education from everywhere. The school librarian ordered some books. I began to write reports on my activities and even leave them around in the teacher's room. Rereading some of them today, I realize how transparently they were defenses. I wanted to be able to stay alive in that school, and to stay alive I needed to be tolerated by some, respected by some, and understood — by even a few.

Lesson plans were not required of the arts team during the first few years. But occasionally I would write up a class plan in such a way that an administrator, stopping in, would be reassured that I did have a direction and purpose compatible with educational objectives.

These are some books and articles I've used in developing my campaign on behalf of Creative Drama in the school:

CHILDREN AND DRAMA. Nellie McCaslin. David McKay, New York, 1975.
CREATIVE POWER: THE EDUCATION OF YOUTH IN THE CREATIVE ARTS. Hughes Mearns. Dover Publications, New York, 1958. For over twenty years this book has been one of my staunchest defenders.
LEARNING IS A HAPPENING. Grace Stanistreet. New Plays, Rowayton, Conn., 1974. Creative Drama teachers are greatly indebted to the thinking of Grace Stanistreet. Open her book and hold dialogue with her.
PUSH BACK THE DESKS. Albert Cullum. Citation Press, New York, 1967. Take courage from his antics on behalf of learning.
ART AND THE INTELLECT. Harold Taylor. Museum of Modern Art, New York. Try opening to page 25.
THE UPSIDEDOWN CURRICULUM. A Ford Foundation pamphlet. Write for free copies to Ford Foundation Office of Reports, 320 East 43rd Street, New York, NY 10017.
PLAY, DRAMA AND THOUGHT. Richard Courtney. Drama Book Specialists, New York, 1975.
GIVE THEM ROOTS AND WINGS. American Theatre Association, Washington, D.C. A curriculum expressed in terms of behavioral objectives and planned-for results.
The Creative Education Foundation, Inc. puts out a journal which will prove supportive through the cross-section of scholarly articles included. Journal of Creative Behavior, State University College at Buffalo, 1300 Elmwood Avenue, Buffalo, NY 14222.

With parents

Brief conversations at parent-teacher meetings made me realize how vital it was to let parents in on what I was doing with their children, so I started issuing reports and notes of explanation to parents of groups that were doing special projects.

As soon as I started sharing that Creative Drama was "more than cream puff stuff," as one father put it; as soon as it became evident to parents that their children were learning viable skills useful to their lives in the Drama room, I gained my strongest support from them.

This meant staying in contact with parents in a number of ways. As a parent myself, I know how I felt when a teacher contacted me about one of our daughters — *not* to complain but to share something positive. Whenever possible, I initiated a mailing to parents to let them know about some special activity their children were involved in. I invited parents in to participate with us in our weekly Court trials, with our International Day preparations, on field trips, for special events.

The Reading teacher, the Art teacher and I set up an evening workshop for parents. Some came with their children. Starting with dessert, they rotated to the Art room, to the new Reading Lab, and to the Drama workshop. They were not lectured to; they participated. It was a learning experience for us teachers as well as for the mothers and fathers.

After this workshop, parents volunteered to help in many ways.

How does one make time for all this?

Teachers in workshops keep asking that question. The most I can answer is, once you get all this rolling, it just continues. When you set your priorities, things do happen. A quick note — dittoed and sent home with students or mailed from the office or in envelopes addressed by the students. It becomes part of your ritual, like preparing individualized reports or submitting lesson plans. Each one of us has a great many more details to our program than we stop to realize — until we write a book about them!

But let's never ignore that the parents are our greatest strength when we want to make changes in education to benefit their children. It was the parents who stood up for our new school at the Board of Education and staved off its dissolution.

With the press

It started almost accidentally. When I initiated "Court," someone mentioned it to a newspaper. The way students were handling their own problems made a good article. A photograph of the students appeared in the largest daily paper in the area. Each student bought a copy, of course. They carried it around and showed it to everyone. It was their faces, in print, doing something that was considered special and wonderful. They were setting their own role models. They seemed to like themselves this way.

From then on I got to know the local news writers. Whenever we did something interesting — interviewing people house to house about the ecology of the city; developing our original play on drug education, dramatizing folklore at the nurseries; whatever it was — I mailed out an article describing it. Sometimes the students wrote the material. Often they made the contacts with the papers. Often the paper sent a photographer to catch them in action.

It was a way of lending status to our new program in Drama that reached the eyes of parents and other members of the community. After our state grants for "Human Beings in our World," and "Drugs and Other Cop-Outs," the news releases and other publicity were evidence that the money was being well used.

I hear some teacher commenting, well, your projects were more newsworthy than a regular classroom is. Well, yes, the state grant was special. But many of the projects we dramatized got in the news because local papers *are* interested in what's going on in education, and local names sell papers. Just be sure to include the name of every student and faculty member participating, helping, or lending endorsement.

With the superintendent

Our first superintendent was a man of profound insights into the needs of the community and the needs of its children. Towards these ends, he dared confront the forces of "keep things like they were fifty years ago; it was good enough then; it's good enough today."

Our pilot school was stage one toward the development of an educational plaza in the city. As most of us on the faculty fully realized, we were on board moving toward a gigantic new reality, one which was already arousing interest in educators all over the nation.

Consistent with his interest in innovation which supported the positive self-image and development of the individual student, he encouraged my program in Creative Drama.

I found it vital to visit him periodically to gain perspective and maintain a larger view of my program's relevance to the larger goals. I gained strength from his thinking and his suggestions. Usually I'd bring a report on one of our projects in Creative Drama, or a proposal I was about to submit. Before he left the system — and a sad tale that is about the forces which split a community and turn it away from innovative planning — he encouraged me to collaborate with our extensive Guidance staff on a drama therapy project within our school.

And a new superintendent

To him, I believe, I was an inheritance of questionable value. By this time, the strong approval by parents and the extent of the publicity for many of my projects and grant awards enhanced my position. I continued to request periodic meetings with him. Although he did little to help me, or even to make me feel secure that Creative Drama would be extended for the next year, he did not eliminate me from the curriculum.

Enter — a new principal!

After five years, educational objectives began to change in our city. Bit by bit, the brave innovation was being chewed away. We had a series of new principals. At a demoralized point of the sixth year, one man was charged with the task of tightening and re-structuring our greatly enlarged school. He walked in to a tough job at a difficult time. But he arrived breathing discipline and power.

One day a group of students were enacting an uproarious scene, in complete seriousness. It was the rest of the class that was rocking with laughter.

The door was flung open. His voice boomed: "This/ is/ an/ academic institution! LAUGHTER does NOT belong/ in an academic institution!"

We froze for a long moment as the door closed after him. Laura let out a long "Wheee. . . . ." Everyone began talking at once, in hushed syllables. "What's wrong with laughing? Whatsa matter can't we be happy and still learn? We weren't fooling around. . .we were doing what we're supposed to do in drama, aren't we?"

The discussion was remarkable. This was a group of students who had been part of the school for two and three years. They'd learned a lot during that time which had nothing to do with curriculum. They'd grown to like themselves; they'd been treated with respect by adults; they'd been given lots of opportunity to make choices about their own lives. THEY HAD DEVELOPED COMMITMENT TO A WAY OF LIFE. Many of them went on to make waves in high school, the kind of waves which demand the best from education and educators.

But, what was I to say to the principal!

I rounded up a new packet of my campaign materials and made an appointment to see him. I tried to explain my procedures and objectives, referring to supportive articles by educators from about the country on benefits of Creative Drama in the schools. I pointed out that the noise he'd heard was related to the lesson. I *was* in control. The students *were* intensely involved. I explained how their increased abilities to express and communicate their ideas and feelings were important preparation for a world which required people to be articulate. I gave evaluations of several of the students and their improved interaction with classmates, their enthusiasm and cooperation.

He listened. But his response implied that our kind of open education was non-productive. City children needed the three R's to "make it" — and a tight outer-directed discipline.

He was considering moving Creative Drama to another part of the building. The sounds were too intense. His office adjoined our room, and visiting parents wondered what kind of education was going on here.

The school began to change. First, scheduling and class sizes. The teachers were pulled in by regular directives from the office. Some teachers left the system, or were dropped during that year. We were no longer consulted as to what we thought was good for the students. Many of my students telephoned me, bewildered about the changes. "Was it our fault, Ms. Wilder?"

In January I requested a leave of absence; my mother was ill. But, had I stayed, I knew I faced some large decisions. After the thrilling rewards of the first five years, could I return to the beginning? Could I even just tread water?

A brave friend, Phyllis Haase, continued the program to be sure that Creative Drama was not dropped from the system, as had been threatened. She met larger groups, in shorter periods for shorter cycles. How I appreciate her persistence and the love she brought to the young people.

When do you quit? Or, if you stay. . .what then?

These are very real questions we confront when we're trying creative teaching in any area.

If you get so chipped away that all the joy is gone out of teaching; if your administration changes to one which opposes all your major beliefs, do you stay to suffer or do you get out?

If you reach an impasse — you've tried and tried and the situation doesn't ease up — are there further compromises you can make and still live with yourself?

If you need that paycheck, and teaching jobs are as scarce as they are now, what choices are there for you?

SHE GOT OUT. One teacher told me she left education that year altogether. She said she thoroughly enjoyed the kids, but she couldn't deal with the administrative changes. The new methodologies imposed on her just didn't make sense to her.

SHE STAYED. I asked a creative teacher who stayed. She said she was given a poor evaluation. She contested it. "It was the hardest year of my life. When the axe was down, I got it from the newer teammates around me. They didn't talk to me. I couldn't take the abuse. Then the principal told me he'd been unfair in his evaluation but it was too late to change it. My teammates suddenly talked to me again. One woman said, "We didn't think you'd make it. We thought you'd have a nervous breakdown."

"So why did you stay?" I persisted.

"I receive ten fold what I give to these students. I feel I have something to offer them. I was not going to be pushed out. And finally I broke through."

Postscript on a positive note

I got a surprise when I showed these pages to the friend who stayed. It seems she had heard the "new principal," some time after he'd settled in to his position at the school, explain to a parent: "The Drama room is noisy, but that's because the children are involved and enthusiastic about going there. The noise is related to what they're doing, and the teacher is in control. They're learning in there how to think on their feet."

"And I wonder," she concluded, "where he got all that from?"

182 Surviving

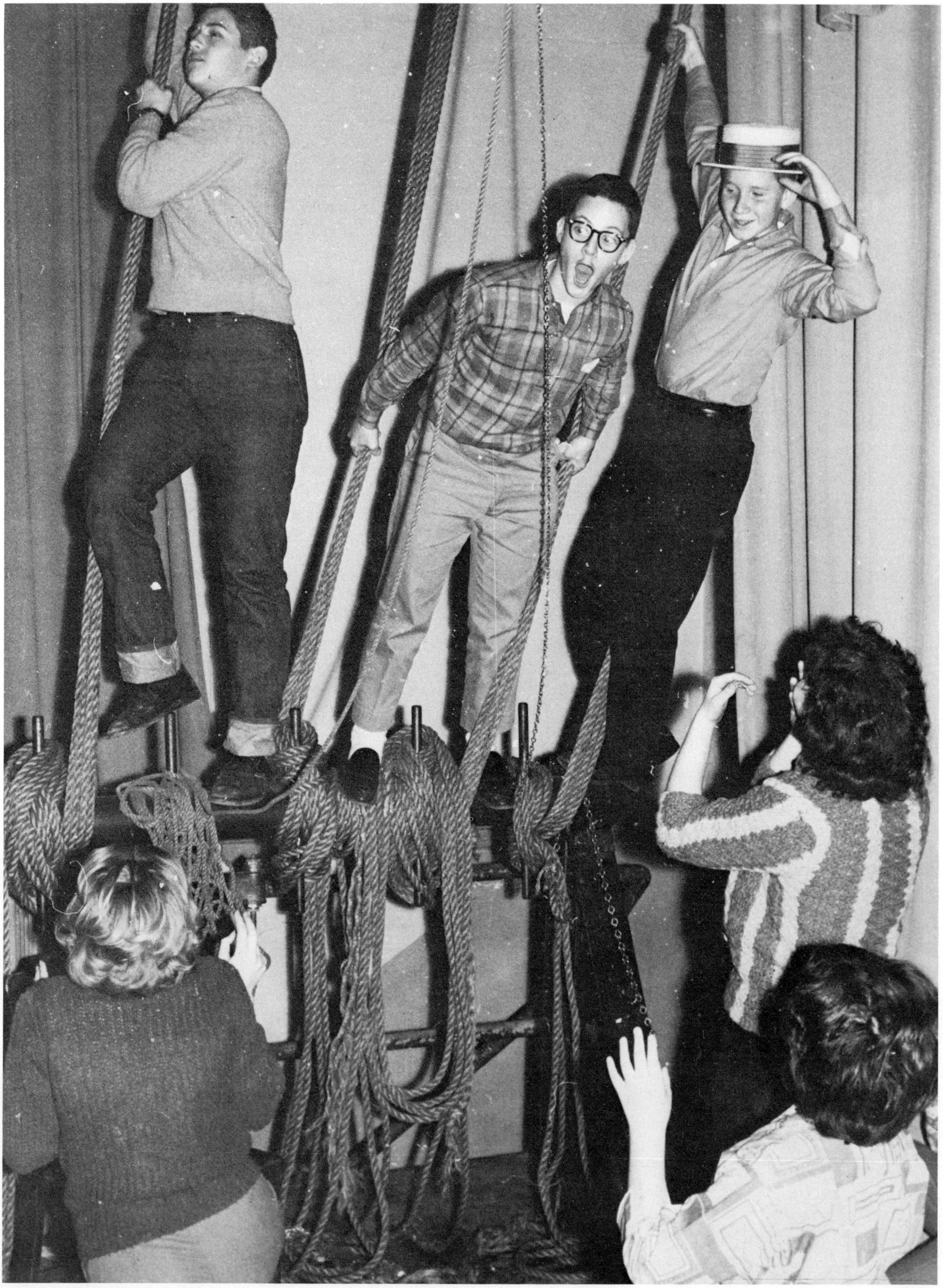

APPRECIATION GOES TO. . . .

A book of this kind evolves. Like a giant vacuum cleaner it sweeps up, encompasses, the many encounters and relationships with people — all of whom contributed to my efforts and understanding. I want to mention a few:

My "Student Advisory Committee" — Janice Anderson, Andrew Brown, Robin Clark, Ea Mingo and Eric Pendleton; and the many students who appear in this book under fictitious names, and their parents.

Teachers-friends-administrators. Barbara Arnay, Jim Garah, Barbara Goodwillie, Phyllis Haase, Barbara Johnson, Ethel Richard, Claire Szeleva and Terry Watson; Superintendent Robert H. Seitzer, Principals Roy N. Young and Arthur Herd. Carol Hyatt, Linda Lewin and my first Drama teacher Edna Eckert. Eldred Harris who still endorses the Drama process.

The New Jersey State Council on the Arts which supported me with an Artist Grant to complete the first draft. The directors at the Upsala College Library, East Orange, N.J. and the Lenox Public Library, Lenox, Massachusetts.

Four people who figure in this book are too soon gone: Eli Jarmel, Professor, Rutgers Law School, Newark, N.J. helped shape "Court;" Burt Scolnick, photographer, shot with an empty camera until the students accepted his third eye; Charles and Elizabeth Weiss, my parents, ever encouraged my work.

My editor-friend, Pat Whitton with whom I shared the process of "growing" a book.

The real Sam and Gilbert behind the composites in this book. At 15 one was in prison. They symbolize many of the youths who walk into our "space" to share a happy spark of themselves as they could become. Sam gave me a tender poem and a noble African King on film for "Let Us Be Free." Gilbert gave me his look of wonderment when he first heard the class approving — of him!

DATE DUE			
MAR 26 1981			
JUN 6 1985			
MAY 24 1991			

HIGHSMITH 45-220